THE SOUL OF DORSET

THE MAYPOLE AT BURTON BRADSTOCK

Design of a picture by Albert Rutherston, in the possession of
M. H. Salaman Esq.

THE
SOUL OF DORSET

BY

F. J. HARVEY DARTON

Frederick Joseph

" This other Eden, demi-paradise. . . .
England, bound in with the triumphant sea."

BOSTON AND NEW YORK
HOUGHTON MIFFLIN COMPANY
1922

Printed in Great Britain at
The Mayflower Press, Plymouth.   William Brendon & Son, Ltd.

TO

RUTH

PREFACE

THIS book has been written as a pleasure to myself over a period of twenty years, in the intervals of a busy life. It began as an attempt to describe, mainly for the use of friends who shared that life, most of them now dead, the admirable fitness of Dorset for walking tours. But the more I walked in that county—and there is only one little corner of it that I have not visited at least once—the more I learnt of England; and I modified my original idea. It seemed to me that here, on the frontier of England (for Dorset was really that until late in the Middle Ages), I had the true story of England; not the extremes of romance and war and politics, but the mean. So I changed my plan, and have tried to do or combine three things in each chapter of the book—to sketch very slightly the main tendency of English history in a series of epochs; to apply that history to its local exhibition in Dorset; and, finally, to describe a string of places, within the compass of a reasonable day's walk, in which some remains of the epoch dealt with are still patent. The Ruttier at the end—"ruttier" is a good old word borrowed from a great English classic, and might well be restored as a shibboleth for alleged patriots—shows how these walks can be combined and worked out in practice. But I have not attempted (God forbid) to write a "gossiping guide," or series of "rambles": my concern is at least as much with my country as with the county in it which I love best.

I do not think I have mentioned any place or building

which in the course of happy years I have not seen for
myself ; not as an antiquary, but as (with exceptions) a
healthy person using his proper legs.   But my personal
knowledge would be small but for certain invaluable
publications, to which I render the warmest thanks : the
Proceedings of the Dorset Field Club, *Somerset and Dorset
Notes and Queries*, the *Victoria County History*, and the
original of them all, Hutchins' *Dorset*. I owe much in the
earlier chapters to Mr. Hadrian Allcroft's *Earthwork of
England*. There are a number of less universal works—
those of Coker, Warne, Roberts, and others—to which the
same general gratitude must be given, as also to national
works of reference of all kinds. It would be tedious to
enumerate the books devoted to special periods or places
which have been of assistance (like Mr. Damon's on Geology,
Mr. Robinson's on Purbeck, Mr. Bayley's on the Civil War,
Mr. Moule's on Dorchester), or the smaller local histories
or pamphlets which in many cases have led me to fuller
investigation. Dorset is rich in competent local historians,
and I hope rather than am certain that I am indebted to
them all. When I have quoted them directly, or when they
seem to be the sole authority for the facts involved, I have
mentioned them by name in the text.

I do not pretend to the status of an historian, any more
than to that of an antiquary. I am quite sure that a
specialist in either kind can condemn me in detail, because
if there is one thing I learnt of my kindly mother, Oxford,
it is that the omniscient scholar cannot and does not exist.
Life would not be worth living if he did exist. What I have
tried to do is to see the chief activities of each successive
age in one English county sympathetically, and to illustrate
them by local facts. I want to dwell upon what he whom
we used to know as Mr. Balfour long ago called subordinate
patriotism. If in my later chapters I have touched with an

apparent lack of proportion on the difficulties of the farmer
and his man, it is because I believe that only in their solution
will England find her true soul. If the agricultural labourer,
under conditions which raise him above the beasts (" beast "
is the Dorset plural) he tends, can really come to have a
pride in the country he has made habitable through centuries
of dumb toil, and a pride likewise in the past hopes and
heroisms I have tried to chronicle, then God prosper
England. But if not, if he is always to be "the
poor," God help us, and forgive those who keep him
in that state.

I am very grateful to friends for help : to Mrs. Ruth
Williams for reading the manuscript and proofs and making
suggestions; to Mr. F. Harcourt Kitchin (seduced from
Devon for a few weeks) for a valuable, if painful, decimation
of the manuscript, and to Mr. Cyril Hurcomb for reading
part of the proofs ; to my publishers, friends of old standing,
for other suggestions as well as for their kindly practical
interest ; to Mr. Albert Rutherston for letting me use a
delightful picture in which, as his original guide to West
Dorset, I may claim almost a god-paternal interest; to Mr.
Charles Aitken, keeper and fosterer of the Tate Gallery,
for leave to reproduce Stevens' portrait of his benefactor,
and for valuable suggestions; to Mr. Wilson Steer and
Mr. Gwynne-Jones for the use of pictures of the county in
which they, too, have been happy ; and to Mr. C. J. Sawyer
for finding and lending some engravings.

The Index is not meant to cover historical periods as
such—the chapters do that—nor special subjects. Whenever a person or place occurs more than once and is given
particular attention, the chief reference is placed first,
irrespectively of order of pagination. The Appendix

PREFACE

(except for one or two necessary entries) is not included in it, because it is so arranged that the itinerary of each chapter coincides with the pictured Ruttier or chapter-heading. These Ruttiers are by Miss Ruth Cobb, to whom I am indebted for her care and adaptability. The prefatory quotations also are not included.

CONTENTS

CONTENTS

CONTENTS

LIST OF ILLUSTRATIONS

I

"Lords and Commons of England, consider what nation it is whereof ye are and whereof ye are the governors ; a nation not slow and dull, but of a quick, ingenious, and piercing spirit, acute to invent, subtle and sinewy to discourse, not beneath the reach of any point, the highest that human capacity can soar to. . . . What could a man require more from a nation so pliant and so prone to seek after knowledge ? What wants there to such a towardly and pregnant soil but wise and faithful labourers, to make a knowing people, a nation of prophets, of sages, and of worthies ?   We reckon more than five months yet to harvest ; there need not be five weeks ; had we but eyes to lift up, the fields are white already."

JOHN MILTON,
Areopagitica.

"This season's Daffodil,
 She never hears,
What change, what chance, what chill,
 Cut down last year's :
But with bold countenance,
 And knowledge small,
Esteems her seven days' continuance
 To be perpetual."

RUDYARD KIPLING,
Songs from Books.

B

I

PEACE

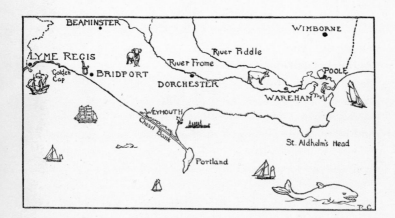

THE England of my dreams is of a magical nature. It appears to me as a green chalk hill, high and strong, running towards the sunset. Far behind you, as you walk westward, lie the smoke and wealth of herded men—who are English, too, but do not live in my dream-country. In the bottoms that run north and south into the long ridge are secret and friendly villages, the homes of those who have made the earth rich by their secular labour. The hill ends in a little forsaken port, where change comes not, nor does any man grow old.

That England is built up partly from my intimate love of one place, Bridport Harbour in Dorset, where the world for me seems to end, and partly from many walks I have taken on the Dorset hills on my way to that haven of rest. Once in particular I seemed to be really in that England of my fantasy. I stood with a companion in great contentment on a great hill, looking out over the blue and golden mists where Bridport lay against the dazzling sea. The earth stretched away into infinite sunshine, and I felt as if I were contemplating the ultimate peace on earth for which the ages have striven, and were a part of it, able to continue in it for ever. Yet as I turned away I knew I must soon go back to less happy places, must face menacing hopes and fears, perform tasks, live and die : not dream.

At the slight suggestion of death there came into my memory an incongruous recollection ; no dream, but a comment upon civilization. I was sitting many years ago in the bar-parlour of an inn at Bridport Harbour, where the mariners and coastguards assembled cheerfully of an evening. Some of us were playing whist, some talking or eating bread and cheese, all drinking from straight mugs. Suddenly a head came round the door, and a voice said " Dick, you're wanted." One of my companions got up and went out, and a moment later summoned a second to join him. They were absent about half an hour, and then came back and resumed beer and whist without delay or explanation.

I asked Dick later why he had been called away. " Old P——'s dead," he replied. " Died in a fit, all hunched up. We had to go and lay him out. He'd got stiff, and I had to sit on his knees to straighten him."

When that scene flickered so irrelevantly across my mind on Eggardon Camp, I wondered idly, as we looked out from the hill towards the sea, whether, five thousand years ago, when perhaps the Camp was first dug, the reason why the Stone Age men were often buried (as they were) " all hunched up " in their barrows was that they had not thought of Dick's simple remedy for *rigor mortis*. His matter-of-fact grimness made our civilization appear a very primitive thing. It made the fancy of a happy England, in which society shall really have become stable and painless, seem a childish invention. And it gave me also the feeling that the development of mankind may have been like a bad cinematograph drama—repetitive, discontinuous, and futile ;

and that our progress may not yet have gone far, if one looks at it honestly.

Yet that night as I stood on the little black wooden pier at West Bay (Bridport Harbour's *alias*), and watched the still beauty of the moonlit sea, the conviction came back to me that there is, after all, something of true peace in an English county—some solid precipitate left after the shaking of the centuries. I thought of other places and experiences in that divine county which had given me the same conviction.

I remembered especially one occasion when I had gone down to the " mother and lover of men, the sea," between that pier and its absurd brother. It was on a coastwise vessel, a squat broad craft of two hundred or three hundred tons, such as the vanished Bridport shipyard used to build a generation ago. Ships have to be warped out to the pier-heads here. You bump, sailless, down between the tiny piers, creaking, rattling : familiar voices cry commands from the ship and from the harbour in turn ; and all the sounds seem separate and ineffably distant, because you are upon a dead hulk, a shell moved by alien hands : a ship being warped out has no soul. But in a little while the last friendly voice dies : the last rope flies curling and flaps upon the drab deck. Blocks squeak, a winch clacks, a few deep orders sound ; the grey lifeless sail climbs slowly and jerkily with its yard, and then, with a quick writhe and a report like a shot, is big and round with the unseen wind. The sea begins to clap its hands upon the curves of the hull. The boat hisses, and leaps, and sways to the tiny song of its tackle. It is born again, a thing of mastery and movement. The pilot goes below and drinks good health to the skipper, and climbs laboriously down the side into his little cockboat ; and soon he too recedes. You are alone upon the curving globe.

The port looks infinitely small now. You see it as with the eye of God—a poor gathering-place of transitory men, busied with petty occasions ; no more ; little, remote, pathetic, like man's life itself. You have come into the real world, the universe where the stars march in their celestial motions. You and your brave ship are your own world, a commonwealth of high adventure.

And yet in the distant, inconsiderable village, that now has become but a few twinkling candles in the strange depth of late twilight, there lingers the necessary and indefinable friendliness of humanity, which the landward look from the sea perceives so clearly. There is no greeting like that of the land to the mariner, no longing like that for port after stormy seas. The familiar fields, those corners and stones and the very puddles that you have so long ago learnt to avoid : the smell of a house : the steadiness of the little quay, the grating shingle, the people watching your coming : so Englishmen have always seen their land, and known peace of soul :

> Oh ! to be there for an hour when the shade draws in beside
>   the hedgerows,
>   And falling apples wake the drowsy noon :
> Oh ! for the hour when the elms grow sombre and human
>   in the twilight,
>   And gardens dream beneath the rising moon.
>
> Only to look once more on the land of the memories of child-
>   hood,
>   Forgetting weary winds and barren foam :
> Only to bid farewell to the combe and the orchard and the
>   moorland,
>   And sleep at last among the fields of home !

The seas and the hills and far-away enchantments may call a man to the ends of the earth. But at the last, before the conclusion of the whole matter, before the final dim adventure, he will cling to those poor, friendly beginnings, and come back, if he may, and be comforted.

That seems to be an eternal thing. Yet is it reality, or only an emotion ? We come back, I say, to our squalor, our splendour, to our hopes and futilities in what we call our home. We take some sort of dwelling-place for granted, and search eagerly for the trivial amenities we have learnt

to love. And yet how have we secured even that much ?
What are the aim and value of all the efforts by generation
after generation to master the riddle of the painful
earth ?

The story of those efforts may point to an answer to the
question, What is peace ? I have tried to imagine some
of its chapters, as they may still be read in broken letters
in a few places in one English county. How long has it
taken a Dorset village to reach its present state, and why
and how have its folk won and kept a hold on life ? What
have been their hopes, fears, successes, failures, century
after century ? That is what I want to guess at in this book
of local happenings.

I will string together, by way of prophecy, so to speak,
some incongruities of the place where I began the book.
They may suggest something of the jumbled romance of
mankind. Bridport itself, a beautiful eighteenth-century
town clustered among hills, and its harbour where every
house seems to be an afterthought, may serve thus as an
epitome of the long story. It contains vestiges of almost the
whole of man's life in Dorset.

The town lies on the most permanent thing in nature—a
river, a very small river, cutting its slow way oceanward
between hills, and dragging down soil to choke its own
mouth ; struggling also against the sea's barrier of cast-up
shingle. As long ago as King John's day, the harbour was
in danger of obliteration. As late as King George V's day,
there was talk of dredging it and deepening it to take a
squadron of motor-boats. There has even been a proposal
to flood the whole valley up to the town, and build a great
breakwater from Thorncombe Beacon, and make a lordly
harbour, rivalling Weymouth and Portland. Man seeks
eternally to subjugate even that little stream. There is
one chapter-heading for the story.

Yet the river will surely survive in its own persistent way.

Consider one of its victories. Thirty years ago, when the little green between the *Bridport Arms* and Pier Terrace was made, they dug up a dead man in the river gravel. He had two great jars round the neck of his skeleton, and he lay in the old river-bed. There is not a word of his story known : whether he was a smuggler, or reveller overcome, or mere carrier fatally belated, or some whimsical trader buried fantastically—no man can tell, nor when he died. He is but bones that carried a jar.

Or go into the *Bridport Arms* and hear other stories from the brook. Stand on the left-hand side of the bar : you are in Symondsbury parish. Stand on the right : you are in Burton Bradstock parish. Nowhere are you in Bridport parish, and yet this is part of Bridport if geography and politics and custom can make it so. The property of the church and a monastery was once divided along that line. In that little detail the dead hand of monasticism and pre-Reformation Church organization is faintly visible, as if striving still to grasp a shadow of power. That is another chapter.

And the parish division, running thus through a house, is an echo of yet another side of history, of geographical facts. Why should it take that line ? Why should the old boundary cut through a venerable inn ? Because Dorset was made without man's leave asked or given : because once, when the parish boundary was determined, the river Brit, which was the boundary, ran along that line. Later it was silted up, after the manner of streams in those parts, and cut itself a new channel. But the old boundary remained on dry land. And that brings us back to the geological chapter.

Look, again, at the buildings of the harbour. All to the east lie great stone barns, some empty, a paradise of hens, some full of timber for the petty commerce of the place. They seem to-day beyond all use in size and stability ; one can peer out under their huge rafters through a bright square of unglazed window as from a prison, the blue sea of freedom shining outside cruelly. They have stood there a hundred years or more. A generation ago, before the railway came and took away the sea trade, they were all full of hemp and jute and rope, and the linchets on the hills up the valley were blue with flax. All the rope for Nelson's ships* was made in Bridport, which for eight hundred years had maintained the same industry, so that " a Bridport dagger " became a proverbial saying. (To be stabbed with that weapon—a halter—was the same thing as falling off a platform while engaged in conversation with a clergyman, and resulted in your dying in your stockings and being put to bed with a shovel.)

There is still great traffic in rope and twine in the clean town itself, two miles away. Its wide streets, because they were made spacious for the drying of yarn on their pavements, are the comeliest in Dorset. But the glory is departed from the barns at the harbour. One ship, before the war, still came specially from Russia every year with hemp : almost all the other boats that blunder between the piers are coasters bringing coal or timber, and going out with the exceeding fine shingle that the inexhaustible sea frets off the Chesil pebbles, and casts up year by year, without diminution, for the streets of cities and the manufacturer of concrete.

And lastly, to continue these haphazard clutches at the past, observe certain chapter-headings in Bridport town itself. Look at the Fives Court wall by the *Fives Court Inn* (now being obscured by a garage), for instance : this was built in 1847 by merchants of the town, who in those days kept, as in Dorchester and Blandford also, a social state of dignity and ordered well-being : they used, for example, to send their Madeira to Newfoundland (a great Dorset trade, three centuries old) and back, in their

* And the rope for King John's ships, and for Henry VIII's ships, and all and sundry ships of England : and much wire netting to catch the evil fish that came out of Germany in 1915 : and likewise lanyards for Jellicoe's bosuns. Moreover, to some extent, flax-growing has been revived : a ripple from the stone thrown into world-markets by the Russian Revolution.

own ships, to mature it. Or the local ironwork railings on the Harbour Road : there is no iron ore near here ; they are a century old. Or the decent Town Hall. Or the magnificent collection of Borough records (Bridport had a mint in the days of Athelstan).* Or the open-air rope-walks. Or the warning, just outside the town, that anyone who damages the county bridge will be transported for life— signed by an official whose family surname under George III began with a capital F, but now begins with ff. Or a thousand other odd and discrepant vestiges of creation.

I want to know what such things mean, and their relative significance in time ; what expression they really are of the spirit of man, and where man has got to in this one piece of England. It seems to me that I may be able to guess more nearly what the progress of mankind has been (if there has been any progress) by visualizing it in a single county (and in a county of which I love every inch) ; by trying to find out with what intention our forefathers built or fought or lived since man came into England, and what kind of Dorset the first man in it and the generations after him have found and altered.

* Almost, but not quite, certainly. It is not determined whether Bredy (up the Bride valley) was not the "town" so honoured, though if so its glory departed very quickly.

II

" It is a question if the exclusive reign of orthodox beauty is not approaching its last quarter. The new Vale of Tempe may be a gaunt waste in Thule : human souls may find themselves in closer and closer harmony with external things wearing a sombreness distasteful to our race when it was young. The time seems near, if it has not actually arrived, when the chastened sublimity of a moor, a sea, or a mountain will be all of nature that is absolutely in keeping with the moods of the more thinking among mankind. And ultimately, to the commonest tourist, spots like Iceland may become what the vineyards and myrtle gardens of South Europe are to him now ; and Heidelberg and Baden be passed unheeded as he hastens from the Alps to the sand-dunes of Scheveningen."

THOMAS HARDY.
The Return of the Native.

" BROADBENT (*stopping to snuff up the hillside air*). Ah ! I like this spot. I like this view. This would be a jolly good place for a hotel and a golf links. Friday to Tuesday, railway ticket and hotel all inclusive."

GEORGE BERNARD SHAW,
John Bull's Other Island.

II

BEFORE THE FLOOD

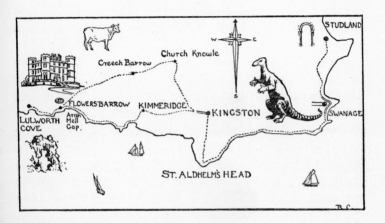

STRICTLY speaking, I suppose, the history of man in Dorset should begin with a conjectural account of the origin of all life—with the atom, the ion, the amœba, the nebular hypothesis, and a view of the (till lately) infinite space where stars grow into worlds. But (praise be!) I know nothing of world-physics, nothing of astronomy, nothing even of astrology; I cannot so much as cast a horoscope, which seemingly almost any clerk in the Middle Ages could achieve. In this book, therefore, I shall speak of the celestial universe (three- or four-dimensioned space and its contents) no further than to point out, upon this opportunity, that the monkish clock in Wimborne Minster is wrong when it alleges in a pantomime, as it has alleged for six hundred years past, that the sun travels round the earth.

But if one pretermits these huge speculations, it is still

impossible to deny all reference to the grim science called
geology ; least of all in a county which has given a world-
name to three notable formations. Moreover, the rocks in
Dorset are a chronicle open and clear. Not only do Dorset
folk use in many ways the stones of the time before the
Flood ; not only do the foundations of the county contain
the tremendous mystery of man's first appearance ; but the
cliffs and the hills and the valleys are themselves a chronicle
of past wonders, now plainly visible. They are as insistent
as an earthwork or a ruined castle. Here, then, shall be a
journey through the old time before our oldest fathers.

The most ancient " rocks " in the county—more venerable
far than man—are the cliffs of Charmouth and Lyme
Regis, and the meadows of Marshwood Vale. The epochs
that went to create them must have been much longer than
all time since. Next upon the stairway of the years stand
the most important of all the county's strata. From
Portland comes the stone that creates the soft shadows of
St. Paul's Cathedral ; from Purbeck the grey columns of
Westminster Abbey, and the splendour of the west front
of Wells Cathedral.

But mankind was not extant when those rocks took shape.
There were thrown up next the glorious chalk hills. On
the chalk the shepherd is able to exercise the first and oldest
art of subjugation. In the high downs—higher, nobler
in Dorset than in the more-praised dominion of Sussex—
rise the scores of streams that the dairies need ; and upon
the sweet turf feed myriads of comely sheep ; the true
horned sheep of Dorset, a valiant and fertile stock with an
old pedigree, the envy of less happier lands, the ornament
and treasure of the green slopes. And in those slopes also
the dominant race of earliest Britain cut its vast and
enduring citadels.

But man was still not born in England even " when first
the hills in order stood." There are clays and sands older
than he. The white earths of Stoborough Heath, which for
generations the Five Towns have drawn from Dorset for

their craft of pottery, were formed ages before the only creature that has learnt how to use a thumb : near here also is the best clay for long churchwarden pipes. Lower down the Dorset slopes, by the rivers and marshes, is the poor kingdom of land that alone is coeval with mankind. There, where still the winds and the streams change by little and little the infirm water-courses, stretches the new-built earth that is man's twin. All else was old and established before any human voice was heard in the fantastic world of continental England.

For that is the unimaginable condition of the beginning of man's life in Dorset—a condition whose results still govern that life. The county lay formerly upon no sea : it was part of a lost Atlantis. How long and how often it was joined to Europe not even the geologists will say with certainty. Twice at least it was submerged beneath the waters, to rise again with land where now the grey warships ride. It was in turn arctic and tropical. Whole generations of living things were born : the earth shook and was opened, and when the torment was past the living things were rock.

At some time in that ebb and flow of terror man appeared in England : Eolithic man. We do not know if he is our direct ancestor : there is in England no link found between him and the later, yet incalculably old, generations of Palæolithic and Neolithic man. We only know that he had to strive against a power we cannot so much as describe : the full might and fury of Nature herself. To Nature fell the victory. Never again in England did she prevail so completely.

Dorset seems to hold a record of that first defeat. Upon the Ordnance Survey's gay and pretty geological map, in the very heart of the county, there is a bright pink speck in the midst of the green stripes that stand for chalk. It is unique, and has a name peculiar to itself. It is called " Elephant Bed of Dewlish " : perhaps the finest achievement of any science in the way of mixed homeliness and romance.

All that is left of the elephants who slept in that bed their last sleep is in Dorchester and Salisbury Museums. The immense curving tusks are over six feet long. They are imperfect : in life they must have measured more than eight feet. The molars are like great lumps of rock. They belonged to the elephant known as *Elephas meridionalis*, the Elephant of the South : by whose presence in our island we know that England must then have had a warm climate. He vanished from the face of the earth in the Pliocene Age.

Close by the remains of these monstrous creatures were found some little chipped flints. They have been thought to be the possessions of Eolithic man. With those feeble weapons he must fight for life against such beasts, with those poor tools he must conquer the hard earth : and but for them we might not know even that he had ever existed in this part of England.*

He vanished, too, like the Elephant of the South. Before Palæolithic man appeared, there was another vast transformation of the earth's face, and England was islanded for a time. Then once more man, Palæolithic man, appears ; in Dorset he has been traced on the Devon border and at Wimborne. Then again came the cold, and the land rose up from the waters, until, by stages not to be numbered certainly, the last great breach with Europe occurred. Man in England had viewed the promised land, but he might not possess it—might not leave upon it the marks which afterwards Neolithic man made ineffaceably in Dorset—until the triumphant sea had torn the cliffs of Purbeck and Portland into walls against itself.

I think the lowest of the many computations I have seen of the duration or evolution of the three Stone Ages in England is 139,000 years. The Neolithic Age ended for us about 2000 years before Christ ; hardly 4000 years ago. If in 135,000 years from now England grew too cold for

* We do not really know, so far as Dorset is concerned. The flints are now said not to have been worked by man. But the Elephant is authentic, and, like the mocking-bird in Mrs. Trimmer's *Robins*, had better remain here " for the sake of the moral."

human life, how much of our civilization would be left for those who at length came back, as perhaps Neolithic man came back, from the warmer zones of the south ? I know that it is a vain speculation ; and the years of geologic time are beyond the mind's comprehension. Yet it is some such indescribable and terrifying immensity as this that the Dewlish flints and Purbeck and Portland stones imply : an immensity containing even the reversal or the dethroning of all that we mean by man's dominion alike over organic and inorganic nature.

Once, from near Dewlish itself, I looked up to the hills and saw as it were a travesty of that antique strife. There was an empty lane climbing the hill between hedges, and the day shone with the hard brightness of spring before the buds have opened. I had grown tired of roads, and looked to the top of the ridge with hope. Suddenly there appeared over the clean line of road the head of a mounted man, with a black cap ; and then a red coat and then the multitudinous waving sterns of hounds ; and after that more red coats and fine horses, ambling easily, first one, then another, and pairs, and at last a host, every one coming into sight like the units of an army—terrible as an army with banners, for had they not killed the fox ? It was a gay sight, a triumphant simplicity, this famous Cattistock Hunt ; and yet it seemed also a parody of that remoter, huger war that had once taken place in those very hills, when all the odds were not upon the hunter. What if the fox, in a million years, had conquered Nature, and made man as the elephants of Dewlish ?

Any man can see in a reasonable walk* most of that geological pageant which I have just suggested ; and he need not trouble himself much about geology, for the places themselves speak in a good comprehensible tongue of their own.

---

* By " reasonable walk," or indeed by " walk " alone, I mean now and hereafter any distance from twelve to thirty miles, according to circumstances. For further details see the Appendix I. In the present case I suggest also the goal of an alternative walk.

c

Begin at Poole Harbour, where the sands and heather and
brambles stretch from the western bank into Studland
Heath and Little Sea. Here, at the outset, the unstable
foreshore performs, by way of forecast, the still unended
miracle of earth-building. A bunch of whin near an inlet
will suddenly hold together a small island of sand : the
wind comes, and lo ! a grass-topped hill in a yellow desert.
The waters slowly push the sand higher, scooping their
own shallow channel a little deeper ; and so, in a few
centuries of minute toil, there is formed a delicate con-
tinent of dunes, whose shape and colour change without
ceasing.

The waters too have simple proofs here of the unhuman,
almost inhuman tasks accomplished by Nature alone.
Poole Harbour, Lytchett Bay, Arne Bay, Wareham Channel
are now pied with islets of stubborn grass, like molehills on
a flat meadow. A gull or a heron may make them his throne
while he rests a few minutes from the search for food,
thinking highly, doubtless, of the Providence that in the last
few years has suddenly set up these inns for his sojourning.
But there is a stranger wonder in the green tufts than the
mere convenience of birds. The grass comes from America,
and with it the New World is rebuilding the Old. A few
seeds of an American grass chanced to come by ship, it is
said, into Southampton Harbour : and by chance, too, they
so fell that they took root ; and now all the flats of water in
that region are filled with the quick-growing sturdy weed,
and the channels are being narrowed and deepened more
securely than man could compass.

It is almost a battlefield, this little strip of coast : sea
against land, man against both. At its westernmost curve
the waves are daily triumphant. Here, beneath Handfast
Point, stands Old Harry. By his side formerly stood also
his long-faithful consort, Old Harry's Wife, a second un-
gainly pillar of chalk. But the subtle, indefatigable sea
plucked at her robes continually, and slid away her foundations, till suddenly she dissolved into the waters, and was

but a heap of diminishing white lumps. Even so will her lorn spouse presently perish.

That cruel deed must have been the revenge of Ocean ; for Studland Heath before that had robbed him not less cruelly. In the waste of sand and lagoons on the Heath, lies the enclosed mere named Little Sea. In Ralph Treswell's Tudor map it is an arm of the great sea, upon which swim swans and ducks and what appear to be pelicans of a pro-digious bigness ; but now the land has imprisoned it, and there are no pelicans. Men say that in its still depths is buried Excalibur, flung there by Sir Bedivere against his will ; and indeed the brown marsh is a ghostly place, where in the twilight the most knightly soul might forget his vows.

There is power in this strange and lovely place : a power not only of beauty beyond description, not only of legend, but of some spiritual force as well. It may be only some trick of light and colour, such as sometimes you get in the Welsh hills or on Romney Marsh. There is contrast enough here for any illusion of the sight : the white cliff of Vectis standing stiffly out at sea, the gold and silver of the sand, the blue and white and grey water, the profound dykes, the heather and pines—all these are played upon by sun and wind and cloud without hindrance to the line of sight, until not twice running will a view appear the same : and in turn the hues play upon the eye of the mind, so that as the wraiths of old chivalry pass dimly, and faint echoes ring in the brain from the forlorn passions and hopes of the knightly years, the whole world and he who regards it from Studland Heath are subdued into a sombre union, an ecstasy of loneliness.

Another legend and another fragment of earth-history lie close at hand. Westward of Little Sea the shaggy heath begins to grow upon clay, coeval with man, and not now shifting and unstable like the sand. In the midst of its wildness are set two great alien stones, the Agglestone and the Puckstone. Legend says that the Devil, having taken a hatred of Corfe Castle, threw these stones at it (from his natural home in some Isle of Wight watering-place), and they fell short. The stories told by scientists are less interesting and not much more plausible. But by any account the Agglestone and the Puckstone are older than their resting-place, and older than man.

From the Heath one comes into the geologically older world of Purbeck. But at this point, he who walks comes upon a serious obstacle. He climbs up to Ballard Down, and sees at his foot a rather large and offensive town, stretching up every valley, full of grievous things : houses built to appear important to unimportant persons ; sham half-timber, eruptive and incongruous glass of many colours, ironwork and paint of the Public Baths and Washhouses Period, cornices that bear no weight, bedizened doors, gables in number like the tents of an army.

Not that Swanage is wholly vile, however. The old pond, and a few grey and white houses of a grave and stubborn homeliness, and the new church, and the harbour, and its seemly Georgian hotel — these have reticence and character.

It is with mixed feelings that after crossing the town one looks back at the unseemly parodies of architecture which climb Durlstone Head. They are, after all, man's victories over Nature in a land where victory has not been easily won. As you pass them, you will see many invitations to the Caves of Tilly Whim. Defy the warning of experience of watering-places : go to these alleged caves. They are not caves :* they too are a battleground. They are disused quarries, worked by the Company of Marblers of Purbeck (a vigorous trade gild or union) many years ago, before they

---

* Nor is Tilly Whim, strictly, their name. They are Tilly's Whim Quarries. Tilly was one of the first to use a crane, or whim, some two hundred years ago : an effort of progress which doubtless Dorset under the Georges regarded placidly as the summit of mechanical skill. But the quarries here have not been worked now for a century past. (See *A Royal Warren*, by C. E. Robinson. Privately printed.)

migrated to other galleries. In the silent workings are all the secrets and all the spirit of an immemorial craft. Men have riven and split the stone in the same way, with the same tools, perhaps since imperial Rome set up marble where before were only the wattle huts of the Celts. There is something indescribably hard and penetrating, yet venerable also, in the grey unchanging masses : they have almost a life—they could speak with the voice of old Time himself, and tell of all the humble hopes, the anger, the joyful strength, the caprices, from which they suffered blows : of all the nameless men now more still than the very dust of the quarry.

Yet even the stones are not wholly dumb. Here have been found many still undefaced records from the dimmest antiquity—fishes of strange shapes, and vast turtles, fit dwellers in such a place and such an epoch as formed Purbeck marble : and one trace of life more romantic, even, than the elephants of Dewlish. It is the footmark of an iguanodon ; one print only, a shamrock-like impress of a huge lizard's foot, twelve inches or so across, left when the rock that now is so painfully carved was but soft mud. It is like the footprint upon Crusoe's island, solitary, un-related, full of terror : but it is from no mere sea that it comes ; it is stamped high and dry above the tide-mark of time itself.

On the lonely hills towards St. Aldhelm's Head, there is a desolation no less suggestive of the beginnings of the earth, though it is in reality a man-made solitude. The coarse grass is strewn with great shaped boulders, like the ruins of a giant's palace. There are strange holes in the turf, de-cayed walls, little deserted stone shelters where once the smaller blocks were shaped and stacked ; brambles and nettles are everywhere, and no smooth surface anywhere. It might be the workshop or rubbish heap of a world-builder. It is but a deserted quarry, left haphazard as though the marblers had fled in some sudden fear. It is strangely full of the atmosphere of awe, like the grisly " chapel " where

once Sir Gawain must abide the three strokes of the Green
Knight :

> " Wild it seemed to him ;
> He saw no sign of resting in that place,
> But high steep rocks on either side the dale,
> Rough knuckled boulders, rugged stones and rocks,
> With shadows full of terror . . .
> ' I wis', quoth Gawain, ' wilderness is here :
> This is an ugly grass-grown place of prayer,
> Where well that Knight in green might pay his vows,
> And do his reverence in the devil's way.' "

At last, after a league of desolation, comes St. Aldhelm's
Head—St. Alban's or St. Aldhelm's, as the Ordnance map
observes punctiliously ; but St. Alban had no commerce
with Wessex. The promontory of the great Saxon bishop
Aldhelm is as it were the pivot or apex of the Isle of Purbeck.
It is an impregnable salient thrust into the sea. Near its
summit the two hard rocks, Purbeck marble and Portland
stone, are broken off ; except for a little strip near Worbarrow Bay, they are not seen again on the coast until
Portland itself rises up at the western end of the wide
curve of the cliffs.

The Headland, perhaps, does not fasten itself upon the
imagination as do certain other seaboard places of Dorset :
at any rate in calm weather. But in the wind and the rain,
when the south-westerly tempest blows clear across the
Atlantic into the narrow groove of the Channel, it is glorious.
The rock seems to join the sea in the war against their
common conqueror. How many tall ships, through the
ages, have been blown safely past the Start, past the terrible
race of Portland, almost into the peace of Christchurch
Bay, to be broken to splinters upon Dancing Ledge or
Anvil Point ?* Out of the innumerable company of their
dead would rise the armadas of nations long vanished, of
empires from whose numb hands sea power departed
countless generations ago. Every race and every tongue

* One almost as I wrote these words.

of Europe would be found there, in ships of strange rig, the little brave creeping ships of the old world.

The low, strong Norman chapel on the headland is by tradition a record of one such disaster. A father, in 1140, it is said, saw his son drowned in a gale before his eyes, and set up this little four-square house of prayer to be at once a beacon-holder and a chantry for the souls of sailors.

There is a change in the pageant of the rocks at the Headland itself. The hard stone ceases and gives place to what seems a more kindly land. Below the cliff is a round blue pool and a gorse-embroidered valley ; beyond, yet another valley, full of trees, and then hill after hill cut short by the sea, until, far away, the cliffs end in a dying fall at the sunset. Instead of the bleak quarries, there comes, after a patch of shale, a great stretch of chalk downs.

If you are walking westwards from here, you can choose either of two routes ; close to the coast, through Kimmeridge, or along the inner chalk ridge, over Creech Barrow. By the Kimmeridge route Encombe Glen (below the House) must be avoided ; ill-behaved trippers have caused it to be closed to the public. But the coast can be reached again near Smedmore, east of Kimmeridge.

The geologist takes great delight in Kimmeridge. The shale ledges are older even than the Purbeck and Portland stones ; and the wrinkled sea that slides over their grey, oily layers hides dreadful things that the earth has done— geological faults, lapses from regularity, highly original sins which make science a ghoulish joy. Are they not recorded and pictured in the Museum of Jermyn Street ?

Man converted the Purbeck and Portland rocks to his use by sheer force. Kimmeridge shale is too subtle for force. This black little piece of coast, grimy, slippery, unfriendly is a record of curious futilities undertaken in many generations. The earliest identifiable men, those of the Stone Age, have left their tokens here. They worked the shale and made ornaments of it ; and made also other things the meaning of which is even now not certainly

known.　Kimmeridge " coal-money " consists of round
discs with symmetrical piercings.　Legend says they are
coins.　They have been found in circumstances that prove
them to be at least pre-Roman.　Some cold-blooded
persons of to-day assert that they are merely the end-cores
thrown aside from the lathe, which was beyond doubt used
by Celt and Roman for making their beautiful vases and
other wares of shale.　But against this is the strange fact
that in many places the " money " has been found carefully stored in cinerary urns.　Here is a riddle set by a
vanished sphinx.　The tokens are almost like what Mr.
Edmund Gosse's father imagined fossils to be—devices
contrived by the Creator, with immemorial prescience, to
tempt later scientists into impious speculation.

That industry, whatever its meaning, was succeeded, two
thousand years or so later, by a less reputable trade.　The
Abbey of Cerne possessed this coast, and with it the right
to benefit from wreckage ; a right which is said to have been
extended, at any rate once, under Henry VII, to the provision of material for its exercise.　And then, in a less
fierce age, came the Clavells of Smedmore, of the lineage of
Walter de Clavile, an authentic comrade of the Conqueror.
Greatest of the family, perhaps, was that Tudor Sir William
who is buried in Kimmeridge Church :

> " Within this marble casket lies
> He who was learned, stout, and wise,
> Who would for no expense conceal
> His projects for the common weal,
> And when disloyal Irish did
> Rebel against the Queen their head,
> Approved valour then did get
> Him the reward of Banneret."

The deeds and customs of the Elizabethan squires of
Dorset are matters for a later chapter.　Here my interest
is only in man's general conquest of the earth's fabric.
Sir William believed that it would be " for the common
weal," to say nothing of his own profit, to work the alum

in the shale. This industry, " by much cost and travail, he
brought to a reasonable perfection." But a monopoly of
alum had been granted to other men, who seized his works.
Thereupon, being one " whom one disaster dismayeth not "
—and he met many disasters of a financial kind—he set
up a glass-house and a salt-house, and made " at his own
charge, with great rocks and stones piled together, a little
quay." A fragment of the little quay long after jutted
forlornly towards the sea, with never a boat or a mariner
to wake the echoes of its stones. Once it was populous with
wild and terrible figures : for Clavell's workmen, by reason
of " the offensive savour and extraordinary blackness " of
the shale they burnt in their furnaces, appeared " more like
furies than men."

The toil and hopes of Clavell died with him, and nearly
two hundred years later even his quay came almost to
nothing ; for the sea beat upon the stones and wrecked the
pier, so that it could no longer be used even for chance
traffic. All the industry that was left to Kimmeridge in
the eighteenth century was the working of the shale as a
kind of coal, which was sold at six shillings a ton. It burnt
hotly ; and it also, in the words of science, " liberated
sulphuretted hydrogen," so that here too Nature had her
revenge. . . .

Yet her enemy was indefatigable. In the nineteenth
century certain Gauls devised a new assault. They built a
little railway, and a fresh quay, and set to work to distil
oil, gas, and ammonia from the shale. They failed : they
could not purify the stubborn substance sufficiently.
Twice or thrice was this effort made, and it is said that now
once more men are to attempt it. But all that the wayfarer on the coast to-day can see is the dismal skeleton of
enterprises long ago disappointed and abandoned, a little
broken fortress of man's hopes, and the sly, slow triumph
of the eternal earth and sea.

From Kimmeridge one comes to Tyneham and Worbarrow, and joins the alternative westward route, which

from St. Aldhelm's Head runs to Kingston. At Kingston the two churches are landmarks: the older one of poor Georgian Gothic, the newer one a masterpiece of the Municipal Style. From this village the way lies due west, through Lord Eldon's park. Take the middle path. West of the park, go across country northwards to Church Knowle. Turn west again, and a little way past a very humble inn you will see a path (unmapped) on the right hand; which brings you to a silver road winding uphill. When you have reached the top of the ridge, Creech Barrow stands up like a mountain.

To reach the summit you must go round a long smooth valley. It is well to refrain from looking at the view until the highest point is attained, for it is then the most perfect of surprises to look suddenly north and east and south and west; but even if you have forfeited that surprise by looking about you as you climbed, you can still look long and behold always new beauty. Once there was a hunting lodge of the Angevin kings here; a few stones are left. Upon Ralph Treswell's map it is shown as it were a spacious temple; and indeed a man might search his soul in solitude upon Creech Barrow, and fall a-worshipping the power that spread the world out beneath his feet; for it is no less than a mirror of the world that stretches every way to the limit of sight—the world that has waited for mankind.

It is to the north and east that old Time is made visible. Here lies a shrunken atomy of the last great earth-cataclysm in the history of England. Far below the green and golden slopes of the hill is a brown wilderness through which, with innumerable tributary streams and isolated pools, run two broad rivers, gleaming strangely in their cold, bright windings. The flats are sombre and still, but the waters, issuing at last together into the Channel, have a quiet power and vitality as of never-ending life.

When those rivers ran in their fullest pride, Dorset was not Dorset, nor England England. Look to the north-west. A long ridge of hill, tree-topped, is the horizon, fifteen miles off. Half-way up the slope, concealed in the blue pale distance, is Dewlish. When man faced the elephant there, the Frome and the Piddle were not silver threads, but a broad flood running into that yet more tremendous stream which is now the English Channel. The Stour, Hampshire Avon, and the Solent were tributaries of that same enormous river : and the rivulets that run north- wards from the ridge, hurried more turbidly past Avalon to a huger Severn. All this land was a causeway of waters roaring to an unimaginable torrent. The shining cliffs of the Isle of Wight stand up like their gateway.

River and heath and sea are still marshalled by the great gesture which swept Dorset into its present shape. The older hills, the chalk and the shale and the limestones, were an amphitheatre for the battle between land and water ; the lowlands seem to be but the shrivelled ramparts and trenches of the conflict itself. When it ended, England was kindly once more. Poole Harbour dwindled into a quiet estuary ; the floods towards Somerset were slowly diminished into marsh-land, and so, at last, within the memory of mankind, into meadows ; the green things that we know familiarly grew upon the earth ; and our veritable father, man from whom we trace unbroken descent, was found in Dorset.

Behold also from Creech Barrow a picture of his kingdom thenceforward to now. Twenty miles away, upon a high hill which yet, in a clear atmosphere, is not the horizon by another twenty miles, is a straight pillar ; it commemorates Nelson's Hardy. Beyond is fold upon fold, the strong kingdom of the fort-building Durotriges, men of power two thousand years ago. Beyond again, on a clear day, Devon can be seen. A little south lies Portland, resting upon the sea like the happy realm of the Phæacians, a shield prone ; or more truly, a stone cold and brutish, justly set apart in the inhospitable ocean.

Follow with your eye the path the sun would tread if he obeyed the Wimborne clock. Lewsdon and Pilsdon, the

one hairy, the other smooth, like Esau and Jacob, stand up
in the north-west, thirty miles distant, and more. East
of them a clump of trees crowns a ridge ; it is High Stoy,
of which Hardy has written that if it had met with an
insistent chronicler, it " might have been numbered among
the scenic celebrities of the century." Where the middle-
north ridge ends, more hills jut out, one behind the other.
The round ball far off is Melbury Down, that looks upon and
is seen magically from the hill-town of Shaftesbury. Walking four miles an hour, you could reach it in seven hours.
To the right is yet another clump of trees on a hill : a holy
place, a grove as high in the story of England as in the county
of Dorset : Badbury Rings, where, maybe, Arthur fell.

And so to newer things again : Charborough Tower,
where Lady Constantine, of *Two on a Tower*, was enchanted by her young astronomer : and that other tower
of Christchurch on the western horizon, whispering faintly
the enchantments that populous trim Bournemouth, near
at hand, can neither recover nor forge. And white and
silver at your very feet gleam the potter's clay-fields, with
their toy railways and their pools of indescribable blue and
green. No authentic sound comes up to the height from
them, and the trains that glide evenly to Corfe and Wareham
move but with a faint ghostly postponed murmur, like an
echo of some more immense labour long ended.

All these things, in one way or another, will come again
into the story now to be written of man's life on the soil of
Dorset : here is but a pageant or prophecy of them. They
are visible enough, emblematically, in Purbeck to-day ;
they stand there for the human victories of æons.

It is hard to leave this noble hill. And yet, leaving it,
be comforted ; for you will see nine-tenths of the same
glorious vision for three miles to come, as you march westward upon the windy edge of space. There is something
in the turf of these chalk downs that quickens life, and
makes the long cool shadow of the valley villages and trees
seem a paltry thing, an artifice of comfort and littleness.

The dry sweet grass tinkles as with a thousand tiny cymbals ; the snail-shells, violet, orange, pink, flaming white, are jewels from Aladdin's cave, the scabious and the daisy coloured stars in a green heaven. Every step, like Antæus his overthrows, gives back some of the earth's own vitality, and one seems to be marching upon a road glistening still with the dews of dawn, made firm with the pride of midday, and ending in the golden sunset gates of a kingdom where youth is for ever lord.

Yet this very exhilaration has behind it something sober and earthy and human, something that dignifies and ennobles rest after toil. There is no ale, no cider, no cheese so good as that in a warm dusky village into which a way-farer stumbles from the heights. There is no tolerance so large and kindly as that which comes from a little ease in such a nest of apparent indolence. Look down upon the hamlets in the valley of Corfe river. There is Barneston Manor ; its stones stood in the same place, the stones of Barneston Manor still, when Edward III was king. There is the old cruciform church of Church Knowle. There is Steeple, where a Tudor squire rests in a complacent tomb, having done his duty quietly and long ; and hard by lies buried an artist-poet of once slightly alarming bodlihead. There is Tyneham, where the old family that built Bond Street still abides. North are other manors, thick copses, white-flagged railway trains ; and a delicious " gate " leading from nowhere to nowhere, built strongly of lime and stone in a German Gothic manner. All these things seem natural and eternal, so beneficent is the highway of the chalk. They are part of a world in which, to a Radical, Conservatism may well appear the creed of Utopia, rather than the abhorred dogma of the Primrose League. The faith is too good to be changed : so it has always been, so it shall always be. Forget the quarries, the waste and horror of the antediluvian earth ; forget the obscene shale, the wrecker monks, the oil-traders. " Allons ! to that which is endless as it was beginningless. . . ."

But in a little while you will find the end comes. Just
beyond Tyneham there is a low gap in the sea-wall, and a
grey knob of cliff protrudes into the sea. Its westernmost
end rises up into a great hill, upon which the coast path from
Kimmeridge and the track from Creech Barrow meet. It
is Ring's Hill, of which the highest part is adorably named
Flowersbarrow (" Flowersbarrow " . . . Are we a prosaic
nation ? Once it may have been called Florus' Byrig).

It is a strange and tremendous hill. On the very top of
it is the last thing you would expect to find in a place so
remote and so inaccessible ; a huge earthwork, five hundred
and sixty-seven feet above a sea which needs no bulwark. It
guards the very end of the Isle of Purbeck. A chalk ram-
part shuts off all the stone and marble formations of the
Isle from the younger clays of the Frome Valley ; the Isle
really is an island, a geological fastness, whatever the
geographers, with their talk of water surrounding land,
may say to the contrary. And Flowersbarrow gives a
most extraordinary vision of that curious self-containment
of Purbeck. Just as from Creech Barrow could be seen the
primal path of the inner waters, so here can be seen, abrupt
and clean, the terrible achievement of the main Channel
stream. Purbeck is cut short, broken off sharp, at Arish
Mell Gap : the old world ends visibly. The sea will not here
give up the dead land.

Go through the camp, climb the three deep western
trenches, and begin to descend the slope. Right in front
stands up what appears, from here, to be a sheer green wall.
In reality, Bindon Hill is not sheer, but simply very steep
indeed. Its white edge is a straight line from the top to the
sea five hundred and fifty feet below. Between it and
Flowersbarrow is a smaller hill, perfectly rounded, like an
inverted bowl girt with a fairy ring. There is a little sheltered
gap at the western curve of this ring ; and from that gap
you look straight across to Portland, the brother land of
Purbeck, now for ever separated from it. There is nothing
between save water and a few grim rocks : Purbeck ends

in a grey blank wall : Portland stands upright eleven miles away : the quiet, insuperable waves hold them apart.

The tiny valley of Arish Mell (an old Celtic name) is a place of warm peace, where kine drift down from the meadows to the seashore itself. Their friendly brown coats are not the brightest colour here. The face of the coast, from Worbarrow Point to Mupe's Rocks, is like a many-hued puzzle, a geological jigsaw. The shingle is yellow and blue-grey : the down turf wears its eternal green : Bindon, its flank dark with pines, has a face of gleaming silver : but Ring's Hill contains every shade from scarlet to purple, while the little headland of Worbarrow is striped with contorted formations, of grey and drab and black. Mupe's dark rocks are of a threatening brown, with the white snow of waves at their base. I do not know whom this desolate and lovely place may most fully satisfy ; the geologist, the artist, the historian, the mere walker may all take delight in it : It satisfies always and fully. There is no emotion with which it is not in sympathy, no happiness which it does not glorify by its kindly peace and its austere beauty.

And so, over the great hill of Bindon along this cliff-edge to West Lulworth, where lobsters die in readiness and numbers for the wayfarer.

There is one other place in Dorset where the Earth's own past obtrudes itself, in a great view, upon one's thoughts about man's past and present. That is the summit of the highest cliff between the Wash and Land's End, Golden Cap. That glorious hill is known and loved by all Dorset men. It stands up with a peculiar boldness : a piled-up sloping mass, and then a bare stretch of yellow earth, crowned with a dark brown plateau. It can be seen from many a Dorset height ; from Blackdown, from Pilsdon, from Hooke, even from great Bulbarrow himself, thirty miles away : always it is the same—a straight flat line cutting the sky proudly, and a golden edge sloping steeply down.

The ascent of Golden Cap is a noble walk from Bridport or from Lyme, or in the journey from one to the other : though if you go the whole way—nine miles or so—you have to climb Charmouth Hill (500 feet), Stonebarrow Hill (500 feet), Golden Cap (619 feet), and Thorncombe Beacon (500 feet)—and descend to sea-level between each. Moreover, the last hundred feet up the Cap, whichever way you choose, is the worst stretch. It grows steepest there, and in summer the face of it is so slippery with desiccated grass, or so prickly with gorse, that the lost agility of Eolithic man would be a boon to-day. Beware also of rabbit snares—wire nooses strongly pegged into the ground. If you come from the east shun the lower undercliff, which looks less arduous as first ; here be quags and (in due season) serpents, as well as primroses and blackthorn and violets and blackberries.

When at last you come to the top, go across the plateau towards the south-west. Cast yourself down at the edge and dream. There are no history-lessons here : only a stillness, a poising of the soul, as of the body, over depths that bring the uttermost wonder of tranquillity. If you can bear it, look down :

> " The crows and choughs that wing the midway air
>   Show scarce so gross as beetles . . .
>   The murmuring surge,
>   That on the unnumbered idle pebbles chafes,
>   Cannot be heard so high."

Or if it can be heard, on this cliff by comparison with which Shakespeare's would be a paltry ledge, the sound is but the caress of a kindly mother visiting your sleep ; a wistful charity in which any man might find peace. What is man in that superb isolation ?

It is always of long-established peace, to me, that Golden Cap whispers. So high, so far, so lonely, you cannot be

LULWORTH COVE

From a painting by Allan Gwynne-Jones

in the world. Why, the very gulls and daws that are floating below you are yet five hundred feet above land. The sea itself could not rage here : the huge arc of cliffs holds out arms to calm it. Portland is not rock now : it is but a grey shadow. West Bay piers look the toys that in truth they are. And inland there is only a glowing ember of the earth's old fires : one of those flushing forests of the fire that hold shepherds and sheep and trees and all pastoral delights. The smooth roundness of Langdon Hill is red with heather and warm with golden gorse : the dark firs are unburnt coal : and there are (or once there were) shining flecks of cold ash—white rabbits at large upon the green and purple : and dead gorse standing for calcined coal. Far off there brood two great beasts, the slow ruminant backs of the Cow and her Calf, as sailors used to name the shapes of Pilsdon and Lewsdon Hills.

But if you go westwards a little you come back to geology, and in its most romantic form. On Golden Cap you have for a moment been on chalk. Then a little way down you are on the Middle Lias, and then on the Lower Lias. You are in the land of dragons. And the cliffs and the shore are full of dead bodies : fossils of all kinds.

These cliffs between Lyme and Golden Cap are unique in the whole world, for here took place a meeting that can never be repeated, a recognition the most uncanny in the history of the earth. In 1811 a child of twelve, daughter of a carpenter and curiosity-monger of Lyme Regis, caught sight of some strange bones in the blue cliff. Having some knowledge of fossils already, Mary Anning caused these bones to be dug out carefully. She was the first known human being, since the very beginning of time, to look upon a fish-lizard, or ichthyosaurus. No man has ever seen one alive : she first saw one dead. A few years later she also first beheld a plesiosaur, and in 1828, a flying dragon, or pterodactyl. Fossils of little creeping things, sponges, waving plants, worm-like curly insects, or humble organisms whose dust is now stone—these man had discovered already.

D

and was beginning to name. But the monstrous beasts of these cliffs were something more, something new—the creatures of a past not merely remote, but wholly alien and terrible. Some perhaps were fierce, as menacing to man, perhaps—had they survived to meet him—as the sabre-toothed tiger or the mammoth. Most of them were probably of a mild nature and unwarlike equipment, ill-fitted for conflict with that puny destroyer. But none survived. The ground quaked : mountains and seas of which no chart can ever be made were confounded : and the earth destroyed her hugest children.

That is the grim vision hidden beneath the primroses on the banks of the little streams below Golden Cap : a vision of a horror more tremendous than the most terrific earthquake or eruption of our calm day—of a fantastic breed of beasts upon a strange earth, and then, in the twinkling of an eye, obliteration : for in this, as in most other geologic changes, death seems to have been abrupt, as of a Roman soldier at Pompeii.

One generation telleth another : but there is no story like that told by the dragons to Mary Anning, for it is the story of all the generations. Look down, when you go over the last hill past Charmouth, upon little Lyme dreaming upon the sea, with its sturdy quiet Cobb and its dignity and decency. It is two and a half centuries since Lyme was in the full stream of history, save for a few hours when the survivors of the *Formidable* struggled ashore there. For twelve centuries and more before Monmouth's landing, strife went to and fro with hardly a break in Lyme, as elsewhere in Dorset. For three hundred years before that, again, there was the Roman peace, that first began for England in the generation of Christ's death. Before Christ there were ages of bronze and stone, while the Iberian and the Celt hammered out their civilization as slowly as one of them might hammer a flint axe. Yet when they strove man was old in England : in his Old Stone Age he had dwelt with and outlived the woolly rhinoceros, the grizzly, the mammoth. And yet again behind his dim shadow is a still dimmer figure—the lonely, tremendous figure of Eolithic man standing against what seemed a hopeless dawn.

The cliffs of Charmouth have seen all that strange pageant. They saw the dragons, too, and their catastrophe. In such a secular chronicle, man's history is but a short page : but in the shops of Lyme the dragons are merchandise.

III

" And it came to pass, when men began to multiply on the face of the
earth . . . that the Lord said, ' My spirit shall not always strive
with man, for that he also is flesh.' "

The Book of Genesis.

" But the iniquity of oblivion blindly scattereth her poppy, and deals
with the memory of men without distinction to merit of perpetuity.
Who can but pity the founder of the pyramids ? Herostratus lives
that burnt the temple of Diana, he is almost lost that built it ; Time
hath spared the epitaph of Adrian's horse, confounded that of himself.
In vain we compute our felicities by the advantage of our good
names, since bad have equal durations ; and Thersites is likely to
live as long as Agamemnon. Who knows whether the best of men be
known, or whether there be not more remarkable persons forgot,
than any that stand remembered in the known account of Time ? "

SIR THOMAS BROWNE,
Hydriotaphia.

THE HILLS OF THE DEAD

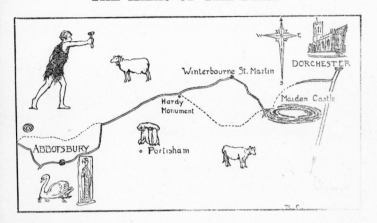

THE story of the rocks does not end with the death of the dragons; but when those monsters have vanished, and Eolithic man also has fallen back into the darkness out of which he rose so mysteriously, the story-teller has a new standpoint. He has to show what man made of the earth, and of himself, rather than what the earth inflicted on man. Man's life and progress are continuous henceforth.

It is at Dorchester, perhaps, more definitely than at any other place in England, that this continuity is visible. It is a town which has been a town ever since towns first were in England. Here every race that has lived in Britain has lived; and when you stand near where now the two railways join one another, you are standing upon a spot than which no place in this island has been for a longer time continuously inhabited.

It is beyond doubt, it seems, that either Maiden Castle (the Celtic Mai Dun, the High Fort) or Dorchester itself is the Dunium spoken of in Trajan's day by Ptolemy the geographer.   Dorchester is a palimpsest.   Its walls are Roman : in them the Roman bricks still inhere.   It is full of Roman pavements.   Maumbury Rings, the amphi- theatre, is in its present form Roman.   But recent excava- tions have shown that its circle was first cut in the Neolithic Age, and that even before that, in the dimmest antiquity, it held a deep Palæolithic shaft.*

Close to the present cemetery is a crowded Roman burial ground.   And Poundbury Camp—" round Pummery " —is said to be Danish : on little evidence, for Celtic and Roman remains have been found in its now rather confused lines : but the Danes once wintered there during a prolonged raid.   One other race also inhabited Pummery.   From 1914 to 1918 it was filled with German prisoners of war. It was curious to come across the hills of the dead round Dorchester, in the utter dark, and see this old fortress of the ravaging Danes blazing with search-lights ;   curious also—to me, in the company of an official propagandist cinematographer—to see sturdy Germans in bizarre patched uniforms laughingly loading sacks into waggons, with the shopkeepers of the eighteenth-century street looking on, and cheerful farm girls in breeches helping them.

Dorchester was a Saxon town after the Romans went, and had a mint under Athelstan.   It was sacked by Sweyn. It was Norman ;   there is a most gentlemanly Norman knight sculptured in Fordington church.   It was the home of men of worship and good lineage in the Middle Ages. The Archduke Philip lay at Sir Thomas Trenchard's house, just outside the town, in 1506.   It aided the Puritan settlers of Massachusetts, whose Dorchester, so to speak, is our Dorchester.   It had the plague as constantly as most

* It is not creditable to our national knowledge and traditions that only the most strenuous exertions at the last moment prevented a railway company from cutting clean through this meeting-place of the generations, and also from demolishing part of Poundbury Camp.

towns, heard the drums and tramplings of the Civil War, and suffered more terribly than any other place under the Bloody Assize. Defoe found it a place of singular dignity and charm. It was the scene of a peculiarly horrible execution in the eighteenth century. It bore a part in the Napoleonic wars. It tried those poor "conspirators" who are known (not quite accurately) as the Dorchester Labourers, and it housed the judges who in 1831 examined the heroes of the last peasants' revolt in England. William Barnes walked its streets, and it is the home of Thomas Hardy. If you seek continuous history, here, as Mr. Squeers said, is richness. The town and its doings will recur constantly in these chapters.

I shall deal later with the different stages in that long and still unended romance. It begins with man of the Old Stone Age. A journey from Dorchester to Abbotsbury and the hills round it shows us the lost kingdoms of the Iberian and the Celt : a kingdom that still can sway the mind of man.

It is when you set out for Maiden Castle, and begin to draw near to that immense stronghold, that the spirit of things very far off, very powerful, falls upon you. There is no time of year, no condition of light and shade, when the vast ramparts do not call up awe and wonder, and even pity : for the people who dug those trenches were a great race, and their power and their glory are utterly gone. But they live in soul. Maiden Castle, a thought made visible for ever, has still almost the strong power of a thought newly uttered into the world. To this day it dominates and hypnotizes.

I remember a certain winter's day when I walked out over the High Fort and was led, it seemed to me, very close to the mighty dead. Snow had fallen, a rare thing in South Dorset, and when I left the broad street where Rome's soldiers once marched, and took the footpath past where they lay asleep, the ice and thin crusted snow crackled under foot like artillery, so clean was the silence. The air

was clear, with the lowering dull glow of storm ; and indeed
before my journey's end I was to suffer many fierce sudden
showers. Now and then pale sunshine flickered for
a moment, but the light nearly all that afternoon
was sombre. There was little wind at first : the
atmosphere was wet and bitter, inimical to the blood of
man. The snow had ceased at midday : there had not been
enough to cause deep drifts, or cover the hills uniformly
with white. But all the corrugations were chalk-white,
and only a few peaks stood out dark where the snow had
not rested.

The northern escarpment of Mai Dun, a mile distant,
rose up like a low strong wall from the smooth-scooped
valley of Fordington Field. The valley itself was full of
mist, a faint luminousness exhaled from the ground after
the storm. It hid everything all round except a tall building
or a tree. Even so the Weald of Kent, seen from a height
on a favourable autumn morning, appears a grey sea with
little clear rocks emerging above it here and there. But
whereas the churches and trees of Kent recall the kindly
habitations of articulate-speaking men, Maiden Castle,
at that magical distance, seemed a very citadel of evil
wizards. Dark and sharp rose the fortified edges : the
streaks of white on the slopes marked out the labyrinthine
dykes with a plainness that was a threat. The fortress had
a personality, a strength not of this world. Even now, I
thought, in that grey stillness (for hardly a farm-hand was
abroad on such a day), strange races, our blood kindred
but the uttermost antagonists of our minds, might be
celebrating there their obscene rites, islanded by the mists
in their cold fortress, and cut off from knowledge of the so
changed world in which I was. They could live there easily
enough, and we in the street of to-day none the wiser.
Their beasts, their households, their prisoners (prisoners
of this century ? were there really no changelings now, no
witches, no demoniac possessions ?)—all alike would be
hidden in that vast arena, secure. The well in the midst

perhaps was frozen : but the slopes, frost-bound, would be unassailable, so that no enemy would come, and daring men might scurry down the steep southern wall to the stream. Only from one quarter, the western spur with its more gradual fall, could foes approach the hill from nearly its own level ; and there, maybe, the royal dead who lay in Clandon Long Barrow would put forth their grim and ghostly might, and give protection.

It is impossible not to feel a sense of awe and even of reverence in this amazing stronghold. It may be simple-minded to be impressed by mere size. But the huge size of Maiden Castle—it is the largest and finest Stone Age earthwork in the world—is a genuine part of its appeal. When the first little group of men who worked upon it began—5000 or more years before Christ—to chip the hard chalk with stone axes, they chose this site because it juts out like a promontory from the higher ridges into the river valley. They had a sure strategic eye. They looked out from the height on to fuller rivers, wider and wetter marshes, through a damper air. Beasts no longer found in England —the wolf, the wild cat, the beaver, the aurochs—were in those marshes. There were forests in many places where now the tamed cattle pasture.* Only in Mai Dun was safety.

There is little doubt that the fort was begun by the Iberian, perhaps in Late Palæolithic days. Generation after generation must have toiled at it ; thousands of hands must have been needed to cut five miles of trenches that for a great part of their three circuits of the hill are sixty feet

---

* Gen. Pitt-Rivers found a curious example of this on the county border, in excavating the Bokerly Dyke (which, however, is not a Stone Age relic, but a Roman-British defence against the Saxons). Its western end is " in the air," as the soldiers would say. When it was dug, however, it rested on the sheltering thickets known as Selwood Forest, now no longer existing except in small patches : it filled the gap between the Forest and Cranborne Chase. These ancient forests lasted long in some cases. Only five hundred years ago, it is said, a squirrel could travel all the five miles from Shaftesbury to Gillingham, by his own airy track from tree to tree, without ever touching the ground (here I use " forest " in the colloquial sense—a wooded place—not in the technical sense).

deep. Very possibly even the eight-fold cross trenches at the main entrance were the separate thoughts of successive chieftains. We know from the gradual betterment of the stone weapons that man was slowly growing into the mastery of mechanical things. But we do not know exactly when or where some unknown Bessemer forged the bronze that was to overcome the stone and give the Celts dominion in England. We know that there was trade with distant lands : amber from the Baltic has been found in Dorset Neolithic graves, and gold (perhaps from Wales) in Clandon Barrow hard by Maiden Castle. Man was beginning to live in society, therefore, not in small hostile units. We know that he could weave flax : linen still adheres to an axe-head found near here. But we cannot guess how quickly or slowly these changes came, nor how they spread, nor what stir they caused in our forefathers' time. We can only look at Maiden Castle, and see, in its symbolic green walls, the age-long wonder of man. " The number of the dead long exceedeth all that shall live."

From Maiden Castle on to Blackdown there are two ways—one by road, through Winterborne St. Martin (Martinstown), the other along the hills, past countless barrows, by a glorious track on soft close down turf. On that winter day I chose the road : the other way, however, is the better : it is one of the three best walks in Southern England.

Martinstown was utterly frigid and desolate. In summer it is very warm, and the little stream that runs along the main street is almost dry. That day the stream was truly a " winter bourne " : squadrons of ducks struggled with its flood. But bare though the wide comely street was, it was more human than the utterly lonely road beyond it. I seemed to be walking alone out of life into—what ? It was just as the stillness became most oppressive that I came upon a strange answer to the half-unasked question. I turned the corner of a high hedge and saw a little black wooden shed. In front of it were two figures standing by a rough table. They were short dark hairy men, in ragged clothes. They had knives in their hands, and they were bending over a third figure stretched upon the table : a naked pink figure.

For the moment I was back in the Stone Ages, looking on the horror of human sacrifice : a natural thing in that kingdom of the dead. But the two peasants were only scraping and cleaning a little pig.

The interminable gritty road seemed emptier than ever after that. Heavy clouds were coming up, and the air grew darker, as the cold wind increased in violence. I came to the last steep stretch up to the summit of the hill, as bare and bleak a place as you could find, where the earth itself is dark and stony and the green turf has almost ceased : only heather and bracken, briars and bilberries, will grow there. At the most exposed point the earth was all at once blotted out by a grey wall of hail.

I ran, battered and wet, to what shelter I could get in the lee of the great column set up in memory of Admiral Hardy. In a few moments the storm was over, and the sun shone suddenly at full strength. I looked out over sea and cliffs and meadows alight with peaceful happiness. I had come back from the dead past into life.

Life—that is what, by some curious inversion of feeling, the hills of the dead round Abbotsbury have always meant to me. The beauty and loneliness of them are informed with some spirit of human continuity, of the splendour and endurance of human effort.

Blackdown, however, is not so full of that spirit as the hills westward. It gives a spectacle of sharp contrasts, natural beauty, and comparatively recent history. The view is magnificent. All Devon down to Start Point can be seen on the clearest day : Dartmoor standing on the very far horizon. Eastward on a few days I have seen the white cliffs of the Isle of Wight, beyond Ringstead Cliff and the hump of Swire Head. North, the view is limited by the equally high ridge which is the backbone of Dorset, some ten or twelve miles away. South, Portland Harbour and its warships, eight miles off, seem on a clear day to be at your feet.

There is something Italian about this part of the coast. Tropical plants grow in the open : azaleas bloom in March : there is an infinite stretch of very blue sea with a very white thin fringe of foam for miles. The lower foothills stand up absurdly like the hills in an early Italian landscape, and the few trees are dark like olives against the bright green fields.

If you look back, you look upon death and desolation. They are still there as you walk westwards from the curiously impressive monument. But now they are directly parallel with country bearing that appearance of bright life which the sudden sunshine gave me on this winter walk : and in summer the contrast is stronger. On your left still lies the brilliant coast and the fertile land behind the Chesil Beach. On the right, as you go westwards from Blackdown, is the dark Valley of Rocks : a singular avenue of stones (I do not know whether they are a natural outcrop or not) which curves all along the floor of a noble valley, leaving a green path in the midst, up to the top of the hollow. They have a look of symmetry, of purposeful arrangement. They lead from a very city of tumuli and prehistoric remains, directly up through the curve (ceasing, however, at its end), towards the stone circle strangely named the Grey Mare and her Colts : and further, if you ignore modern plantations and fields (which here, in practice, I have found it to be difficult and painful to do, not to speak of illegality), to Abbotsbury Camp.

Past the Valley of Stones, you continue, as so often in Dorset, on a high ridgeway, with the same enchanting view, the same contrasting hills and valleys, on either side. You come above Portisham to a vast natural amphitheatre —one of the largest scoops in a chalk ridge I have ever seen. The road then curves down into Abbotsbury. But it is better to leave it and continue by an almost disused track along the southern edge of the ridge. This brings you within sight of (and finally beyond) Abbotsbury village and that beautiful Tudor seamark, St. Catherine's Chapel, and leads eventually to Abbotsbury Camp.

The Camp is an irregular triangle, following the contours in the main. A road has been cut at one end which may possibly have obliterated some of its original line : east of this road there are confused trenches and hummocks which look as if man might have shaped them. The lines of trench are fairly clear still, but their true depth and strength are hard to determine. Heather, bracken, and gorse have here had unlimited power. There is little turf. The rabbit is incredibly plentiful. My Bedlington once spent six hours continuously in chase : one down, t'other come on : to my great content. I say this without shame : he was doing national service. It is wrong that so splendid an earthwork should be let decay so heedlessly. The Camp is simply a rabbit warren with a covert or two planted just below it. The rabbits are mining it to atoms. The neglect can serve no useful purpose. There is no production here. The two or three slopes which look as if they might once have been cultivated have been allowed to revert to wilderness (one is a blue sheet of wild borage in the summer). It is true that a farm a little westward, close to the shore, on the lowest slope is called Labour in Vain. But at Abbotsbury Camp there can have been no labour, vain or fruitful, for long past, except for a little digging of flints.

Here, by the way, I was once granted the privilege of seeing and hearing the cuckoo sing both at rest and in flight. I testify that one did so before my eyes, perching in the copse north of the Camp and flying south-west over my head, all the time garrulous.

The Camp itself is to me almost the best-loved place in Dorset. Here one can lie in a nest of bracken and heather and dream all day in utter happiness. Even in winter there is a gentleness about the rough worn walls of the fort. In summer, when the whole West Bay sleeps in the sunshine, the loveliness and peace would bring rest to the most troubled mind.   Even if you look inland, instead of at the glorious curve of foam from Portland to Devon, the citadels of the Iberian and the Celt, the hills covered with trenches, tumuli, monoliths, stone and earthen circles, seem less grim. You can see from here almost the whole extent of the chief domain of the fort-building Durotriges, with whom even Vespasian (only a sub-commander then) had to fight many pitched battles before victory.   But the hills are no longer menacing.   The battles are over, the old races vanished save in our bodies and souls.   Bexington and Labour-in-Vain farms, the white-walled coastguard station, the tower of Abbotsbury Church are what we have reached after the centuries of strife and toil.

Yet are they after all greater and more stable achievements than this ruinous citadel that looks down on their apparent prosperity ?   Anywhere between here and Swyre you can trace the outline of fields once rich with crops, now conquered again by gorse and bracken : and likewise on the steep road down into Abbotsbury.   In Abbotsbury itself there are a hundred emblems of stranded pride.   The church has a Saxon carving of the Trinity : where is the Saxon Church ?   Where is its predecessor, the Celtic Church that the priest Bertufus, " in the verie infancie of Christianitie among the Britains," built at the bidding of St. Peter in a vision ?   Where is the monastery that when it was surrendered in 1539 was valued at over £400 a year ? Some of it is visibly built into the cottages of the village. Part is used as a stable.   Only the stone coffins of the Abbots and the noble Tithe Barn and the carp pond testify to its former greatness.   Even its customs are obscured.   The Barn has a chamber over the great door with windows looking both inwards and outwards—obviously for an overseer or clerk to tally the incoming tithes and keep the accounts.   " That's where the Monks starved themselves," I was told.

Where again to-day are the uses of St. Catherine's Chapel ? It is a seamark, true.   But who pays for masses for sailors

ST. CATHERINE'S CHAPEL, ABBOTSBURY

From a drawing by C. Dayes, 1802

in it ? Who in Abbotsbury knows anything now of the saint whose face shines so gravely and graciously in a piece of old glass in the church ?

There must have been among the Durotriges eager builders, fervent priests, fighting men who violated holy places as Abbotsbury Church was violated during the Parliamentary wars. There must have been humble toilers, happy lovers. Were they relatively (and that means absolutely, too) less happy, less prosperous, less comfortable than we ? Perhaps some later century will know : perhaps there may even be proof in the space between them and us, which I am now to traverse. Meanwhile the sunlight and the heather and bracken on the Camp can do away with all emotions but present happiness.

E

IV

" Excudent alii spirantia mollius aera
  (Cedo equidem), vivos ducent de marmore voltus,
  Orabunt causas melius, coelique meatus
  Describent radio et surgentia sidera dicent :
  Tu regere imperio populos, Romane, memento
  (Haec tibi erunt artes) pacique imponere morem,
  Parcere subjectis et debellare superbos . . .
  Sunt geminae Somni portae. . . ."

$$\text{PUBLIUS VERGILIUS MARO,}$$
Aeneis VI.

" Your new-caught, sullen peoples,
  Half-devil and half-child."

$$\text{RUDYARD KIPLING,}$$
The White Man's Burden.

IV

THE GREEN ROADS

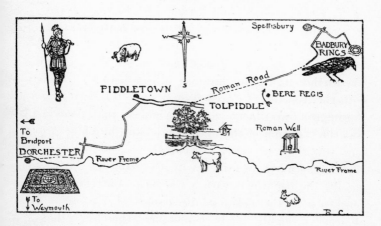

THE Roman roads in Dorset are curiously eloquent of the present as well as of the past. They show, because of their comparative unimportance in the strategic and commercial aspects, just what was real to Rome as to us. The chief Roman city in the county, Dorchester, was never of the first importance, nor was the great road that ran through it the main highway to the last outpost of the Empire in the west. There was, perhaps, a certain settlement of Romans in the county : but quota portio faecis Achaei ? How many were true Romans, how many adventurers of the outer races drawn into the Roman army, cannot be known. Apart from the idiosyncrasies of the roads, to which I shall return, the significant features of the Roman period in Dorset are three : the farm settlement in Cranborne Chase excavated by that great archæologist, Gen. Pitt-Rivers : the Bokerly

Dyke, which is neither pure Roman nor pre-Roman : and
the Chi-Rho symbol—the first two letters of the name of
Christ, in a monogram—in the mosaic floor uncovered at
Frampton.

It is perhaps simplest, from an historical point of view,
to start with the Chi-Rho. That emblem of Christianity
almost certainly shows that between the death of Christ
and about A.D. 400—probably between 200 and 400 after
Christ, when the Roman order had become apparently
permanent in South Britain—there was a Roman-Christian
household in Dorset. If only a tiny fraction of the Glastonbury legends is true, that is not in the least incredible.
The further arguments, however, which deduce a connection
with the Apostles of Christ from a stone fragment found at
Fordington, are much more ingenious than convincing.
But the tradition of the Celtic-Christian Church at Abbotsbury seems to be fairly trustworthy. And the stones in
Wareham Church inscribed with the name of Cattug may
possibly be connected with a Cattug or Cattogus who was
concerned in the Pelagian discussions of A.D. 430. It is
at least a highly likely conjecture, therefore, that the
exotic religion from Palestine had some foothold in Roman
Dorset.

Cæsar arrived in 55 B.C. His excursions into the Home
Counties can hardly have touched Dorset. But echoes
of the clash with the great civilization of Rome must have
reached even the far-off Durotriges. It must be remembered
that they were not savages. They may have used woad
and worn skins : I have seen blue face-powder and furs in
London to-day. They may have burnt prisoners in wicker
cages (that is one theory of the origin of the giant at Cerne).
But they were probably part of the third wave of immigrant
Celts, and they had come themselves, far back, from the
Europe with which, if only because of the gold and amber
which I have mentioned, they were still in habitual contact.
They used a Greek design for their coins, that of the well-
known Macedonian stater, of which Dorset examples are

preserved in the County museum. They had certainly some sort of ordered civilization of their own, however loosely knit. And they had rendered the soil of England in some degree hospitable to man's needs—they, and the Iberian before them. There was thus the result of five thousand years of purposeful work, undertaken not by eccentric units but by communities, upon which Rome could readily impose her greater order and peace.

Practically nothing is known of the real conquest in A.D. 43. It is pretty certain that the Durotriges—the real border folk of the Celtic race in the south-west just as the Dorsaetas later were the march folk of Saxondom—must have fought stoutly. It may be conjectured, perhaps, that as Claudius' army of occupation had the eastern end of Southampton Water for its base, Dorset was entered from the south-east rather than the north-east (the same problem arises in connection with the Saxon invasion). One of the pitched battles was in all probability fought on Hod Hill, a wonderful eminence above the Stour, where a Roman camp of the regulation square type has been cut in a corner of the much larger British contour fort. Possibly another encounter took place—the evidence suggests it—on Pilsdon Pen. It must have needed all Rome's military efficiency and startling rapidity of movement to subdue the sturdy people of the green forts.

Consider now the lines of the proved Roman roads in Dorset.* They enter the county from east-central England. The main trunk road, which probably determines all the rest, was that which ran from Sarum (Salisbury, as near as no matter) through Badbury Rings to Dorchester, possibly Bridport, and Exeter. The direction of the vicinal roads branching from it may be significant.

It is not known when, nor exactly why, this main road was built. There are no records of strife or important events in the West after the first conquest, even when, with a first-rate British heretic in Pelagius, and an emperor of

* See Codrington's *Roman Roads in Britain* (3rd Ed., 1918 : S.P.C.K.)

an enterprising and unusual type—the first British admiral—
in Carausius, and the death of a Roman Emperor, Con-
stantius, at York, England seemed to be well in the main
current of European history. The road was in all probability at once a precaution against risings, a direct route
to the Celtic frontier west of Exeter, and a commercial
necessity. The striking thing about it is that it follows the
line of a string of Celtic or British forts.

From Old Sarum (Celtic) it swings, after some miles in
a south-westerly direction, south-west of south at the county
border. It passes close by a cluster of Celtic and Iberian
tumuli on Handley Down, where there is a Roman British
farm and villa, just under the upstanding Celtic earthwork
of Pentridge (whence a very noble view of the road, and the
Bokerly Dyke, and Cranborne Chase, and Grim's Dyke, and
half Wiltshire, can be gained). It goes straight to Badbury
Rings, one of the most beautiful as well as most famous of
Celtic works. It swings again westwards to the Celtic
Crawford Castle (Spettisbury Rings). It keeps along the
ridge to the British village above Bere Regis. It passes
close under the earthworks and tumuli of Rainbarrow.
It goes direct to within half a mile of the greatest of all
forts, Dunium, and the Palæolithic work at Maumbury
Rings. It runs then in an almost straight line westwards
to the splendid fort of Eggardon. And then——

Well, then, according to the archæologists, it becomes
non-Celtic. It drops to Bridport, and is no longer a ridgeway track. It leaves Dorset, however, close by the Celtic
earthwork at Lambert's Castle: and so on to Exeter.
The evidence for the stretch from Eggardon westwards is
not strong.

If the good engineering of an easy road were the sole
aim of the road-makers, this latter non-Celtic stretch was
their most sensible effort. But if their object was either
to move troops to tribal centres or to link those centres up,
the portion up to Eggardon was the most successful, and
the remainder useless. For west of Eggardon the road

neglects the earthworks at Cattistock, and the British villages above Cerne, the camps above Beaminster and at Pilsdon Pen : and it does not proceed, if the Bridport route is correctly judged to be the main one, by that principle of sight-survey which Mr. Belloc expounds so convincingly in *The Stane Street.* The view-points, the long glimpses from peak to peak, are lost by the Bridport route. And some portions at least of the Bridport route must have provided very heavy going in damp weather, with rivers fuller than now (the spring-level was 80 feet higher) : the present road is not infrequently flooded.

There might be several explanations of this seeming change of purpose in the road-builders. The track may even have been wrongly mapped by modern experts. The last effort of British resistance may have been on Eggardon, though Pilsdon Pen's earthworks are so strong, and the height so commanding, that it would seem almost essential for Rome to be able to reach it by a good transport route.

The branch roads are also interesting. One runs from Badbury Rings to near Hamworthy, on Poole Harbour. It is believed that Rome had a port there. Another connects Dorchester with Weymouth, which, from the Roman remains found, was also probably a port even then. The earthworks at Flowersbarrow and Bindon Hill, where, apart from those two names, the Celtic name Arish Mell also survives, are not linked up at all with the Roman road system. There is evidence of a track running northwards from Badbury to Shaftesbury, along or near the line of earthworks above the Stour valley. But there seems to be no trace of a road along the real central ridge, west and north of Bere Regis, where the noble camp of Rawlsbury commands the Dorsetshire Gap. The road from Dorchester to Ilchester, on the other hand, runs through territory clearly inhabited and fortified by the Celts.

The position, therefore, seems to be that the chief road in the county, so far west as Eggardon Hill, was planned to fit existing British settlements ; and its chief local branch-

road was the cross-cut to the great west main road at
Ilchester. The cross-cuts to the ports of Hamworthy and
Weymouth—both, perhaps, non-Celtic—seem, however, to
show the new world-standpoint. If the Celts in Dorset
used a port at all, it was likely to be at Arish Mell Gap,
where the chalk in which they loved to build touches the
sea, and where their names and forts still live ; whereas
Rome, building with an economic outlook of European
scope, chose the natural harbours on Poole estuary and
Weymouth Bay, and linked them up artificially with a road-
system adapted to the tribal population. But she thought
it safe, apparently, to leave the minor Celtic centres in the
county unconnected with the main arteries.

The nature of the Roman settlement is probably seen
most accurately in Cranborne Chase, rather than in the
more highly and perhaps more artificially civilized town of
Dorchester. Gen. Pitt-Rivers excavated remains of an
extensive farm or farm-colony near Woodyates. His finds
are suggestively various. There are a few pieces of fine
pottery, good ornaments and trinkets, studs of blue and
yellow enamel on fibulæ, decorated furniture of imported
Spanish wood, an elaborate system of central heating,* coins
covering the reigns of many emperors ; and alongside
these things, which a Roman colonist (say, a retired captain
or sergeant-major) would take care to possess in a so distant
and savage spot, many remains of farm tools, some well
finished and clearly imported, but others rough and primitive,
like native products. The farm might well be like an up-
country station in Rhodesia to-day.

"The people of these parts," says Gen. Pitt-Rivers,†
" in Roman times were much shorter than they are at
present, shorter than they afterwards became when the
Teutonic element was introduced. . . . They were not
hunters, but lived a peaceful agricultural life, surrounded

---

* The skeletons discovered show that the inhabitants suffered from
rheumatoid arthritis.
  † *Excavations in Cranborne Chase.*

by their flocks and herds. . . . They spun thread, and wove
it on the spot, and sewed with iron needles." They kept
horses, oxen, sheep (all of small breeds), mastiffs, terriers,
and dogs of a dachshund type, roedeer, red deer, swine.
They ate horse and dog, though not so much as beef. They
had apparently none of those snails which Rome is said
to have introduced into Britain. Their wheat was of
high quality, as might be expected when Britain was a
granary of the Empire. The labourers seem to have lived
in wattle and daub huts.

Dorchester, on the other hand, would be nearer akin to
the older Pretoria (it was not, however, a Colonia, nor the
seat of a legion, though very likely troops—companies or
even only a platoon—were stationed there from time to
time). It had its still-preserved walls, its fine amphitheatre,
a score or more villas of a good standard of provincial
luxury, its cemetery, its water supply from Compton
Valence. A little way off, at Weymouth, there was a temple.
And it may even have had, as has been said, devotees
of the new and eventually fashionable religion called
Christianity.

There are abundant tokens of the dead past in such a
place. I was at Maumbury Rings in one of the years during
which it was excavated. The chalk was cleanly cut into
tiers of seats. There was a trench between them and the
central ring, perhaps for safety. The socket-holes that must
have held barrier posts were still brown with the dye of
damp wood. The den at the far end had clearly contained
beasts. And two soldiers of Rome, disinterred once, lie
again at rest beneath one of the green curves.

So the Roman-British pursued, in the contentment
reared and strengthened through ten generations of man's
life, those arts of peace which an island with no enemies,
under the shield of a vast Empire, might enjoy. Doubtless,
as I have said, they heard of the doings that troubled great
Rome—of wars upon distant and to them unimaginable
frontiers : of the new Eastern religion that Constantine,

whom in Britain they knew so nearly, had thrust upon the dominions won by the soldiers of older gods : of the heresies and radical faiths that shook that young established Church, and more particularly of that heresy of Pelagius the Briton. There would come to them, slowly and unnoticeably and with easy acceptance, as it came to us also, the knowledge of little technical improvements of life : better nails, a finer earthenware, a cheap imitation of the red luxurious Samian, a new art in pot-shaping. There would come also the alien splendours of the Roman official : the fine stone houses he built, the delicate shining coins he decreed to be current over the rough native mintings, the stoves that even poor settlers' houses might expect, the intricate wonders of his mosaic pavements, the wide paved causeways. They could gradually work their finer artistic sensibility into the heavy Roman work.

There must have been strange memories in the Dorchester of those days for men who had been young in the war with Vespasian, and for their sons and grandsons. For a thousand years their fathers had trodden the ancient tracks from hill to hill, from fort to fort. They had walked upon the path from Badbury to Mai Dun, from Mai Dun to Eggar Dun : they had been wont to flee from the valleys into those great strongholds where a whole tribe could live securely. And now the narrow old footways upon the green hills were paved and made wide and firm, and there was no longer war, and the bright chalk trenches grew green with disuse : in Mai Dun itself arose a rich man's house of lime and stone. Warriors who before would have fought their very kinsmen in that land of tribal wars sailed now to the Oversea Dominions, to uphold there by their strength and skill the power to which they had yielded, the peace in which their houses were henceforth set. Upon the ancient wells of generations too old even for folk-memory, the rulers had traced the circle of a circus, for a spectacle in which Britons fought, after the manner of men, with beasts which once they had hunted precariously. The ships came trafficking

to Hamworthy : news and merchandise went to and fro
with regularity. We to-day have to conceive of a national
strike, or of utter severance from friends across many
seas, before we can imagine what augmentation of comfort
the establishment of routine government from an all-
powerful centre meant to these distant provinces.

Yet it is in the singular appeal of the great roads that
Rome seems nearest. I stood once, not long after Belgium
was first invaded in 1914, above Cattistock, where the
road is inexorably straight and very lonely. Suddenly the
unique carillon at Cattistock began playing a hymn tune,
and I remembered that the thirty-two bells were cast at
Louvain, then lately ravaged, and that one of the chief
of them bore the motto " Grant peace in our time, O Lord."
Peace was Rome's gift to Celtic England. There was longer
peace in England then than at any time since : a peace
stretching as long as from the last of the Tudors to the House
of Windsor.

There are many wonderful stretches of these noble roads
in Dorset. The structure of the road itself is nowhere
better seen in England than where it enters the county from
the north-east. It runs, a broad high dark ridge, four or
five feet above the down-surface, as inflexibly and as enduringly as the fine modern coach-road from which at this
point it separates. The modern road goes to the rich little
valley towns. The old road makes straight for the hill
fortress of Badbury, whose trees can be seen from many
other distant hills. The ridge of its actual formation is
visible also in the stretch a little east of Spettisbury Camp,
and again near the Milbornes. The road was strongly and
purposefully engineered : its purpose of peace is still
visible.

The portion just north of Badbury Rings, if one comes
(contrariwise) to it from the west, brings the ages before one
in a curious jumble. Behind that fir-topped hill lies a wood.
The road curves past the green ramparts—hardly less, in
places, than the terrific defences of Maiden Castle—and,

almost invisible, across some cultivated land : and then there opens suddenly a pathway among trees so fantastically venerable that they seem older even than that ancient trackway. Huge wych-elms they are, grey and twisted with the deformity of naked time : year after year has gripped them, and bent a fibre or turned a shoot, until their old arms are the very emblems of unabated agony. Ivy crawls upon them, and between grow thick brambles and unpruned hawthorns that might guard a Sleeping Beauty —if the strange awe of the place did not suggest rather a sleeping dragon.

Chivalry, with its capricious romance, its heroism of loneliness, was born in the welter of Rome's death. In this little acre of meagre forest, where the old Rome's road still runs, knights of the new Rome might well have ridden on their first adventures. Here a man jingling on a clumsy horse might have seen rough bearded knaves in ambush, or a maiden tied to a tree : or lions or unicorns or dragons or monstrous boars, wherein the world was then putatively rich. Guy might meet here a three-headed giant, or Arviragus encounter the wizard who could remove rocks from the sea : or that student might wander who in a dream saw his fellow killed in a stable. Among these trees any legend might be true : and yet there is enough of reality left in the road to make the sweat and the dirt as plain as the romance. If men in the past did fare here upon strange errands, nevertheless they hoped or feared as we do. They saw the same world, the same incommunicable life of other organisms : stepped in the same mud, stumbled over the same tree-roots, startled the same race of squawking blackbirds. The old tracks are the very vehicle of time : this grassy way has been trodden for a millennium and a half, and every blade of grass in it, every twig, even the very worm-cast mould, is of an ancestry as splendid as man's. If it be preserved only by so little as one wayfarer's steps in a year, it is still the authentic and undiminished chronicle of stories that have become our minds.

It was here, I like to think (and not without some historical warrant), that the last stand of Roman Britain against the heathen Saxon was made. Badbury may well be the Mons Badonicus on which Arthur fought and died : for the historians seem agreed that Arthur may really have lived, that he checked the Saxons by his final victory, and that " the last great battle in the West " took place either here or near Bath.

From Badbury onwards, if one goes eastwards through the enchanted forest, the road is like many another ancient way for some distance—a path maintained for no very clear reason save its antiquity. It runs, as the Winchester Pilgrim's Way often does, between high hedges, through whose interstices there are sometimes views of a pleasant spaciousness. Its line is straight : it has the directness which popular scholarship ascribes to Rome's ways, though it has not often the bare visible strength. It is, in fact, a hedged track of no marked character. It crosses a few lanes, and is joined by a few others. After many parasangs it reaches, with an annoying deviation from its straightness, a hamlet populous and great which the Ordnance Map shyly refuses to name, and which I decline to incriminate. This place is very strange : it is like a loose end of, say, Beckenham, cut off and transplanted. Its contents are : (1) a gabled, bow-windowed studio-villa-parish-room (large enough and comprehensive enough for all those functions), which, it is to be hoped, will crumble before posterity labels it typical of any period of English architecture (it suggests the soul of a retired advertisement contractor, with a taste for Birket Foster and bad water colours) : (2) a few long low stucco buildings hardly of the decent proportions which stucco demands : (3) some ordinary ugly cottages which look like 1890 : (4) some buildings which simply *are* 1890 suburban villas, and nothing else. Quite a number of houses, no shops, no purpose, no character : a phenomenon rare in Dorset.

The wayfarer must here continue along what, by the straight-line method, is the obvious Roman way, past the uninteresting cottages. At the top, in a wood, a gate to the right bears a threatening notice about privacy. The path beyond it leads . . . however. . . . Well, at any rate . . . the fact is, it is quite possible here to walk across the park without directly disregarding *any* notice : and the Roman road (a path of decent ancestry, after all : older even than a nineteenth-century peerage) runs right through the park, close by the great house.

Its track continues thence undeviatingly, across the stream at Gussage All Saints, up through tumuli over Gussage Down —one of the alleged sites of Vindogladia, an imperfectly identified Roman-British settlement—and over the crest of Bottlebush Down, where it joins the modern road, near a still greater host of tumuli, under Pentridge Hill ; and so out of the county : in its way touching the Ox Drove across the Wiltshire hills.

The Ancient Britons, our forefathers—not cut off sharp from us either by Julius Cæsar or by William the twentieth or thirtieth Conqueror—were no doubt subject to the emotions of joy, pity, and terror much as we are. Their lives were less secure and more volatile than ours. They lived in what are more like the lower portions of our basement houses of the nineteenth century than anything else since : half-buried huts, of which many traces remain on or near this great road. They used successively stone, possibly iron, and bronze. They secluded flocks and herds of sheep and cattle in their vast citadels. They made linen, they ate much the same food as, in our simpler moments, we eat. They had an organized religion. They did not know the potato, the hop, the cherry, root crops, or a hundred other pleasant things familiar to us. They had in the course of centuries exterminated the beaver, and had at last got the better of the wolf, though he still existed in the woods. The terrible semi-tropical beasts that Palæolithic man had to face were never their enemies. Our sheep and cattle of to-day, like the valley sheep of the ballad, are fatter than theirs, which must have been lean, strong, and nearer to a wild type. "The number of cattle is very great," said Cæsar. The turf was infinitely less rich, and there were no meadows or hedges. Very probably, in fact, a fastidious modern verdict on the Britons would be the familiar "manners none, customs beastly."

That would be the application of a wrong standard. Cæsar thought Kent "the civillest place in all this isle." We have not his opinion on Dorset, since he never visited it ; nor have we Vespasian's. But at least this is tolerably certain, that the Durotriges were not to Rome as the Australian aborigines were to Captain Cook. Their vestiges show a civilization nearly as high as that which Cæsar underestimated in Kent. They had long ceased to jabber uncouthly, to struggle hard for a bare existence, to be unaware of other folk. On the other hand, they had tribal wars. They had had torrents of invasion (fresh hordes of Celts) unknown to us except by vague conjecture. They knew a great civilization lay east of them.

Did the coming of Rome seem different from their other wars, except in that it was more highly organized, more permanent in effect ? As they hurried the herds along the hidden way of the Ox Drove, or scuttled hastily, women, children, cattle, and domestic implements all confused (or perhaps marshalled orderly by preconceived plan), into Badbury Rings or Maiden Castle, had they any sense of destiny ? Pretty certainly not. They were just afraid and angry. Very likely they did not even think they were being wronged. But we cannot anyhow get back veritably into their minds. That is the suprème defect of archæology as compared with documented history. And we must leave it at that. There is only the end of an immense epoch to be recorded : an end violent in its early stages, but not ungentle in its results, not a catastrophic and final conclusion. The settlement at Woodyates (like that at Rockbourne Down, a little way off, just over the present Hampshire

F

border) means coalescence, not absorption, nor suppression ;
a few Romans, Roman law, Roman conveniences, greater
security, a number of small changes (for the good) in daily
habits, better houses, better tools, and life as before—birth,
love, marriage, death, with the old trees behind Arthur's
battlefield outlasting them all.

What did the incoming Roman think ? He must have
worked and made others work unceasingly to repair the
damage of his invasion and render life safe for himself and
the conquered. Merchants, missionaries of Empire, must
have come quickly for the fine British gladiators, the large
British dogs, the bursting British grain sacks. (We know
from Cicero's letters how in remote Cilicia Pompey and
Brutus, high financiers and low money-lenders, had swiftly
got greedy fingers into the work of Empire development).
Later, the feeling must have been to some extent reversed.
Priests and politicians and soldiers of fortune came from
the most distant outposts to disturb the central decadence
at Rome itself : as it might be a financier from South Africa
or Canada in London to-day.

But in the early days, when the first legionary stood
on Spettisbury Rings, what emotion was in his mind ?
Probably none, except a certain pride and sense of adventure.
He could not see, as we see now, the distant towers of
Wimborne Minster. Yet his Eternal City alone made the
Minster possible. He could not look out over the sunset,
and see the few twinkling lights of the village below, or
hear a train roaring through the cutting in the chalk walls
which he may have had to storm, and think (as we might
like him to have thought), " Here am I on the edge of the
world : all the universe is spinning round me in the twilight,
and it will change and die : I, Rome, alone am immortal,
because I am an idea."

He was probably very tired, and not a Roman at all, but
some countrified lad from Spain or Africa. All he wanted
was a good meal and sleep. The next day he must get up
early and go on to " the next of these beastly barbarian

villages " (he who may so lately have been a barbarian himself) : " more fighting, perhaps : Ibernium, Ivernio, some such outlandish name." (The correct spelling would be settled by the scholars five or six generations later.) " Quite a lot of those Brythons there." And a spring, it was said—better than the swamp he had just crossed below Badbury (for to-day's lovely old bridge at Spettisbury was not built till fifteen hundred years later). Ibernium seemed healthy when he got there : a good place for a properly sunk well. And so to-day, if you lean on your stick at the green hut circles above Bere Regis, it may suddenly vanish into the soft moss where Rome made the well for the Roman-British village.

And thus on to the famous town of Dunium, which Rome had really heard of : to be rechristened Durnovaria and provide Thomas Hardy with one of his unerring fictitious names. As the Roman marched over the last stretch of track, he trod land probably unchanged from then till now —Hardy's Egdon, the noble brown Rainbarrow. He could see the marshes of Dorchester before him, and the high menacing Ridgeway beyond to the south and west ; could discern, as we can still, the notch in the Purbeck skyline which is Flowersbarrow camp ; could see far away the gap in the hills which Corfe Castle once guarded—long after his time, long before ours ; and in front of him the huge white trenches of Mai Dun.

And after Dunium ? Prisoners probably told of the other great forts at Abbotsbury (its Celtic name has not survived) and Eggar Dun and Pils Dun. The troops, with their amazing celerity of movement, their perfect and compact equipment, must hurry on to the sunset, along the British track that the inhabitants would soon have to turn into a proper paved road. It leaves to-day's turnpike-era road about three miles west of Dorchester, and goes straight up the hill to the next view-point. It is a grass-grown lane between hedges now ; sometimes unhedged, swinging with the topmost line of the hills, still, somehow or other, preserved ; in some places curiously fenced by slabs of stone that might once have been its own pavement.

It climbs steadily on for several miles, a little up or down as the hills run, following the ridge with unyielding certainty. There is no life on it at all but that which has always been there—gorse and bramble and hawthorn, harebell and fox-glove, toad-flax and scabious : green generations that may outlive us, their younger brother. So deserted is the track that in all my wanderings upon it I have but once met another person—a solitary postman. He appeared to be going nowhere in particular : but he seemed somehow symbolic, a unit of the organization that was just coming to its first birth in England when the road itself was first paved. The Roman posts ran along that road.

Rome is apt to stand out in the mind as a self-contained thing. But, as the excavations in Cranborne Chase prove, here in Britain there was the half-fluid life of a frontier. Here in this last plain stretch of the Roman Road in Dorset one gains a geographical vision, as it were, of the limits of the far-flung Empire. The lonely track takes a final slight bend and runs between thick bramble hedges, where families of stoats play openly, almost deriding the multitudinous rabbit. (A hawk once chased and was in turn chased by my dog here, so aloof and unsophisticated is the place.) Then the hedge ends, and the sea suddenly blazes on your left, as though the Channel were a vast heliograph. The Devon coast is before you. A curving promontory, bare but for one little tree,* ridged with trenches, stretches westwards for forty score yards, and ends abruptly. You are on Eggardon Hill, one of the greatest and perhaps the most nobly placed of all the Neolithic fortresses of the West. With it ends the chalk backbone of England. Save for Marshwood Vale, the rest is Devon and Cornwall—Dyvnaint, the country of the " Welsh." Dorset, as I have said, is the real English frontier—the place where invasions and con-

---

* A smuggler once made a plantation of trees there, to be a sea-mark for his trade ; but an unsympathetic government cut it down.

quests weakened into fusion : beyond are the purer, older races, the blacker, older faiths.

When they had taken Eggardon—and they approached, one can hardly doubt, from the only direction from which it *could* be taken by force, for all the sides other than the eastern are precipices, up which even a terrier after rabbits must go slowly—the Romans looked out towards the uttermost west to which they ever penetrated. On Pilsdon Pen alone is there a western prospect comparable to this, and that view is inferior because it does not include the same vision of Golden Cap, nor the same bare deep wide cleft made by the tiny Bridport rivers.

It is a magical vision, that from Eggardon. You are looking into sunset kingdoms into which you must almost fear to enter, lest there be in them enchantments from which you cannot escape : but happy enchantments. You see, as elsewhere in England, the " coloured counties," the whole of several huge valleys parcelled like a map. You see depths of shade, of luminous mist, spaces of blazing sea, clean-outlined hills, billowing in waves to a horizon thirty or more miles away ; and at the same time you have fields almost under you—but several hundred feet beneath you. Nowhere in Dorset, nowhere, for that matter, in the south of England, have I felt (and resisted) so strongly the call to the West that has made European civilization.

I say resisted, for here to me England, except for a little necessary stretch of foothills, ends. Here, on this glorious headland, is all the happiness and peace I can ever desire. Here I can look out and be sure that in the end I shall attain to Tier-nan-Oge, as my forefathers the Ancient Britons hoped—to fortunate isles " beyond the baths of all the western stars." I can look down on life hence, as I look down on the lane below, and say " I am on the heights : I have lost the whole world and gained my own soul."

V

"Some, therefore, of the miserable remnant, being taken in the mountains, were murdered in great numbers ; others, constrained by famine, came and yielded themselves to be slaves for ever to their foes, running the risk of being instantly slain, which truly was the greatest favour that could be offered them : some others passed beyond the sea with loud lamentations instead of the voice of exhortation. 'Thou hast given us as sheep to be slaughtered, and among the Gentiles hast thou dispersed us.' Others, committing the safeguard of their lives, which were in continual jeopardy, to the mountains, precipices, thickly wooded forests, and to the rocks of the seas (albeit with trembling hearts), remained still in their country."

THE EPISTLE OF GILDAS THE WISE
(Ed. J. A. Giles).

"In the meantime, [Alfred] the King, during the frequent wars and other trammels of this present life, the invasion of the pagans, and his own daily infirmities of body, continued to carry on the government, and to exercise hunting in all its branches ; to teach his workers in gold and artificers of all kinds, his falconers, hawkers, and dog-keepers ; to build houses majestic and good, beyond all the precedents of his ancestors, by his new mechanical inventions ; to recite the Saxon books, and especially to learn by heart the Saxon poems, and to make others learn them ; and he alone never desisted from the mass and other daily services of religion ; he was frequent in psalm singing and prayer, at the hours both of the day and the night. He also went to the churches in the night time to pray, secretly, and unknown to his courtiers ; he bestowed alms and largesses on both natives and foreigners of all countries ; he was affable and pleasant to all, and curiously eager to investigate things unknown."

ASSER'S *LIFE OF ALFRED* (Ed. J. A. Giles).

V

THE HEATHEN CONQUERORS

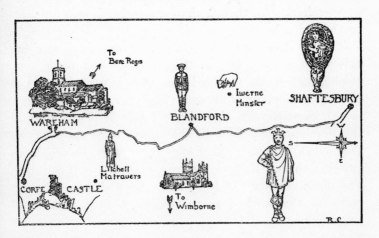

WHEN Rome went, peace went. Peace herself
had indeed already set about going, for the
barbarians had long been raiding Britain as
well as the inner Empire. But the withdrawal of the
legions, and with them of authoritative central government, meant that organization (which may be much more
important than plausible peace) also disappeared. The
picture given by all the chroniclers, whatever their value,
and however great their discrepancies, is of a country
disorganized, frightened, incoherent : not so much of civil
war, though that may also have taken place, as of civil
dissolution.

It is not agreed how or when Dorset became Saxon.
The battle of Mons Badonicus, whether it took place at
Badbury Rings or not, was probably fought in 516. It

seems likely that the invaders left Dorset alone (save for peaceful penetration) until, proceeding westwards from Salisbury, they conquered Somerset in the days of King Ine.

By then, however, the county had a strong Saxon tinge. Ine's own sister founded Wimborne Minster in 705, and his Bishop Aldhelm Sherborne Abbey : Aldhelm had also associations with the Isle of Purbeck. There was a monastery at Wareham, too, though the Saxon church still standing on the walls there may not have been built till much later.

It must have seemed, indeed, under the beneficent episcopate of Aldhelm, as though order and peace were coming back to the troubled county, now veritably part of the strong kingdom of Wessex. But two generations later, in 787, came the first sign of new torment. Three ships of the Northmen appeared off the Dorset coast (probably at Weymouth) and slew the King's reeve when he sought to question them. He was the first Englishman they killed. The ninth century was to suffer worse and more frequent raids, as the Anglo-Saxon Chronicle records with blunt accuracy :—

" A.D. 833. This year fought King Egbert with thirty-five pirates at Charmouth, where a great slaughter was made, and the Danes remained masters of the field. . . .

" A.D. 837. Alderman Ethelhelm, with the men of Dorset-shire, fought with the Danish army in Portland Isle, and for a good while put them to flight : but in the end the Danes became masters of the field, and slew the Alderman. . . .

" A.D. 840. This year King Ethelwulf fought at Char-mouth with thirty-five ship's crews, and the Danes remained masters of the place."

Before the tenth century ended, to sack Wareham had become almost an annual pastime with the pirates. It took an Alfred to deal with them.

From the time when he buried at Wimborne the brother whom he succeeded, till the last year of the ninth century, when he himself was laid to rest at Winchester, Alfred must have been constantly in Dorset. So also, unhappily for Dorset, were the Danes : " the greater part of that province was depopulated by them." They lay much of one whole winter at Dorchester (very probably in Poundbury). But in 876 their fleet of 120 vessels was caught in a mist and storm off Swanage, and utterly destroyed. Yet through all those years of trouble Ælfric was at Cerne Abbas, making it a centre of learning for half England.

The next century and a half was as full of tragedy as Alfred's reign was of splendid romance. Immediately on his death his nephew seized Wimborne : and though he was easily suppressed by Alfred's son Edward, his attempt was prophetic of the domestic strife to come. The Wessex Kings of all England were at constant war with Mercia or the Danes or their own kin. Under Edward's son, Athelstan, however, Dorset may have enjoyed greater peace. He established four mints there—at Shaftesbury, Wareham, Dorchester, and Bridport—and his connection with the county, apart from his foundation of Milton Abbey, seems to have been close. In his reign, it is probable, the bones of St. Wite or Candida were brought in their leaden reliquary to Whitchurch Canonicorum, where they still rest.

For some little time Dorset itself was untroubled, though it may well be that her sons had to perform their military service with the Fyrd in the north, where most of the fighting took place. And then, in 978, occurred the event which stirred the imagination of England as well as of Dorset, and helped to give Shaftesbury in years to come a glory that spread far beyond England : the murder of the boy King Edward at Corfe by his stepmother.

It will be convenient, before considering the direct effect of that crime on Dorset, to look forward to the uneasy period that ended with the coming of " King Norman." The chroniclers say that it was ushered in with portents : " this same year (979) was seen a bloody welkin oft-times in the likeness of fire : and that was most apparent at midnight, and so in misty beams was shown : but when it began to dawn, then it glided away." Three years later "the pirates" landed and plundered Portland. In 998 they encamped at Frome-mouth, "and went up everywhere, as widely as they would, into Dorsetshire." In 1001 they marched through Hampshire and Dorset into Devon and back, burning and laying waste. In 1003 Sweyn ravaged the land from Devon to Hampshire. In 1006 all the population from Wessex was called up and "lay out all the harvest under arms against the enemy." In 1015 Canute himself encamped at Wareham, "and then plundered in Dorset and in Wiltshire and in Somerset"; and there was a battle near Gillingham the next year, in which the Danes were defeated.

When Canute became King of all England, there was greater peace, and by the time he died at Shaftesbury in 1035, Dorset may well have recovered from the incessant ravaging. It was his steward Orc who founded the abbey of Abbotsbury (where still the Saxon carving of the Trinity survives), and Orc's wife Tola had possessions in mid-Dorset, where her name lives in Tolpiddle. The mother of the Confessor owned Dorset land, and the great Earls Godwin and Harold held estates there. Godwin was frequently at Portland, from which base he harried the south coast in 1052. Brihtric is recorded to have held many hides. Aiulf the Sheriff had estates at Durweston and Marshwood, growing vines, according to his fancy, in the almost forgotten Celtic way (he alone in the county suffered little loss of lands at the Norman Conquest). But save for a few names like that, there is little direct evidence of the country's activities after 1015 until in 1066, "very many" Dorset men fell fighting round Harold under the Dragon Flag at Hastings.

There were, then, in this corner of Wessex, three main factors at work in the five or six centuries after the Roman peace crumbled: the wars of races and eventually of dynasties: the slow progress of the resettlement of agriculture, with the obscure gradual birth of what we still call the agricultural labourer—a greater figure, a greater problem, than any dynasty: and the solemn, sincere vision and growing power of Holy Church. They were all to become dominant in turn: the labourer not till the Black Death altered economic conditions, and then only for a moment; the dynasts as soon as the strong rule of the Conqueror ended.

The Church, made strong in the West by Aldhelm and Alfred and Dunstan, was to hold men's imaginations for six centuries more, under the impulse of such scenes as were inspired by the murder of Edward. Follow the path of the martyr from Corfe to Shaftesbury.

The story of the murder is simple and well known.* The boy-king had reigned three years and eight months, when, having hunted in the woods round Wareham (" now only a few bushes," says the chronicler, writing perhaps in the twelfth century), he remembered that his younger brother Ethelred lay at Corfe a few miles away (" where now "—and by implication not then—" a large castle has been built."). He loved Ethelred with a pure and sincere heart. He dismissed his attendants, and rode to Corfe alone, fearing no one, since not even in the least thing was he aware that he had offended any man.

Word of his approach was brought to Elfrida, his step-mother, who, " full of wicked plans and guile," rejoiced at the opportunity of obtaining her desire, and hastened to meet him and offer him hospitality. He said he had but come to see his brother, whereupon she invited him to refresh himself with drink. As the cup touched his lips, one of her servants, " bolder in spirit and more vile in crime " than others, stabbed him from behind. He fell dead, " changing his earthly kingdom for a heavenly one, his transitory crown of a day for the unfading diadem of eternal happiness."

The body was hurriedly carried for concealment to a cottage (local tradition says it was thrown into a well)†.

* The account here given is freely adapted from the St. John's College, Oxford, MS. life in monkish Latin, first printed by the present Dean of Winchester in 1903. Mr. W. H. Hudson has given a fine romantic version of the story in *Dead Man's Plack*.

† The chronicler states that a spring of pure water broke out from the place where the body was cast later.

But that night the woman of the cottage, old, and blind from birth, a pensioner of the Queen's, watching by the body, had a vision : the glory of the Lord filled her hovel with a great splendour, and she recovered her sight and saw that which she guarded. When the Queen heard of this, she was struck with terror, and had the body cast out into the marshes that lie between Corfe and Wareham. Herself she went hastily to her house at Bere Regis, northward across the Heath, taking the new king, Ethelred the Redeless, with her. He, poor boy, gave way to grief, and did not cease to weep and lament. But Elfrida, driven to fury, beat him with candles so savagely (" she had no other weapon to her hand ") that ever after he could not bear candle-light.

But her bitterness could not prevail to hide her deed. In a short time, the legend says, a column of fire stood over the spot where the body had been thrown down. Certain devout men of Wareham perceived it, found the body, and bore it to their town, amid a great concourse of people mourning as it were with one voice. They carried it past the Priory to the church of Lady St. Mary, and laid it in a rude shrine there. The shrine still stands, in part, at the south-east of that gracious and beautifully placed house of God ; and still St. Edward's stone coffin rests in the church.

The divine pillar of light must have shone down on the same brown heathlands of Stoborough (mother-town of old Wareham, it is said) as the sun looks down upon to-day. Had the devout men had our book-learning, they might have had a vision of another old chieftain, a nameless king of the Neolithic Age, who lay buried in a deer-skin near their path : they might have remembered those strange British or Danish Christian chieftains whose memorial stones, in Wareham Church, were plainer then, perhaps, than in the poor fragments left to-day. They must have seen the almost newly built castle by the river as they crossed it to go to the shrine, and have thought of this fresh renewal of the terror their town seemed to have passed through—not knowing

CORFE CASTLE

From a painting by P. Wilson Steer

that worse was to come. Their act, however, was perhaps just what the chronicler calls it—devout, a duty of religion and the expression of human grief.

There were other miracles during the year the body rested at Wareham in its simple shrine : and at last, after the end of the year, it was exhumed and found to be yet incorrupt. It was lifted by the hands of reverent men and set on a bier, and borne with a great following of clergy and people to Shaftesbury, to the famous abbey of Mary the Mother of God.

It is not difficult to see that procession : stately enough, may be, for ravaged Wessex, but poor beside the splendour that the martyr was soon to bring to his last resting-place. The brown figures, straggling over roads or tracks that even now in April (the month of the translation) are none too easy, must have taken more than one day over the twenty-mile journey. We cannot tell which track they followed : all the roads north lead in the end to Shaftesbury. I like to think that they chose that beautiful deserted byway across the open heath, from which to-day there is a magical prospect of Corfe Castle, in its gap, and the shining clear ridge of Purbeck. The red and green fungi fringe would star the brown earth then as now, the bog myrtle scent the air.

Thence, in time, I think, the pilgrims would cross the Stour and climb to the dry clean ridge that runs from Blandford due north. Leaving the valleys, even the Minster's chapel at Iwerne, on their left, they would come at last to a place behind Fontmell and Melbury Downs where the ancient Ox Drove from the east vanishes. There a black copse makes a cleavage in the green to right and left. The trees sink abruptly into a steep valley. For a mile or more this valley runs low and slim, interrupted, at almost regular intervals, by long transverse slopes and hollows, whose denuded flanks show a peculiar cold blue soil. The ghostly deeps are folded regularly, like the narrow central trackways formed if one interlaces the fingers of the two hands, knuckles

upwards. At the end a huge round hill blocks the channel.
Along the right-hand ridge the Ox Drove begins or ends
its course, and a view of other slopes and uplands to the
north is opened.

Hitherto the western edge of the hills has, at most points,
kept the outer western prospect invisible. And as one looks
to the east from behind Melbury Down, it seems as if a man
might walk for ever, as in Purbeck, poised over void space,
silent, remote, never beholding the dark, patient folk who
live below among trees and streams. And then suddenly the
long track falters. The hills drop all away, and the wide
scroll of Blackmore Vale lies open—" a deep country, full
of pasture, yielding plenty of well-fed beeves, muttons, and
milch kine." Mile upon mile of trim rich land, mapped out
into fields like the pieces of a dissected puzzle, fall and rise
until, half a day's long walk away, they reach the central
ridge of the county, nine hundred feet high. This fertile
country stretches west and south-west almost without
bound : and the eye travels over it equably, to be arrested
only by isolated heights to the south and north : to the
south, those along which the pilgrims' track had already
curved : to the north by Shaftesbury—still Shaston on the
milestones—the legendary British town of Palladour.

It is this northern height which holds the attention most
magically. Here truly is a city set on a hill : neither Rye
nor Glastonbury Tor stands up more sharply from the plain.
A dark skyline of trees, a shining square tower, blue wreaths
of smoke, clustered golden houses all hung upon a green
precipice—that is the city of Palladour. A city of dreams,
the perfect description by a great writer calls it : dreams of
the dead, for whom the multitudinous sad-toned sheep-
bells of the downs seem to be for ever ringing lamentably.
Men live and move and have their being in Palladour busily
enough to-day. It is as comfortable and pleasing a country
town as any in England. Its civic spirit and corporate
activities are vigorous, and its dwellers prosper. But in the
old time before them it was no mere country town. It

was a city of prophets, priests, and kings, "dear for its reputation through the world," a habitation of pride and beauty and immemorial legend : of which magnificence to-day even the legend is only a dimly remembered dream, recorded in a few half-buried stones. Shaftesbury seems to stand up out of the valley mists like a city of ghosts.

Not less aerial does it appear from within. If from the plain it climbs skyward with a sudden gleaming aspiration, from its own ancient terraces it is still a place apart, hung delicately above the gross earth by the art of Merlin : a haven of the fabled Isle of Gramarye itself.

For a thousand years Palladour was a place of reverence. Its antiquity is wild myth. Lud built here his city Palladour, says one monkish chronicler : and Lud was eighth in the line from the no less fabulous Brute himself. A certain Cicuber, says another, founded at Palladour three temples, "and placed in them flamens" : but this scribe, rashly precise, gives Cicuber a date many generations older than the order of flamens. Yet a third speaks of Hudibras, and a fourth of Cassibelan. The exact truth of such tales matters not. They are our English counterpart of the Heracleid pedigree—the assimilation and adaptation and handing on in their chronicles, by the conquering Saxon immigrants, of the still dominant traditions of the conquered. It is probable that Romans or Roman-Britons dwelt at Palladour. It is not established that there was any town there before them.

It is in 888 that the greatness of Shaston really begins, when Alfred rebuilt the city and established the Abbey, endowing it with many acres of rich land, "with the men and other appurtenances, as they now are, and my daughter Ethelgiva." He dedicated it to the Virgin. A century later, when the body of Edward the Martyr was brought hither, St. Edward was joined to St. Mary in the patronage of the growing house. Thereafter, with the holy shrine of the Martyr to glorify it, it increased rapidly in wealth

G

and power, so as to overshadow all the abbeys of South
Wessex, and give ground for the saying that if its abbess
(it was a Benedictine nunnery) could marry the abbot of
Glastonbury, " their heir would hold more land than the
King of England." But for all the nunnery's wealth, even
the King of England himself still held land upon precarious
tenure, as a gift to the Abbey shows. In 1001, when the
Danes were burning and reburning the ports of Dorset, and
holding territory far inland in other regions, Ethelred the
King bestowed on the nuns a " monastery and vill " a
dozen miles away to the north-west, to be a safe refuge
from foes he could not repel. By an irony of history,
King Canute himself died in the Abbey thirty-four years
later.

By Domesday Shaston, even then a borough, stood high
among the towns of the south. It had three mints, sixty-
six houses in the King's demesne, and one hundred and
eleven in the abbess's. That powerful lady could command
one hundred and fifty-one bordars, and owned, besides
the various Abbey buildings, " a garden, value sixty-five
shillings." With the King she halved the manor of Palladour,
and continued in that possession till the Dissolution. Her
house ranked among the first four nunneries of England ;
within the boundaries of the borough were twelve churches,
certain chantries, two hospitals, and a small priory. The
number of the nuns ranged at various periods from fifty-
five to one hundred and twenty. At the Dissolution, the
income of the Abbey was £1300 a year : none too much for
the upkeep of such state as included, among other buildings,
" the great bakehouse, the pastry house, the breadhouse,
the Long Stable, the three great base courts, the laundry
house, the star-chamber, the wardrobe chamber, the green
chamber, the second great stable, the millhouse, the malt-
house, the brewhouse, the hay-house, the larder-house,
the wool-house, the gardens, the park, the dovehouse."
Truly, as a stout Protestant historian admits, " the town
made a very great figure in times of popery."

Yet it may well be that such magnificence defeated its own ends. There is hardly a word of notable events between the Norman Conquest and the Dissolution. One Sir Osbert Gifford was stripped and whipped in Shaston "for three Sundays together in the market-place and parish church," in 1285, for stealing two nuns from Wilton. Elizabeth, wife of the Bruce, was lodged here civilly, as a royal prisoner, in 1313 and 1314. And that, except the rites and levies of the Church, the arrival and departure of countless pilgrims, and the lawsuits and commerce of the citizens, seems to be all that took place in Shaston in five hundred years. It was a shrine of the blessed dead, and the home of plain-living Englishmen; no more. Its glory, when Wessex was no longer a separate unit in the English polity, was too great for it. Long before the Reformation its twelve churches were too heavy a burden, and many began to fall into decay. Not the most discreet and tolerant behaviour of the last abbess could persuade Henry VIII that Alfred's house still served a need. In 1553 it was dissolved, care being taken that the nuns suffered no worldly discomfort; and in a very short time the fabric vanished. Its stones are the dust of Wessex roads, or the walls of later houses; sometimes put to strange uses, as when a tomb canopy became a burgher's chimney-piece. The bones of St. Edward are lost, the gold and jewels of his resting-place dissipated over the world. A few gravestones, the base of a column or two, a thin layer of wall here and there, a little fragment of what may even be the authentic record of Alfred's own foundation, a leaden bull cast aside in a cellar, where the writ of the Vicar of God no longer runs—that is now the Abbey Church of St. Mary the Virgin and St. Edward the Martyr in Palladour. A huge wall still stands, a wonder of architecture and strength to this day; it is but a poor piece of the boundary of the Abbey Park.

It was not only the great house that disappeared. The churches, already in 1553 falling into disuse, fell also into misuse. Of the twelve within the borough, one alone

(St. Trinity) is now left to maintain continuity and celebrate daily the religion of Western Europe. One other, a venerable and gracious building of the fifteenth century, is preserved, an empty but lovely shell, with a noble peal of bells still rung upon occasion. They do their best to recall the time when all Blackmore Vale must have resounded with the glad sounds from the high hill ; when a man could inscribe in the belfry his conviction that

> "Of all the music that is played or sung,
> There is none like bells if they are well rung."

In this desolate church are sad memorials—some fine oak and a little old glass, gravely beautiful ; recesses, doors, pillars, now void of meaning ; and in a crypt-cellar below, traces of a former altar. This cellar—lately re-acquired for the church—not long ago belonged to a neighbouring tavern ; and within living memory there ascended into the church above, during the services, the fumes of ale and tobacco.

The fall of the Abbey, though it was not, in Shaston any more than elsewhere, the definite end of Roman Catholicism there, or the definite birth of Protestantism, meant to the borough an obvious depreciation of life. Thenceforth it must live for itself alone. It became local, not national. There was no longer any reason for travellers to visit it except in passing. The great past was lost, whatever memories it may have left for a few generations. Its former splendour is to-day not so much forgotten as obliterated. Palladour, to that extent, is not the city of Hudibras and Alfred and Canute, but a mere market town. A stronger thread of unbroken life, however, runs in the families of its inhabitants, whose names have changed little in the secular progression. One house in particular still preserves a pure lineage. There are to-day X——'s in and near Palladour. They have a pedigree traceable beyond doubt, step by step without intermission, to 1243. The name is in Domesday, and it was old then. For ten centuries

X——'s have dwelt on the same acre of England : their dust is the very soil of Shaftesbury.

Less ancient, but not much less, and apparently not less permanent, are other local names and usages. The non-conforming community (now diverse, but formerly uniform) is continuous to so far back as the reign of Henry VIII ; it is one of the oldest in the country ; it is in a sense the natural offspring of Alfred's Abbey. The street names in many cases are exactly as they are in court-leet rolls of Edward IV. The market of the borough is still held (as it was held under Elizabeth, and before her, under that almost queen, the Lady Abbess) on the seventh day of the week, and on the same spot ; and still on Saturdays the awkward kine are frightened this way and that by barbarous devices, much as they were frightened by Britons and Saxons and Normans. The market house, rebuilt, like most of the habitations of corporate life in the borough, in the early nineteenth century, stands on the site of the old stocks, the bull-ring, the whipping-post : an evolution, if not exactly a direct succession. It preserves, in certain features, the last decencies of the Georgian Era—pleasant domestic pro-portions, a delicious canopy for the mayor's seat, some portraits and records. It preserves also older things, like the standard bushel measure of the place, dated 1670. Best of all, it houses the byzant or besant of Shaston : an emblem of singular suggestiveness.

Briefly and strictly, the besant—a vernacular form of " besom "—is a relic of the past. This gracious object offers to us one of those vestigial fictions so abundant in English law and custom. It is the symbol of a practice that died not a century ago. It must be premised that until recently Shaftesbury was dependent upon its lowlands for water. Geology, in giving it, by isolation, strategic and æsthetic advantages, has denied it the office of a watershed. So its folk must go to the springs on the lower slopes, especially to Enmore Green, half a mile away. Within living memory donkeys plodded to and fro with barrels, for hire. But Enmore Green is in neither the borough nor the manor of Shaston. The town, therefore, may not draw water there as of right, but only upon leave given. And that leave was formerly to be won, not by purchase nor by service, but by the yearly ritual of a solemn dance, wherein burgesses must move fantastically round " a staff or besom adorned with feathers, pieces of gold rings, and other jewels, called a prize besom." For one whole hour by the clock " there they shall dance, with their minstrels and mirth of game " ; and they must give to the bailiff who witnessed this duty, a penny loaf, a gallon of ale, a raw calf's head, and a pair of gloves ; which if they do not, " then the said bailiff and his men shall stop the water of the wells of Enmore from the borough of Palladour."

What that ceremony may have meant originally is beyond guess. In the indenture just quoted, it is mentioned as a custom set up " time out of remembrance and mind " ; and that document itself was signed in 18 Henry VIII. From the day appointed for the rite, it might have been a combination of May Day observance (itself antique beyond the memory of man) and the rendering of symbolic dues. It is said that two persons called the Lord and the Lady were noteworthy figures in the procession.* At any rate, it was a binding ceremony. Even as late as the beginning of the nineteenth century, a failure to carry it out *did* cause the water of the wells of Enmore to be stopped from the borough of Palladour. In 1830 the custom ceased, by permission of the Lord of the Manor ; it had become not merely unmeaning, but expensive—the decoration of the besom and the gay trappings of the dance alone cost the corporation twenty pounds or more. And so another immemorial simplicity was broken. Only the besom survives—a delicious gilt pineapple on a short pole, in a glass

* I am reminded by my mother that the Lord and Lady were habitual and important persons in the chimney-sweep's May Day ceremony, which personally I just remember seeing as a small boy. They accompanied the Jack-in-the-green.

case in the Town Hall parlour ; a more ancient emblem, perhaps, than either of the town's superb maces.

Such, then, is the profounder past of Palladour ; a past which many an English country town might envy, and yet which many such towns might parallel. A birth in primal mists ; five hundred years of a fame that spread even over Europe ; then a shrinking to the interests of a twenty-mile circle. From 1553 onwards the town lay outside the middle current of great things ; seldom indeed, did even the outer ripples touch it. Its greatest activity was typical of its history after the Dissolution : it tried not to have any history. Palladour was the head-quarters of the un-fortunate Clubmen, of whom I speak later.

There was one other episode in the town's story, however, which resounded beyond Blackmore Vale, even into West-minster Hall itself, in 1778. Shaston decided that two " nabobs " (persons suitably enriched at the expense of India) should represent it in the House of Commons. Unhappily it came to this decision upon questionable grounds. The voters of this earlier Eatanswill were not entirely free and independent (there were, apparently, less than two-score freeholders). The nabobs were returned by what was afterwards called, in Parliament, " the shame-ful venality of this town." The procedure, it was alleged, was as follows : " A person concealed under a ludicrous and fantastical disguise, and called by the name of Punch, was placed in a small apartment, and through a hole in the door delivered out to the voters parcels containing twenty guineas each, upon which they were conducted to another apartment in the same house, where they found another person called Punch's secretary, who required them to sign notes for the value received : these notes were made payable to another imaginary character, to whom was given the name of Glenbucket." The affairs of the constituency occupied the House of Commons for some time, and the Law Courts for more : but one conclusion all the various verdicts amounted to was that the nabobs were

improperly elected. Their exploit affords evidence, with
an interesting fulness of detail, of what the poll in a rotten
borough meant. At present, it is to be feared, Palladour
does not elect two members, nor even one ; it is but a centre
of a county division.

For the rest, it is to-day a comely town, full of that
pleasant, busy English peace which Jews might respect and
Americans adore. Men brew good ale there. They live
decently and prosperously, tilling the valley lands, pasturing
their sheep on the hills, and trafficking in cattle. Agriculture
has not changed much, even if, after God knows how many
thousand years of slowly growing experience, science may
be altering the husbandman's implements. But the soul
of a people changes. Perhaps some day Palladour will
lose the world and regain its soul. Perhaps it will remember
the sundial motto translated on one of its own house-walls—
Pereant et imputantur ; "So speed we, but the reckoning
bideth." In the twentieth century the old faith has gone,
with all its monstrous abuses ; but there is no new faith in
its place—no common hope that can make Everyman's
spirit fill the whole world and rejoice that the stars are his
jewels. In Palladour there is no vision, save perhaps one
that was given me by the eyes of a man of the Naval
Division, trained hard by, who told me, with a face of horror
that had got past grief or fear, of what he had seen at
Gallipoli. Yet hither to Shaftesbury, if ghosts could dream,
their thoughts would surely wander, till the gleaming hill
became populous with the innumerable dead. Here they
would stand looking out, south, and east, and west, as of old
they stood, watching for the dim hope or danger or the
departing joy far below in the weald. There is no scene
which the imagination may not readily picture, whether it
be Alfred coming from Wareham in triumph to found his
Abbey ; or the hasty messenger from Corfe with tidings
that a king was murdered ; or the sad and splendid cavalcade
of the martyr's reinterment ; or that other mourning
procession that bore away the great Danish king to his tomb

at Camelot ; or tithe-waggons creeping up to the rich Abbey, summoners jingling forth to expedite the reluctant ; pilgrims as gay as Chaucer's climbing the last slope of their journey, the black mud of the valley on their feet now chequered with the white of the hill ; mirth and solace at the many inns. So might our forefathers renew old laughter and old tears ; saddened, perhaps, and yet rejoicing that Palladour still stands, that still in their hill-town human hearts, their sons' hearts, beat with the same frailty, the same strength, the same eternal striving.

VI

" If any person wishes to know what kind of man he was, or what honour
he had, or of how many lands he was lord, then will we write about
him as well as we understood him ; we who often looked upon him,
and lived somewhile in his court. This King William then that we
speak about was a very wise man, and very rich ; more splendid and
powerful than any of his predecessors were. He was mild to the good
men that loved God, and beyond all measure severe to the men that
gainsaid his will. . . . Amongst other things is not to be forgotten
that good peace that he made in this land ; so that a man of any
account might go over his kingdom unhurt with his bosom full of
gold. . . . Assuredly in his time had men much distress, and very
many sorrows. Castles he let men build, and miserably swink the
poor. The king himself was so very rigid, and extorted from his
subjects many marks of gold, and many hundred pounds of silver ;
which he took of his people, for little need, by right and by unright.
He was fallen into covetousness, and greediness he loved withal.
He made many deer-parks, and he established laws therewith ; so that
whosoever slew a hart or a hind should be deprived of his eyesight.
As he forbade men to kill the harts, so also the boars ; and he loved
the tall deer as if he were their father. Likewise he decreed by the
hares, that they should go free. His rich men bemoaned it, and the
poor shuddered at it. But he was so stern that he recked not the
hatred of them all ; for they must follow withal the King's will, if
they would live, or have land or possessions, or even his peace."

THE ANGLO-SAXON CHRONICLE.

" ' Mr. Clare is one of the most rebellest rozums you ever knowed—not a
bit like the rest of the family ; and if there's one thing that he do
hate more than another 'tis the notion of what's called a' old family.
He says that it stands to reason that old families have done their
part of work in past days, and can't have anything left in 'em now.
There's the Billetts, and the Drenkhards, and the Greys and the St.
Quintins and the Hardys and the Goulds, who used to own the lands
for miles down this valley ; you could buy 'em all up now for an old
song a'most. Why, our little Betty Priddle here, you know, is one
of the Paridelles—the old family that used to own lots o' the lands
out by King's-Hintock now owned by the Earl o' Wessex, afore even
he or his was heared of. Well, Mr. Clare found this out, and spoke
quite scornful to the poor girl for days. " Ah ! " he says to her,
" you'll never make a good dairymaid ! All your skill was used up
ages ago in Palestine, and you must lie fallow for a thousand
years to git strength for more deeds ! " ' "

THOMAS HARDY,
Tess of the D'Urbervilles.

THE CHRISTIAN CONQUERORS

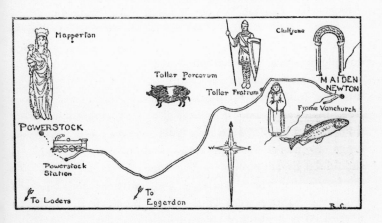

THE great and famous Mr. John Durbeyfield, of
Marlott, in the county of Dorset, was led to believe
that his family reached "all back long before
Oliver Grumble's time," even to the very days of "King
Norman." I have heard the walls of Wareham ascribed to
this same potentate, acting in collusion, apparently, with
Queen Elizabeth and King Napoleon. Such is the deep,
blurred impress of a great personality.

It is beyond doubt that John Durbeyfield's singular
boast of high lineage and low fall therefrom could be upheld
no less justly by many Dorset peasant families. In the
lowlier classes, and among the yeomanry above them, even
more than in the higher ranks of to-day, names are found
which go back, discontinuously, yet persistently, from
generation to generation, from century to century, to the
Conqueror's time. A few stretch yet further into the waste

of Saxon years. But that year of climacteric, 1066, is a real turning-point in English life. Duke William was the last great racial whirlwind to set in turmoil this troubled island.

Yet conquest is always a relative thing. Except by sheer annihilation or expulsion, a conquered race is not blotted out. The language we speak to-day—the language which can still be heard in strong and simple purity in the Dorset villages—is English,* not French nor Scandinavian : the victims have passively conquered the victors. And even at the moment of conquest the invaders did not set up a completely new fabric of life. The towns of England, for the most part, were towns before the Normans came. The humbler folk lived on in their squalor and hardship, less free, politically, but in material circumstances not very differently placed. It was a chief concern of the Norman kings to assert that the laws and customs of England should be as they were in the time of King Edward the Confessor, in whose amiable and cultured half-Norman reign the Saxons were thus led to perceive the hitherto unrealized perfection of their own social order.

The stir of this new governance of England, however, must have been tumultuous in detail. Even in the negative picture of Dorset's share in it the shadows of the great change can be discerned.

So far as Dorset is directly concerned, after Hastings there is a brief darkness. Fifteen months later, Western England rose, and William, who " let his men always plunder all the country that they went over " marched to Devonshire and beset the city of Exeter. No doubt the non-combatant folk of Dorset then saw for the first time, in many a hamlet, what conquest meant. But there seems to be no definite ground† for Freeman's belief that the towns of Dorset (especially the four royal boroughs) banded themselves

---

* Barnes pointed out that only the choice of London as capital instead of Winchester prevented it from being Dorset's English.

† See Exton on the Dorset Domesday and Round's *Domesday Studies*.

together at the call of Exeter, and were ruthlessly despoiled. They were to suffer in time of peace. " Between the Conquest and Domesday (1086) more than half the houses in Wareham and in Dorchester were utterly destroyed." And the majority are stated to have been destroyed " since the time of Fitz Grip "—Hugh, son of Grip, a sinister figure who, with his wife, stands rather for the predatory than the civilizing aspect of the Norman Conquest.*

The division of the spoils was not without significance. Thirty-six and a half parts of the county were taken by the King (who seized Harold's estates " by escheat ") ; one hundred and two belonged to Sarum and the monasteries ; ninety-eight to Earls, Barons, and the greater lords ; and only twenty-eight and a half to lesser men. Out of one hundred and twenty pre-Conquest landholders only twenty continued in possession. The English, however, were for the most part bound to the soil, not to the soil's lord ; they became in fact what the poorer of them had already tended to become—immovable forced labourers paid in kind. The whole population of the county is estimated at about nine thousand.

The Turbervilles of Wool and Bere Regis, the de Claviles (Clavells) of Smedmore, the Trenchards, the Martins, the Gollops of Strode, the Mohuns of Blackmore Vale, de Aquila of Wynford Eagle, and many another family rich and powerful in the generations to come, were among the newcomers, in William's reign or a little later. They were to hold their lands till the days of the *nouveaux riches*—till the Wars of the Roses had worn them out and the Tudor

---

* The wife of Hugh may perhaps have been the more voracious, but they both appear (with mysterious frequency) in Domesday as acquisitive. " To this manor (Abbotsbury) belongs one virgate of land which Hugh, son of Grip, unjustly took ; and his wife still holds it by force. This, in King Edward's time, was for the sustenance of the monks. . . . Hugh held this land of the Abbot of Abbotsbury, as his vassals say, but the Abbot denies it. . . . With this manor (Winterbourne), the same Hugh holds one virgate of land unjustly, which belongs to William de Moione (Mohun). . . . Hugh gave this hide (at Orchard) to the Church of Cranborne for his soul, it is worth twenty shillings. But the wife (widow) of Hugh holds the half hide."

tradesmen bought them up. The old names, as Hardy says, lasted on. There was a Norman Bonvile de Bredy (Bridport) : a prosperous garage at Bridport to-day is Bonfields. A Norman, de Moulham, was granted quarrying rights in Purbeck. It was a quarryman of Swanage who in the nineteenth century founded the great contracting firm of Mowlem.

To the peasant, perhaps, except for the severity of the forest laws, life under the new lords was not much more unpleasant than before. To the former free Saxon land-holders, if the chronicles are a true guide, the impression the conquerors gave was one of ruthless strength, of controlled and controlling force—as well as of extrusion. As the Norman architecture was stronger and more spacious than the Saxon, though akin to it in essentials, so the Norman rule was stronger and more capacious than that which it succeeded and developed.

There is to me a human quality in the majesty of Norman architecture, and conversely something impressive in the often crude humour of its details. The beautiful little Norman church at Studland still seems to breathe its builders' steady purpose. The leaden font at Wareham, the arches at Wareham and Whitchurch Canonicorum and Iwerne, the victorious horseman in Fordington porch, the grotesques on the pillars at Bere Regis, are evidences of a simple sincerity which was itself strength. And in the transition arches of Wimborne and Bere Regis (so alike that they might well be by the same architect) there is what almost appears to be a weakening into beauty.

There is much of that architecture in the county. To me, apart from the places already named, there seems always to be something left of the Norman spirit, and, most of all, of the spirit of the Conqueror's great peace, in the country between Maiden Newton and Powerstock.

" Waleran himself holds Maiden Newton. Alward held it in King Edward's time, and it was taxed for six hides. There is land to seven ploughs. Of this there is half a hide in the demesne, and therein two ploughs and five bondmen : and seven villeins and fourteen bordars with five ploughs. Two mills pay twenty shillings : and there are eighteen acres of meadow. Pasture fourteen quarentons long, and seven quarentons broad. Wood five quarentons long, and three quarentons broad. It is worth ten pounds."

So there were no free Englishmen in Maiden Newton in 1085. Where was Alward ? Dead at Hastings ? Fled overseas as many Saxons are said to have fled ? Or had he become one of the villeins, working perhaps half the year for Waleran the Norman, and the rest of the year toiling for himself on the land to which he was bound ? Even so, he would be better off than the bordars, his own former underlings, who might swink three quarters of their lives for their conquerors.

It is a long stretch from that abjectness, in which arose the fine Norman arch of Maiden Newton church, to the gild of bell-ringers whose rules and rhymes are to-day in the church tower. The coming of the Normans to some extent stabilized and strengthened the one agency in England which, whatever its faults in the direction of repression, gave men hope and beauty. This village church is full of the purposefulness of Holy Church herself. The Norman arch was part of a strong house of God. The double " squints " of two centuries later, cut through the Norman work, let more peasants approach Him than ever before. The fine Perpendicular porch, with its wonderful gargoyles, gave a new entrance into the invisible Church through the visible. The Faith is seen growing as the building and the people grow.

There is only one mill at Maiden Newton now. But it has one of the comeliest mill-houses imaginable, lying on arches across the smooth Frome, whose waters, full of trout, tempt the back doors of half the village. If you follow that gracious stream you will come (but few know it) to another Norman arch, in the tiny little church of Frome Vauchurch, which might well join the company of claimants to the ex-

H

treme of smallness. With its early English work, its Norman font and door, its fine modern copy of a Dutch painting, its sense of confined intimacy, it seems almost to boast that there always have been and always will be two or three country folk gathered together in that same spot at hours of worship.

There are two Fromes in Domesday, but it is not clear which is Frome Vauchurch, Frome St. Quintin, Frome Belet, or even Chilfrome. But "Alward held it in King Edward's time, and it was taxed for four hides." Alward again. . . . He held many lands in Dorset, and every one a Norman holds in Domesday. The Earl of Moreton* held this Frome, one Bretel holding a hide of it from him. Formerly the land was worth forty shillings : " now sixty shillings." Who created and who earned that increment in the rich pastures where now the lovely dairy farms of Notton and Cruxton lie ? Alward, or the Earl, or Bretel ?

All round here the Normans were populous. At Wynford Eagle was that de Aquila whom Mr. Kipling has rightly placed at Pevensey also. At Toller (whether of the Brothers or of the Pigs is not clear : Pig Toller has a Jacobean manor-house, Brother Toller an alleged Roman but probably Saxon font). The Earl of Moreton held Toller also, and Drogo held it of him. " Almar held it in King Edward's time." But Waleran also held a Toller, and Olger held it from him. " Alward——" he too held land in this Toller in King Edward's time. " It was worth three pounds : now four pounds." The same story.

And it is the same story at the other Frome. William de Mohun held it, and Robert held it of him. " Alward held it in King Edward's time. . . ." Three thanes also had held land there in King Edward's time, but two of William's vassals held their lands in the Domesday record.

As you leave Maiden Newton behind and across the stream (where eels congregate and trouble the water), and

---

* William's half-brother : " a man of crass and slow wits," according to William of Malmesbury.

climb the hill past the manor-house, you come into a deserted
" forest " that can have changed little in the last thousand
years. Pasture land lies on its fringes, where it slopes down
to the many brooks. But the uplands are much as they were
when King John hunted here : a waste of gorse, heather,
broom, and bramble, aflame in due season with foxglove
and loosestrife, yellow iris and scabious, filled with gigantic
blackberries, the home of innumerable birds and rabbits.
You will not meet a soul as you go along the bypath from
one Toller to the other. There may be a few people in the
straggling street of Toller Porcorum (Great Toller : great
as compared with Little Toller, Toller Fratrum, where are
but five or six houses). But as you go deviously back into
the " forest " and climb towards Eggardon, the loneliness
descends again, and a serene desolate beauty meets the eye
on all sides.

Even Eggardon fell into other hands under the Conqueror.
William de Braose held the cultivated lands under the great
hill, and Hunfrid held it from him, and there were six villeins
there, instead of the five thanes of Edward's time. As you
stand once more on the hill and look west, you face other near
hamlets where the old order changed. William de Mohun
held South Mapperton, with six bondsmen, six villeins,
seven bordars. " Elmer held it in King Edward's time."
Further on is Broadwindsor, under the same William :
" Alward held it in King Edward's time." Mapperton itself
was held by Ernulf de Hesding, instead of seven thanes :
and he held likewise North Poorton, in place of other seven
thanes (the Abbey of Tavistock held land there also, and at
Askerswell). At Loders again was the Earl of Moreton,
with lands that in Edward's time had belonged to Brihtric :
and the wife of Hugh, son of Grip, held a hide there in place
of two thanes.

But there is a pageant of other things in Powerstock,
a village visible only from Eggardon, and hard to discover
even to those who know the country. From the camp
there are two secret lanes to it, high-hedged winding tracks

such as lovers use. One of them goes past the station, where a beautiful golden cottage crouches under the embankment. Take the path in front of the cottage, cross the rails, and you will see a path leading into an orchard, a path of eternal peace.

In the season of apple-blossom that path is the loveliest in the world. It winds among the trees, streams tinkling alongside, the rich grass consecrated to the calm horned sheep, a few golden cottages asleep by little footbridges. It is like that orchard of ecstasy in Virgil's eclogue :—

> " Jam fragiles poteram a terra contingere ramos . . .
> Ut vidi, ut perii, ut me malus abstulit error ! "

High above, on the right, is a steep hill. On top of it are mounds and trenches upon which you can look down from Eggardon. " Roger Arundel holds Poorstock, and Hugh holds of Roger. Ailmar held it in King Edward's time. . . . There are two ploughs and a half in the demesne, and five bondsmen : and two villeins and nine bordars with two ploughs and a half. Two mills pay three shillings. . . . It was worth four pounds : now six pounds." Those mounds are all that are left of Roger Arundel's pride of power. He or one of his immediate successors built a towering motte-and-bailey castle there, to which in due time King John repaired when he came to hunt in the forest. Now the village children play on the grass-covered foundations.

You have touched the Roman road on Celtic Eggardon : you have crossed to-day's railway, you have seen an outpost of monasticism at Toller Fratrum turned into a squire's manor-house, you see the broken Norman strength above your path. The track widens into a little open meadow, and the secret village lies before you, on a terrace, as it were a battlemented City of God, with its bright walls of golden stone, its roofs of thatch of paler gold, its gay gardens slipping down to the silver stream, and in the midst the yellow tower of the church.

The church itself, on a platform covered with trim grass, is one of the most attractive in Dorset. It has a handsome Early English tower, and a porch. Inside the porch, over the door into the church proper, are niches wherein still stand golden images—images not of gleaming metal, but of the gentler rich-hued stone of West Dorset. By some chance, like the more numerous sculptures at Beaminster, these figures have escaped the " slighter " : no Puritan Dowsing come to Poorstock to cast down idolatry. One or two other shapes are missing, but there remain two royal saints, and above them the Queen of Heaven bearing the infant Christ. Time and the generous stone have mingled to give the Virgin an exquisite grace and simplicity. She has stood there, I suppose (for the niches appear to be Perpendicular work), for four or five centuries, her form growing ever more tender, her mien more kindly, as the observances of faith, and perhaps faith itself, grew colder and more cold. " Books for the simple people," an inquisitor of Spain called images to a stout Protestant English prisoner with whom he was arguing. This book may still be read.

Within the church are other memories. Once, clearly, there was a rood loft. There is a double " squint," and in a pillar or buttress between the tower arch and the south aisle a curious door-opening which now serves no purpose, leading nowhither, unnecessary. If these vestiges of architectural creation could be deciphered, and the minds of builders and the defacers known, we should, it may be, learn much of the English religious temper. Who thought it would be a good thing to have that little door, and to what did it give special access ? In what state was the rest of the church at the time ? Who consented, whose feelings were hurt by the innovation that is now so old ? Every church in England, almost, asks these riddles ; seldom are there documents enough left even for a conjectural answer.

Inside the tower is an old memorial slab, commonplace

enough in its pathetic claim upon generations unborn, yet equally suggestive by reason of the things it cannot tell us :

> " Here lyeth the body of Thomas Larcombe of South Porton, desesed the 31 Day of August anno 1610 (1670 ?)
>
> > ' All those that turne aside my tombe to see,
> > Think of your end and warning take by me.' "

It is easy to read between the lines of pompous falsehood in an eighteenth-century epitaph, or to realize a life from the account of a soldier's death : but Thomas Larcombe has not even a character in the census of the dead.

But the chief glory of this perfect little church, apart from the images, is the Norman chancel arch. It is very heavy, almost as if it had once supported a huge strain : and it is all askew—not, it seems, from pressure, but because Roger Arundel's humble architect could not achieve the pure arch, and built, as his best, this lopsided curve that even mathematics could not name. It has four layers of decorations—loops, spirals, chevrons, and leaves : all perfectly preserved.

Bowed and twisted, yet beautiful in a strangely intimate way, this homely arch in a tiny parish church seems to speak like a sudden voice in a still place. Here is something of the Norman secret. We English, when William came, were no mean race. After the Roman peace, we had had six centuries of strife and hardship to make men of us : and yet these fierce kinsmen of the Dane could conquer us, and write our possessions in a book, and make our laws. We swallowed them up : English prevailed. But sometimes, as in an old legal phrase, or a piece of land tenure, or a few well-mortared walls, the masterful Norman lives again with startling clearness. Here in the stones of Poorstock church there is much later history written : but the Norman stands out, unique, plain, individual : a step in the succession, but not native to it. The ideals and the splendour of a race are revealed ; and while here the castle, in its pride of strength, has perished, beauty and faith endure.

Opposite the church is the inn, a place of good local cider.* It is the only modern building in the village—the only unsimplicity. But the hearts of those who use it are simple. An old blind bob-tailed sheep-dog blundered in one day as I sat there : he stumbled against chairs. " Poor old dog," said the landlady ; " I want Dad to shoot 'un, but he won't. He says he can't lift his hand to a maimed thing like that." " You gi' I the gun, Mother," said an old labourer ; " I'll shoot 'un for 'ee." " It do seem hard," she continued, " life is sweet, we know that, but I wouldn't want to go on living if I went blind." " No : I'll shoot 'un for 'ee. Life is sweet, so we do know, but I'd shoot mysen if I went blind "—he looked out at the bright sunlight— " after seeing *that*."

Life is sweet, even to the hardest-worked class on earth ? Is that the faith that the Conquerors bequeathed to us ? Or did the people of England hold it even then ?

---

* If you wish to injure the feelings of the kindly landlady, ask her if it is Netherbury cider—Netherbury being a noted cider village a few miles away—and hear her indignant reply.

VII

"O God of battles! steel my soldiers' hearts;
Possess them not with fear; take from them now
The sense of reckoning, if the opposed numbers
Pluck their hearts from them. Not to-day, O Lord,
O, not to-day, think not upon the fault
My father made in compassing the crown!
I Richard's body have interred new;
And on it have bestowed more contrite tears
Than from it issued forced drops of blood:
Five hundred poor have I in yearly pay,
Who twice a day their withered hands hold up
Toward heaven, to pardon blood; and I have built
Two chantries, where the sad and solemn priests
Sing still for Richard's soul."

WILLIAM SHAKESPEARE,
The Life of King Henry the Fifth.

"A.D. 1137. . . . They had done him [Stephen] homage, and sworn oaths, but they no truth maintained. They were all forsworn, and forgetful of their troth; for every rich man built his castles, which they held against him: and they filled the land full of castles. They cruelly oppressed the wretched men of the land with castle-works; and when the castles were made, they filled them with devils and evil men. Then took they those whom they supposed to have any goods, both by night and by day, labouring men and women, and threw them into prison for their gold and silver, and inflicted on them unutterable tortures; for never were any martyrs so tortured as they were. . . . When the wretched men had no more to give, then they plundered and burned all the towns. . . . After a time, they spared neither church nor churchyard, but took all the goods that were therein, and then burned the church and all together."

THE ANGLO-SAXON CHRONICLE.

"Indeed, it had been no error to say that this building was one that appealed to the imagination; it did more—it carried both imagination and judgment by storm. It was an epic in stone and marble, and so powerful was the effect it produced on me, that as I beheld it I was charmed and melted. I felt more conscious of the existence of a remote past. One knows of this always, but the knowledge is never so living as in the actual presence of some witness to the life of bygone ages. I felt how short a space of human life was the period of our own existence. I was more impressed with my own littleness, and much more inclinable to believe that the people whose sense of the fitness of things was equal to the raising of so serene a handiwork, were hardly likely to be wrong in the conclusions they might come to upon any subject."

SAMUEL BUTLER,
Erewhon.

THE GREAT ABBEYS AND THE AGE OF FAITH

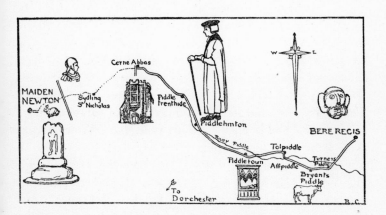

THE period between the Normans and the Tudors, from a purely historical point of view, is full of important details ; and historians look at those details with different aims. The older school saw most prominently the romantic flight of Matilda, the Crusades, the wars in France, the long War of the Roses. The stern political historians are interested in the relations of the sovereign to his nobles, the evolution of Parliament and the judicial system. The economist dwells on the Black Death, the Statutes of Labourers, the Peasants' Revolt ; while the modern religious historian laments to-day's loss of the reverence that built the great abbeys and beautified the many churches that now are seldom filled.

This book would be too long if I were to attempt a continuous chronicle of each of these four branches of progress (if progress there was), or to divide the Middle Age centuries

into more than one period. My reason for keeping them in
one is that the Conquest ended one quite clear and separate
chapter of English history, and the Dissolution of the
Monasteries began another equally distinct and new : in
between was constant and perplexing change. So I shall
only string together a few typical events in the life of Dorset
within those years before turning to some of their vestiges.

And first of war. Wareham, the often-sacked, fared ill
in the collapse of order which followed soon after the
masterful hand of William was withdrawn by death. Bald-
win de Redvers landed there in 1139 " with a full and strong
host of soldiers," and went to Corfe. In 1142 Robert of
Gloucester besieged and took Wareham castle, and " did
other annoying things " ; but Stephen came and " ravaged
cruelly with fire and sword, plundering and carrying off all
he could lay hands upon." Four years later Prince Henry
made it his port for escaping to France. And then there is
comparative silence until John's fondness for Dorset made
him discover the value of Corfe Castle. Here he imprisoned
and let starve twenty-two noble knights of France ; and
here too lay the wretched Peter of Pontefract :—

> " Here's a prophet that I brought with me
> From forth the streets of Pomfret, whom I found
> With many hundreds treading on his heels ;
> To whom he sung, in rude harsh-sounding rhymes,
> That, ere the next Ascension-day at noon,
> Your highness should deliver up your crown."

King John imprisoned him at Corfe ; and when the
prophecy came true, the wretched man was drawn on a
hurdle thence to Wareham, and back again, and hanged.

The story of the twelfth century is almost a repetition of
the grim record of the Saxon invasion. " At this time
(1143) England was troubled in many diverse ways ; here
sorely straitened by the King and his partisans, there
suffering grievously from the Count of Gloucester ; ever and
always commotion and desolation. Some, their love of the
fatherland turned to bitterness, sought distant lands ;

others round the Churches, in the hope of sanctuary, built lowly huts, to lead a life of fear and misery. Food ran short (for famine spread terribly over all England), and some lived on the forbidden and unwonted food of horses and dogs, while others were driven to subsist on roots and grasses. Hosts died of want. Old and famous towns, all the inhabitants of every age and sex dead, lay desolate and empty." " If ever upon the way one spied another, he feared and fled into a wood or other by-way."

On the other hand, these centuries also saw events that are a faint prelude to Dorset's long connection with English sea power. By 1300 or so Wareham was declining from its position of one of the chief towns of the county; but Poole and Weymouth were rising. They were opposing—forcibly— the Cinque Ports' quasi-monopoly of English shipping.

The next century produced the singular naval happening of Poole's private war, conducted by an almost fabulous hero. Arripay—thus does a Spanish chronicler, as it were a Cockney, render the great name of Harry Page—was a seaman of no common mould. In the naval warfare of Henry IV—a mere matter of piracy and resolution, as a rule, but calling for a proud heart if it was adopted as a profession —he harried Flanders and Brittany and Spain with address, pertinacity, and even fury. He was at first the lieutenant of the hardly less bellicose Lord Berkeley; but he appears speedily to have become lustrous as an individual. Poole, said a gentleman of Spain, " belongs to a knight named Arripay, who scours the seas, as a corsair, with many ships, plundering all the Spanish and French vessels that he could meet with. This Arripay came often upon the coast of Castille, and carried away many ships and barks; and he scoured the channel of Flanders so powerfully, that no vessel could pass that way without being taken. This Arripay burnt Gijon and Finisterra, and carried off the crucifix from Santa Maria de Finisterra, which was famous as being the holiest in all these parts (as in truth it was, for I have seen it), and much more damage he did in Castille, taking many prisoners, and exacting ransoms ; and though other armed ships were there from England likewise, he it was who came oftenest " (Sydenham, *History of Poole*).

The Dons liked him so little that, upon opportunity, they paid a special visit to Poole, and slew Arripay's brother ; but they were forced to retreat. In token also of their opinion of Page, they on this occasion suspended for the time being whatever of international law was then operative —that a Christian soldier was not to murder prisoners, nor injure refugees, nor rob churches, nor burn houses or crops, nor do violence to women : " these rules Pedro Nino ordered to be observed everywhere, except in Arripay's country, because he had burnt houses in Castile."

There is not much information of a definite kind about the Dorset seafarers of this period, except for that vivid little chapter of truculence. Inference from a few recorded facts, however, shows living and active continuity. John ordered rope in a hurry from Bridport in 1213. He and other kings demanded ships for the French and Scottish wars. Lyme (its Cobb, built in Edward I's reign, a wonder to all, and its standing enhanced by his charter of 1284), Weymouth and Melcombe, Poole and Wareham furnished vessels from time to time, just as the abbeys and landowners furnished land service and gave hospitality to the King's horses, men, and prisoners. There were raids and counter-raids from France and Spain and even visits from Barbary pirates. A system of beacons—a natural anticipation of 1805 and 1914—was set up to guard against invasion.

In the midst of the foreign and domestic tumult kings came to and fro. The strategy of castles bade them keep a watchful eye on all parts of their kingdom, and Dorset was still something of a sea-gateway from France and Spain to the West and Middle-West of England. There were castles at Corfe, Portland, Lulworth, Sherborne, Wareham, Powerstock, and possibly three or four others of less importance. The King constantly addressed to his Dorset officers and subjects open letters—letters patent of favour,

of armistice, of protection : " The King to all his bailiffs
and faithful subjects, greeting . . . know ye that we have
taken under our safe conduct " some fortunate person who
could produce this document. Often enough he warned the
guardians of his coasts to be watchful and responsible, or
ordered his bailiffs " to select immediately the best and
strongest men of your ports, and those who are well armed,
to man our vessels, at our cost and for our service."

John visited the county with some frequency. He
afforested* the whole of Purbeck—wrongfully, so the monks
of Cerne claimed : they owned rights in the isle, already
mentioned. In almost every year from 1204 to the end of
his reign he lay a night or two at some Dorset manor or
castle—Dorchester, Bridport, Gillingham (the ruins of his
house there are but green mounds), Powerstock, Corfe,
Bere Regis, Sherborne, Cranborne, and other places all
saw him : Corfe and Gillingham most often. Powerstock
Castle was either rebuilt or reinforced : there is an entry
of £104 spent on it, and of 100,000 nails brought thither for
the work. There is, too, a suggestive entry in the Patent
Rolls about Corfe :

" Teste 11 July, at Corfe. Know, that we received at
Corfe on Tuesday, the Translation of St. Benedict, in the
18th year of our reign, from the hands of Agatha Trussebut,
wife of William de Albeny, and her chaplain William,
500 marks for the ransom of this said William de Albeny."

Poor Agatha ; and poor tenants of Agatha and William !

Edward I was another frequent visitor to much the same
places as John, except that he seemed to be specially fond
of Bindon Abbey, which William of Newburgh had refounded in 1172. Piers Gaveston was thought to be a refugee
in the county in 1311, and Edward II was imprisoned at
Corfe before he was removed to his murder at Berkeley
Castle ; while Margaret of Anjou, befriended by Cardinal
Moreton of Bere—a former monk of Cerne—rested at Cerne

* Put under the Forest Laws : not planted trees.

on one of her vain attempts to secure the crown for her son.

The Dorset abbots and friars who took so large a share in the public life of the country, in service to the King, in education and in improving the land, have left, thanks to the Dissolution and the passing of the monastic buildings into the hands of Henry VIII's favourites, few visible remains of their greatness, except in three glorious buildings still in use—Wimborne Minster, Sherborne Abbey, and Milton Abbey. Wimborne—a royal chapel and college of secular canons—contains not only Norman and Transition work, but an Early English east window of great beauty, and the grave of Athelstan. Milton has some splendour of the Decorated period, and keeps a little of the gay hues that once made the great churches a marvel of rich colour : while the fan-tracery of Sherborne is an unsurpassed glory.

Cerne—like Abbotsbury, Sherborne, and Milton, a Benedictine house—is but a fragment : Abbotsbury, save for the noble barn, little more : Shaftesbury not as much : while Bindon, a Cistercian foundation, is the most pathetic forlorn ghost of grave beauty imaginable. Of it Mr. Moule, the Dorchester antiquarian, wrote feelingly : " You cannot wall in the free heart : you cannot wall out the world ; but the place where the effort was made is no common ground." It suffered a curious irony in its death. It was dissolved among the smaller monasteries in 1536, refounded by Henry VIII himself in 1537, and again dissolved in 1539.

The priories, minor houses, and hospitals—there were many lazar houses—have almost entirely vanished.

We can, however, guess at a little of the local vigour and sincerity of that life when religion was real and vital to conduct as well as to salvation. Much of the beauty of Sherborne is due to a desperately earnest quarrel. The people of the place in 1436 had a bitter dispute with the monks about the position of the font and their own entry into the church. They came to blows, a riot ensued, and the

CERNE ABBEY GATEWAY

Engraved from a drawing by J. W. Upham

old fabric was very seriously damaged by fire : the rebuilding gave us much of to-day's loveliness.

That was a case of religious ardour. On the other hand, the abbot of Abbotsbury of a century or so before, Walter de Stokes, behaved like the traditional predatory abbot of fiction, and a long enquiry into his conduct would probably have ended in scandal but for his death.*

Of the glories of Shaftesbury I have already spoken. In contrast to that world-wide fame is the gentle seclusion of the Cistercian nuns at Tarrant Keynes, to whom a famous treatise in Middle English was probably addressed—the *Ancren Riwle*, or Anchoresses' Handbook, said to have been composed for them about 1200 by Richard Poore, Bishop of Salisbury. The Abbey was but a little house : at the surrender in 1539 it contained an abbess and eighteen nuns. When the *Riwle* was written, it was the refuge of three sisters of gentle birth, with lay sisters and servants. Among the reasons why they fled the world the writer gives these :

" It is a proof of nobleness and liberality. Noblemen and gentlemen do not carry packs, nor go about trussed with bundles, nor with purses. It belongs to beggars to bear bag on back, and to burgesses to bear purses, and not to God's spouse, who is the Lady of Heaven. Bundles, purses, bags, and packs are all earthly wealth and worldly revenues. . . . Ye take no thought for food or clothing, neither for yourselves nor for your maidens. Each of you hath from one friend all that she requireth ; nor need that maiden seek either bread, or that which is eaten with bread, further than at his hall. . . . The sorcerer would fain with flattery render you perverse, if ye were less gentle and docile. There is much talk of you, how gentle women you are ; for your

* The last abbot also is alleged to have given offence, according to a document quoted by Hutchins : " Whereas the Abbot taketh to his own use and hath made great waste of wood sales wrongfully sold from his brothers and their tenants, and also hath sent out of the treasury certain jewels more than half (whereas we cannot judge the true value of the same) and hath sold it. . . . He hath an abominable rule with keeping of women, not with i, ii, or iii, but with many more than I do write of, and also no religion he keepeth nor by day neither by night." Not proven, says the *Victoria County History*, in effect.

I

goodness and nobility of mind beloved of many ; and sisters of one father and one mother ; having, in the bloom of your youth, forsaken all the pleasures of the world and become anchoresses."*

All their daily customs, religious and lay alike, were expounded to them in this generous-minded homily ; how they were not to be liberal with other people's alms ; not to buy nor sell (" a buyer and seller selleth her soul to the chapman of hell ") ; not to use too harsh a discipline of their bodies ; to have blood let four times a year (thereafter resting : " talk with your maidens, and divert yourselves together with instructive tales ") ; and " ye shall not possess any beast, dear sisters, except only a cat."

That fine piece of South-Western dialect English gives some hint of what was coming to pass in England. The nation was becoming English, and so was its language. The peasants saw the world in the great wars : they learnt at Agincourt and Creçy their own strength. The men of Dorset fought on St. Crispin's day under their own banner of a silver tower on a red ground. They had come gradually to be part of an organism not merely local, their terms of service secured by national, not local justice. But until the long wars brought their inevitable penalties on Europe, the English peasant had no real chance of freedom. It was in Dorset, through the seaport intercourse with France and the Channel Islands, that the greatest economic change of this long period commenced. The Black Death broke out at Melcombe Regis in 1348. Within three years " the inhabitants remaining are not sufficiently numerous to protect (the coast) against our foreign enemies."†

It was upon the poor, living in squalor, that the plague fell most heavily. But it had its compensations. In a short time, instead of being bound ineluctably to forced toil, the peasants, through the reduction in their numbers, could sell their labour at a high price, and employers had to compete for it, and did compete for it, in spite of the

* Camden Society's translation.   † Gasquet, *The Black Death.*

successive Statutes of Labourers which tried to fix the conditions.*   The wages system had arrived, though with
many local variations and survivals of the old tenures and
compulsions.   And one result of this weakening of compulsion was that within two or three generations English
was perforce the common language of all classes.

Whether the wages system made for the real happiness
of the poorest labourers, or not, can be better judged when
we come to the revolts of five centuries later.   A hundred
small hardships and injustices, not easily remedied when all
the real force was in the hands of those who wore armour,
embittered the relations between the villagers and the lords ;
and in 1381 the Peasants' Revolt flamed out.   It was easily
put down, after a dangerous but sporadic success.   Dorset
seems to have taken no great part in it, unless a reported
local increase of crime is an outer ripple of the whirlpool.

It is in walking through a tract of deserted churches and
lonely villages, it seems to me, that something of the multi-
farious, excitable life of this time (Chaucer's pilgrims were
always at the zenith of their personalities) can be recaptured.
Start again at Maiden Newton, from what was once the
revered village cross : it is now a centre of children's
games and a leaning-post for those who await the opening
of licensed houses.   Hither came the Abbot of Milton's
corn to market, borne by his forced labourers ; and Cerne
Abbey held a third of the manor.   Go past the station by
the white track, steeply uphill.   Near the top cross the
fields to the left : you will walk over a British village : if
haply you have a dog, he will go down to the annals of
innumerable rabbits as a sudden piratical raid which caused
great terror.   A little further west, you cross the Roman
road from Dorchester to Ilchester, a lovely grass-grown
straight track filled with eternal peace.   Down a path

* Some striking but not always exact parallels may be found between
these Statutes (and their intentions) and the arguments in use at the
present moment in regard to the deceased Agricultural Wages Board.
Prof. Oman, in his standard work, makes a quotation from *Piers Plowman*
about the greedy labourers which might come from a retrograde farmer
to-day.

westwards which hardly exists,* you come to an odd hedged lane leading nowhere, with a private walk alongside : some vanished or disused idea never fully carried out : and so to Sydling St. Nicholas, where are a fine Tudor barn and a sturdy church and as many Georgian houses, deliciously spaced, as could well be desired ; and streams and ducks all down the wide pretty street.

The church itself is curiously impressive in its historical gaps. It is an immensely strong building, shored up by very heavy buttresses, and mostly Perpendicular in style. It has large grotesque gargoyles, a fine tower—and inside, a number of monuments to eighteenth and early nineteenth century London aldermen and their families. On the tithe barn are cut the initials of the wife of Elizabeth's Secretary, Walsingham, who held the manor from Winchester College. Imagination tends to dwell on what is not there, rather than on what is. The village is so neat, so quiet, so primevally domestic, that there ought to be visible evidence of the period when the church was first built.

Sydling may well claim to be one of the half-dozen most beautiful villages in Dorset†—or even in England. It lies in a deep valley in the chalk, well watered, full of sheep. North there is a noble walk to the main ridge. But the way now lies past a well, where it is good to sit and hear running water, and over the high hills again. And as at last you descend, you see on a hill opposite the Cerne Giant.

When I last sat on the slope and looked at the Giant, I felt myself back in a scene of a year before. I was then in the Town Hall at Dorchester. It was full, quite full, of farmers, with a sprinkling of gentry and humbler folk, and a few obvious agents : a gathering huge by the side of the coteries of Sotheby's or Christie's. I had in my hand a monstrous fine folio book about Cerne, which the auctioneers

---

* Across the Roman road, immediately opposite your track : close along a hedge which must be kept on the right.

† Other claimants in Dorset are Corfe Castle (without recent additions), Affpuddle, Burton Bradstock, Rampisham, Chideock (except the inn and a building opposite), and Milton Abbas, and Hammoon, and Okeford Fitzpaine, and—but this is becoming a gazetteer.

had bestowed upon me for nothing. An austere man with a little white pointed beard and a monotonous voice was saying, " Any advance on £700 ?   £750.   Any advance on £750 ? Going at £750 . . . going. . . . Gone at £750. Mr. X. Bought by the tenant." There was hardly even an inflexion in his colourless voice as he asked " any advance ? "   But in the audience there was a subdued undercurrent of feeling which could not be mistaken : it broke out in cheers when a tenant bid successfully.

For a whole village was changing hands. I had been into some of the cottages a few days before. There were holes in almost every ceiling : most of the walls were perishing : slugs of the Giant's kin were in many rooms—they were exhibited with a kind of pride. The Abbey Farm was shut and deserted :* the lovely orchard behind it many feet deep in grass and nettles, the little fabric of beauty in the old gateway and the oriel window in the barn losing its mortar and drawing still nearer to final decay.

If Goldsmith wanted to write a new *Deserted Village*, or W. H. Hudson an even more sombre *Shepherd's Life*, Cerne Abbas might be the inspiration. The wide street is always empty, save when charabancs vomit incongruous crowds. There seems to be hardly even the ordinary tiny activity of a general shop—though there are several shops, in point of fact. I doubt if a man could get drunk in the inns : they are too desolate. If anyone lives in the two or three comely private houses, it must surely be some aloof Mrs. Sparsit. Even on the streams of the village, to which I was told (my informant wearing an air of shy half-credulity) the Giant came down to drink at nights, there are few ducks, and those meagrely loquacious.

The church is a beautiful skeleton. Outside it has little flying pinnacles of a lovely design, in yellow stone, niches with some saints still inhabitant, a fine tall tower. Inside

---

* I should like to say here that the present tenant of the farm, who is working strenuously with his own hands to repair the property, very rightly resents wholesale intrusion on his orchard and field. The Gateway ruin can be seen by decent people who ask decently and behave decently.

it is as frigid as a neglected museum. There were at one time recently no less than three fonts in it : one venerable, of the Middle Age (so simple in design as to have no marked characteristic) ; one modern, of which the less said the better, for it is ugly ; and one delightful absurdity of the Georgian era—a sort of small hand-basin on a leg, composed of wood or some composition painted to look like marble. As at Batcombe, there is a stone rood-screen. As at Abbotsbury, there is a good seventeenth-century pulpit. There is a decent pompous wooden screen, also, at the west end of the nave. The Perpendicular east window is remarkably large. The church is a spacious building.

One of its exhibits (I *must* use the word : the church does not " show off," but it is not instinct with any reality) is a stone coffin. There are plenty of others in Dorset. But I cannot quite conceive the mind which thus preserves a void grave, out of its designed place, and insignificant, in an edifice dedicated to public worship. It can hardly be doubted that some successor of Ælfric, some abbot or high officer of Cerne Abbey, lay in this massive bed : dead, in the faith of Christ. We know that stone was used for coffins, and we know (at least, we are always told so) that churches *are* places of worship, not museums. We should inspect empty stone coffins, therefore, as exhibits, in a real museum : not at the spot where their vanished tenants were once buried with the rites of Holy Church. Would any vicar, any parishioner, prop up to-day against a wall, for a show, the empty oak box that recently held his grandfather's decaying flesh and bones ? Antiquity is no defence. What do a few centuries matter to the principle ? It might be argued that the remains of the pious dead, or their relics, should abide at or near the place where they were committed to the mercy of God. But their mortal bodies, in such cases as this, are not there to await the resurrection. The " sad and solemn priests " sing no longer for their souls. The tomb or chantry of a dead man, his perpetual ornament, a piece of architecture, remains rightly part of the church in which he worshipped,

was buried or commemorated. But here the empty re-
ceptacle of his person is made a show.

I think the most human thing in Cerne church is one of
its two or three interesting epitaphs. " Here lies the body
of Robert White, who died Jan. 6th, 1753, aged 46 : having
been upwards of 20 years in Antigua in South America,
and returning home with a good character, which is well
known by the best sort of people in that island." The exile
from the little village, with a good character vouched for by
the best people . . . I am sure his character was truly good.

Yet life here must have been real once. Consider the
legend of the name Cerne Abbas. You will find (if you go
about it in the right way), near the gate-house of the
old Abbey and the orchard, a well—St. Austin's or St.
Augustine's well. A stone step of its superstructure, in
Hutchin's time, bore five Latin words—" Of Thomas Corton
thirty-fourth abbot." Corton was the last Abbot of Cerne.
He preserved a continuity which by tradition went back to
him after whom the well is named. St. Augustine is said
to have come hither and to have been mocked by the
inhabitants. They tied fishes' tails (some say the tails of
cows) to the skirts of himself and his followers and drove
them out. But the saint immediately in a vision saw their
destiny, and called out, in a loud voice, " I see God (cerno
Deum), Who will pour into them a better spirit." The men
of Cerne in a short time repented and asked him for forgive-
ness and begged him to return. Cerne is the place of the
vision of God.

There are other explanations, not less credible, of the
founding of the Abbey. It is probably at least a ninth-
century creation. It owned many manors. To-day there
are left of it some stones in the dead village, many in the
fine Abbey Farm, an oriel in one of the farm buildings, and
the lovely gate-house. But like Bindon Abbey, it holds the
soul of man. When at one time before the farm was reoccupied I went through its empty deep-grassed orchard,
saw the ever-running well-stream, the dim green lines

behind the Gate-house which showed where once the
structure of beauty and worship had confronted the world,
the place seemed populous with futile, baffled ghosts. It
was a little house, maybe, as abbeys go.

The Giant—" ithyphallic and clavigerous "—may have
watched with a cynical eye many generations of peasants,
and a few great men. He saw—if the explanations of him
are true—he saw the Romans on the hills near him, and the
Celt driving the Iberian out of the dens that mottle the
green turf still. He saw Brichtuin holding the land in the
Confessor's time, and under William : and no more than the
Giant was Brichtuin allowed to " depart from the land."
He saw the monks at work upon their famous Book and
Cartulary. Even when there was a fanatical Protestant
or a no less fanatical malignant swaying the village, humble
lovers must still have looked with a curious wonder upon his
shameful form. The coaches of the turnpike era let inquisitive
passengers ask questions about him. The smugglers exchanged their goods in his secret mart : and if he had not
preferred the village streams, so numerous and pretty, the
Giant might here have quenched his thirst with " a beer
superior perhaps to any liquor of the kind ever known ":
so its fame ran of old.

From Cerne go up over Black Hill to Piddletrenthide,
by a lovely road giving wonderful views. Piddletrenthide
is a long village of pleasant houses and cottages. In its
church, more beautiful without than within, is a modern
window showing a figure of a man in khaki—the earliest
I have seen to perpetuate thus the Great War. I wonder
why (colour apart) the uniform looks so ignoble by that of
the saints and other warriors in the same window ? Is it
the humbug of ancientry that makes armour seem more
beautiful ? It was a clumsy garment at best.

Follow still the byroad, due south. You will come shortly
to the straggling village of Piddlehinton. The church here
has that curious thing, a palimpsest brass—or rather, one
which has been used on both sides. There is also a remark-

able brass of a vicar with a walking-stick : he is Thomas
Browne, " parson of this place seven and twenty years,"
who died in 1617. The registers of the church contain much
interesting matter which has not been published : how
stranded sailors (so far inland) were relieved, how a grocer
of London whose house had been burnt was given a small
dole, and the like. Oddly enough, I met that grocer long
ago at Oxford : it was exactly the same yarn.

From here the road curves south-east to Piddletown.
And here the church again is to be venerated. It contains
all the life of England, and that not, in its atmosphere of
preservation, in the manner of a dead survival. The font
is Saxon or possibly Norman, with a fine interlacing design.
It stands under a seventeenth-century gallery, from whose
floor depend canvas buckets of 1805, the property of a
Bath insurance company. The east end has been altered ;
but the roof is good. There is the greater part of a carved
three-decker pulpit. And if you go through the Martin
chapel, in the south aisle, into the vestry, you will find the
flutes of the village choir of a generation ago.

The Martin or Athelhampton chapel is a glory of the
county. Here are buried knights and ladies of that notable
family, the colour still rich on some of their tombs, the
supine figures still little harmed by the slighter. " Pray
for their souls," one inscription bids us, " with hearty
desire, that they both may be sure of eternal light."

This little homely chapel holds some of the last enchantments of the knightly years. It is impossible here not to
believe that the Faith was real. Those who wrought the
Purbeck stone into shapes so enduringly gracious, those who
touched them with gay blue and red, those who engraved so
carefully, with so sure a sense of proportion, the strong
brass, had some quality few possess to-day. I think the last
of the Martins preserves it in an epitaph of 1595 now lost
(recorded by Hutchins) : " Nicholas ye first, and Martin
ye last. Good night, Nicholas." A long night, whose dawn
may never break.

Piddletown church, it also seems to me, is one where the past and the present veritably overlap from day to day, even to our own time, and are not cut off, shut apart, one from another. Its simplicity and its beauty have always belonged to this one village, grown with it, formed part of its people's lives. Here, more certainly than in any glorious abbey or cathedral, the Word of God might remain flesh.

From Piddletown follow byroads or paths, which the map shows adequately, to the three divine villages hidden a little way from the main road—three river hamlets, Aff-piddle, Turner's and Brian's Piddle. You can, if you prefer, go along the main road to Tolpiddle and turn off there. You will see a handsome church, the " martyrs' tree," and a monument to those martyrs, of whom I speak later (see Chap. XIII).

Affpiddle has a very handsome church very beautifully situated. It was built, probably, at any rate so far as the tower goes, by the same monk-artist who designed the tower at Cerne. It has the same lovely little flying pinnacles, the same lofty grace. The interior contains splendid wood-work—a pulpit and a number of carved pew-ends—also by a Cerne monk : one of the pew-ends and the pulpit are dated 1547.

The village is pure Dorset : low thatched cottages of yellow mud and plaster, with a little wood and stone : jasmine and fuchsia and veronica creeping shaggily round the windows and doors : unexpected little streams and patches of grass. A few years ago it was more beautiful than encouraging : for the cottages were in grievous dis-repair, the mud walls often gaping or falling, the timber rotting in the damp valley air. But Mr. Debenham has done wonders of restoration of late, and has added, to the ex-cellence of model farming, a striking new farm-cottage architecture which deserves to live alongside the old.

Bryant's Piddle—the Piddle manor of Brian de Turber-ville—is much the same as Affpiddle, but smaller. The last of these three villages is the most exquisite. Toner's (Turner's) Piddle was once the manor of the Toneres, or de Toneres, Norman lords of whom little is known : they rendered service to the crown of Edward I, and that is about all their history. If their lives were as retired and obscure as their record, they can have chosen no more satisfying place of retreat than this tiny hamlet. To-day it consists of a little gracious farmhouse, two or three cottages, and a toy church, so small and compact and neat that it should hardly be more than a cathedral for Lilliput. Small though it is, it yet contains a Norman font—a last relic of departed strength.

There is no Norman air about Toner's Piddle. It is just a little farm set in rich deep water meadows below the huge brown heath which breaks out immediately behind the barton. It is in a place of streams, a maze of fords and foot-bridges : bright with yellow iris and meadowsweet, willow-herb and loosestrife, a haunt of moorhens and herons.*

Take the sandy path alongside the farm, up the hill. You will come out on one of the noblest stretches of " Egdon " Heath. From its height Corfe Castle can be seen guarding its gap, Purbeck keeping back the sea, the chimneys of the secret war-factory at Holton Heath, and of the pottery works not far away : between you and the horizon the grim brown waste undulates in big and little hollows, a few firs here and there, a copse in a valley, the light ever changing.

That is the best way to come to Bere Regis : most of all if you can contrive to reach your end about dusk. You come from the mysterious glooms of the Heath down into a little leaf-hedged path, past a modern cemetery whose stones in the crepuscular half-light are white ghosts ; over a little bridge where all day long you can watch the fat voles

---

* I think the most startling event in Nature is the sudden unexpected uprising of a heron a foot or two away from one. The enormous spread of wing, the first heavy uplift, the long clattering beak, all seem exaggerated, as if the thing were a pterodactyl. So my dog thought on his first putting a heron up at Turner's Piddle, for he ran away for dear life.

at play, or washing their comfortable persons. And so to the imminent church—standing up, from there by the bridge, like a glorious cathedral, hanging over the stream and the few cottages by its side with a dominance of both power and beauty.

The tower is finely decorated : the body of the church has excellent gargoyles. But it is the windows which, if you come from without when they are lit up from within, will stab your imagination. At the east end the light shines through three beautiful Early English lancets (inside they are framed in slender dark Purbeck columns). On the south wall the Turberville arms glow in the many panels of a perfect window in the Perpendicular style. At the east end of that aisle is a glorious little flowing Decorated framework ; an easy, sinuous rhythm in stone that the light transforms into a flower.

There is the whole peace of humanity here. Here, among the works of men, as amid the work of God on Eggardon Hill, I can find the ultimate rest. There is nothing in the church itself which does not suggest a permanent ideal of life. The Turberville aisle has those Decorated and other empty tombs where once poor Tess took refuge. The old local ironwork in the squint has a peculiar homely beauty. The Tudor squire and his wife in the chancel *ought* to be buried there : it is theirs. The " puzzle " brass, in some sort of dog English-Latin, is a proper idiosyncrasy of a little secluded civilization. The pages from the records (showing the authentic Turberville signature), the old and lovely font, the late Norman arches, the grotesque faces upon them, the ancient local tiles and woodwork, the myriad pottery vases for to-day's floral services—there is a chain of life more continuous here than even at Piddletown.

The roof is the wonder of the place. It was brought from Flanders by Cardinal Moreton, it is said. It is a noble arrangement of beams from whose every end juts out a gaily painted figure—severely humorous like the Norman faces in the arches below. The central boss—said traditionally to represent John the Baptist—carries a vast round bearded face, like a Cruikshank illustration to " Jack the Giant Killer." They keep the colours fresh. The roof remains eternally young, eternally real : witnessing to the simple sincerity of a faith that was confident enough to laugh at itself ; witnessing to a temper of mind that was not too self-conscious to mind ridicule if it were in earnest.

When I was last in the church, during the war, the altar bore no flowers ; instead, there were set up small flags of all the Allies—Japan, Serbia, the United States, France, and all of us. I was reminded by them of a war-time scene a friend had described to me.

It took place at the cross-roads at Bere. My friend was staying at the admirable inn there in the summer of 1915, to complete some work and recover his health. He heard the usual noise of passers-by, farm-carts, motors : but it was suddenly broken, in the late afternoon, by a more tumultuous sound. After a time he looked out. A flushed woman of thirty or so, once very pretty and still not wholly unbeautiful, was leaning against a cottage wall opposite. Round her, at some distance, were the louts of the village. They were all arguing angrily. The woman—obviously of a certain profession, a " leaguer-wench," and rather drunk—was taunting them for not going to the front. In that respect, they were good lads : they had tried, and had been forbidden ; farm-labour was too precious. Many of their friends had gone and fallen ; they themselves were to be scraped off the hungry land later. They, on the other hand, starting by jeering at her drunkenness, had come to inflame their jeers with anger at her profession, which they soon guessed. They would not leave her alone. She was afraid to turn her back and go on. Their numbers increased, until perhaps a couple of hundred people—men had now joined the group—stood in a menacing circle round her. No one yet offered active violence, but the temper of the crowd was clearly ugly. My friend went out and spoke to the seeming chief man there. He got nothing but angry words. He spoke to the woman ; she said, sobbing in a horrible drunken way, " I daren't turn my back on them— they'll stone me." She was now pretty nearly sober and ready to moderate her bitter tongue : but he felt her words were true. He turned and talked savagely to the crowd at large ; a mistake, for their anger was not abated by shame. Then he tried persuasion. He spoke to the senior men quietly and said he would take the woman himself to the constable's house—three-quarters of a mile away—if they would keep the crowd in order. They agreed, and he told the crowd what he meant to do, saying that it was the right way to deal with such a person. Then the wretched woman was induced to cling to his arm and turn her back —and he turned his, not without genuine fear—and they went off on the long street, the crowd following ten yards or so behind, watching, it seemed, for a moment's lapse or weakness. Several times the woman broke down and refused to go any farther, and he had to prevent her reviling the people incoherently ; often there were sinister cries of opprobrium behind his back ; until at last they came to the constable's cottage, and gave the poor wretch to his kind wife for a night's lodging. She was following the camp from Weymouth to Blandford : she could not have walked another mile.

It was not her profession, nor the precise exchange of taunts, that interested my friend. It was the fear he himself felt, " in his bones," of the crowd. It seemed like a recrudescence of mediæval horror—of witch-hunting, heresy-hunting, torture, all the animal ferocity of man let loose. There was a force here that the modern mind might not be able to tame : a morality (resentful and perverted, doubtless) that would stick at nothing. He had been lately in that calm and beautiful church, where all the ages, even to-day's, seem to be in happy communion. Here in the twilit village street, with the rough threatening pleasantries, the hysterical woman's sobs, in his ears, he seemed to have reached a dreadful continuity of evil in man ; or not so much of evil as of cruel faith in an unreal good.

They burnt a woman in Dorchester in 1706. They ducked scolds there in 1630. They branded a woman in London in 1751. In my own life-time, not a quarter of a century ago, I have heard " rough music " administered, and the skimmity-riding of " The Mayor of Casterbridge " is only just obsolete. I have seen an otherwise humane fisherman in the last year or so set his dog to worry live crabs, and laugh hilariously when a claw or leg was tugged off. Perhaps eternal beauty needs that face-to-face knowledge of beastliness. " O God of battles, steel my soldiers' hearts. . . ."

VIII

"In this channel under a marble stone doe lye the bodies of Francis Chaldecot Esq., and Edith his wife, younger daut^r. and coheire of William Chaldecot of Quarrellston, in Dorset, esq., who were liberal constant housekeepers; bountiful releivers of the poore; carefull breeders of their children in piety and vertue; diligent and devout comers to the church, though it were very painfull unto them in their latter times, by means of age and other infirmity: 53 yeares and upwards they lovingly lived in chast wedlocke, and had issue 15 children, whereof 3 sons and 7 daughters came to mature age, and were most of them in the life times of their parents matched into ancient families of worship, most of them having fayre issues.

"Thus having lived to see their children to ye third generation, they meekly dyed in ye feare and favor of their God.

"He on Thursday ye 19th of May, 1636, aged 85. She on Thursday ye 23 August, 1638, aged 75."

Epitaph in Steeple Church, Isle of Purbeck.

"A.D. 1588. A letter to Sir Richard Rogers, Knight, and others the Commysion(ers) appointed for the Musters in the Isle of Purbecke, that where(as) their Lordships are given to understand that divers persons of habylytie that have landes in the said Isle had of late absented them selves from thence, and did dwell uppon their own livinges in other partes of the Realme, whereby bothe that Island (being a place of no small importance) was unfurnished of men of habylytie and calling, and did want the succor of that necessary contrybucion for publique services: therefore they were required and aucthoryzed by vertue hereof to cause such a reasonable taxe and chardge to be laied and levyed upon the landes of soche persons so absenting them selves and not resydent there, as should be fytt to be imployed uppon muskettes and other necessary provysion."

Acts of the Privy Council of England. New Series, Vol. XVI.

"O eloquent, just and mighty death, whom none could advise, thou hast persuaded; what none hath presumed, thou hast done; and whom all the world hath flattered, thou hast cast out of the world and despised; thou hast drawn together all the extravagant greatness, all the pride, cruelty and ambition of man, and covered all over with two narrow words: *Hic jacet.*"

SIR WALTER RALEIGH,
The History of the World.

K

VIII

THE NEW RICH

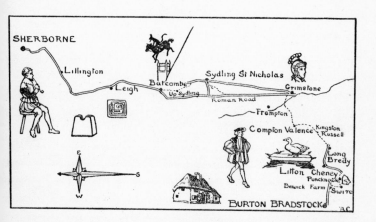

THE Cardinal Archbishop who set up the bright-
hued roof in Bere church was in many ways like
great men of other times. He had eminent
virtues of statecraft and administration. He brought two
sovereigns—Margaret and Henry VII—to England from
overseas : he was the rightly trusted adviser of each. He
encouraged the young Thomas More, and saw in him signs
of future greatness. He held many livings (several at once,
as a rule) and filled many high offices. But the life he had
lived in Dorset was soon to vanish and not return. If he
could have looked into the future, he might have said, with
Mr. Turveydrop, " We gentlemen are few : I see nothing to
succeed us but a race of weavers."

It would have been a curiously apt statement. For one
great change in country life that came in with the Tudors
was due in a large measure to the development of the cloth

industry. It was due also to other causes which will be mentioned. But under Henry VIII the sheep emerged to give rural England wealth, and to consolidate the growing tendency to the holding of private property in land.

Henry VIII himself took note of that tendency. In the preamble to an Act of his twenty-fifth year of rule, he complained of the way in which his subjects were scheming " how they might accumulate and gather together into few hands, as well great multitude of farms as great plenty of cattle, and in especial sheep." A few years earlier he had observed that " vagabonds and beggars have of long time increased and daily do increase," and he initiated the long series of vagrancy laws.

It is not certain that the noble creature of the Dorset hills to-day was itself one of the agents of this change. But the Dorset Horn sheep—the Dorset Down being apparently a later breed—is as least very ancient, very famous, very strong ; so strong and fierce-looking, at times, that delicate females have been observed to show fear in the presence even of the ewes. The lady sheep has horns and a Roman nose, and a great thickset body. See how haughtily she looks down that nose at you, with what menacing pride she draws herself up to confront you. She fears nor man nor dog. Let the terrier approach, she stands superb : she frowns, she stamps her foot : she stamps it again. If the terrier quails, she chases him. But if, after the manner of terriers, he blench not. . . .

I once saw about three hundred of these gracious dames in a big green valley. They were fussing together like a swarm of ants. I could not understand why, until I caught sight of what looked like a bright brown leaf blown about round the flock. The leaf danced methodically ; and when its caperings had got the sheep neatly herded in a dense mass, it stood at the end of the valley and regarded them triumphantly, its plumed tail waving over its back like a banner ; for it was a small and infinitely pugnacious Lion Dog of Pekin.

No, the Dorset ewe is not really braver than other sheep, though handsomer. But the ram is another matter. He is a great barrel of a fellow, with a head like a bull's. And he is not content with the simple Ionic curve of his spouses' horns : he has coil upon coil gloriously wreathed.

The offspring of these mates (whose hardy vigour often produces two families in a year) are perhaps the most interesting lambs known to our fortunate isles. Not only are they delicious food; they are Nature's most successful attempt to live up to Art. The ideal lamb of Art, of course, is the woolly toy of the nursery. The Dorset lamb is an excellent imitation of it. Its nascent horns give it the breadth of forehead necessary to make the features at once perfectly innocent and perfectly foolish. Its eyes are small and properly overshadowed by wool, its nose a mere pink speck in a white plain. It ought to be mounted on a little crimson stand with wheels, and to squeak when pinched. I have never pinched one, but its bleat is thin, in contrast to the deep poignant voice of its mother.*

But the land-grabbers of the sixteenth century were not concerned with the æsthetics of sheep-keeping. They had too many interests for that. The Dissolution of the Monasteries brought wealth to many of the sovereign's supporters ; and they had a very good idea of business. I do not find the days of great Elizabeth particularly spacious : as a rule they are intensely concentrated, and often narrow. What an Elizabethan Englishman did was usually for his own advantage, and he did it with all his might. And he certainly, if he had the means, was " a liberal constant housekeeper," like Chaldecot of Steeple. I am not sure that the Elizabethan and Jacobean manor-houses are not finer survivals of the best life of the time than all but the greatest of its literature.

Dorset is peculiarly rich in such houses. Of those not to be dwelt upon much hereafter Athelhampton (begun perhaps in 1503), Cranborne, the house of the Cecils (of much

* Cf. Elizabeth Prig.

the same period), Melbury, whose builder is shown in a brass
of 1532 in the church close by, Poxwell (Jacobean), Mapperton (late sixteenth century—a most lovely secluded house),
Parnham (one of the largest and most beautiful buildings
in the stone and red-brick Tudor style), Chantmarle (1619
—lately restored to its old perfection), and Bingham's
Melcombe (Henry VIII, for the most part, but older in places)
rouse feelings much like those Butler experienced, in a
different way, in the presence of the cathedrals : their
builders must have been right in any conclusions they
reached about life. And scores of little hidden farms, of
the same period and of the same inspiration, but now en-
joying no manorial rights, add to the conviction that nothing
in the way of the adaptation of beauty to the then domestic
life remained to be learnt by the Tudor landowners.

It is a reflection on our life of to-day that whereas a
house built by a newly enriched person at any time in the
present or just past generation is more than likely to be
vulgar, the homes built by the new rich of Henry and
Elizabeth and James cannot have seemed seriously in contrast with the abbeys out of whose stones they were so often
constructed. The monastic buildings were noble models.
The stone was good and well cut. It was put to many
uses, for habitations of all kinds, as has been said already.
I wonder what sort of queer pride a man who had made a
fortune felt when he saw the material of the former sacred
foundation rising, block by block, into the cosy mansion
in which he and his wife (or his second or third wife) would
eat their enormous rich spiced meals and beget their ten
or twenty children ?

Yet when the first vigour of our renaissance had gone, the
uglier side of it shows. A Dorset parson throws a little
personal light on the change. Thomas Bastard, born at
Blandford in 1566, Vicar of Bere Regis and Rector of Almer
for most of his adult life, wrote a book of epigrams—
Chrestoleros—of more than average merit. He suffered
himself, it seems, from poverty : an epistle of 1603 (accord-

ing to his admirable editor, Dr. Grosart) addressed to King James I, speaks of his "extreme poverty and toiling wretchedness." In an epigram on a chance meeting with a "wantcatcher," he puns upon the double meaning of the mole's old name :—

> " ' Then you have left no more ? ' ' No more ? ' quoth he,
> ' Sir, I can show you more : the more the worse.'
> And to his work he went. But 'twould not be—
> For all the wants were crept into my purse.
> ' Farewell, friend wantcatcher, since 'twill not be—
> Thou canst not catch the wants, but they catch me.' "

In another he speaks of his needing £100, and being unable to make it by his books.* There may have been good reason for his poverty. Dr. Grosart thinks he was " a genial, not to say jovial parson, after the type of Robert Herrick." He seems to have been unhappily married, and his end was lamentable : " being towards his latter end crazed, and thereupon brought into debt, (he) was at length committed to the prison in Allhallows parish in Dorchester," and what that means the baiting of the alleged lunatic Malvolio may suggest—" where dying very obscurely and in a mean condition, he was buried in the church-yard belonging to that parish on 19th April, 1618." An unkind brother epigrammatist wrote to him that :—

> " Preaching would do more good
> If preachers wallowed less in flesh and blood."

And as a young man he got into trouble at Oxford and had to resign his fellowship of New College, " being much guilty of the vices belonging to poets, and addicted to libelling."

But whatever his virtues or vices, he loved Dorset and its " green joy," and above all the good trout-fishing at Bere.† And he evidently was on intimate terms with the

---

* On Feb. 6, 1922, a single copy of the first edition of *Chrestoleros*, one of four or five known copies, was sold at Sotheby's to the representative of a great American book collector for £155.

† " My little Bere dwells on a hill,
Under whose foot the silver trout doth swim."

local gentry—Strangways and Moretons. He saw little
good in the new order : he foresaw a wonderful scarcity

> " Of bankers and bakers, of all such as brew
>   Of tanners, of tailors, of smiths and the rest—"

because they would all have become gentlemen. And
again :—

> "Never so many masters any knew,
>   And so few gentlemen in such a crew,
>   Never so many houses, so small spending,
>   Never such store of coin, so little lending.
>   Never so many cousins, so few kind.
>   Goodmorrows plenty, good wills hard to find,
>   Never so many clerks, ne'er learning less,
>   Many religions, but least godliness."

The words have a curiously modern ring. And again,
he complains of the multitude of usurers—yet not enough,
for they were all so busy lending to " gentlemen, merchants,
nobles of the land " that poor men got no chance to deal with
them. He found it hard even to write consistently ; for

> " How shall men's or manners' form appear
>   Which while I write do change from what they were ? "

Not that one need seriously regret the disappearance of
the great religious houses and the established order of which
they were part. They stood for a certain dependence of
life which was becoming foreign to the English temper.
As a consequence, the Dissolution shared with the wool
trade the responsibility for the increase of vagrancy. Not
only were hundreds of monks and nuns and servants of
the religious houses deprived of occupation—it should be
remembered, by the way, that many were pensioned—but
the whole administration of charity and much of the
organization of agricultural work vanished when these
centres were destroyed.

The direct result was the Elizabethan Poor Law, of which
we are not yet rid. I am not going to argue for or against
the various proposals for dealing with the problems the Poor
Law was meant to solve. The effect, so far as the country

labourer in Tudor times is concerned, was to keep wages low
—because the parish could be brought in to supplement
them—and to tie to the parish the worker who at the time
almost seemed, by the process of economic evolution, to
have got free of the chains that bound him to the soil.

But to dwell on purely agricultural questions alone
would be to ignore a large part of the bustling Tudor life.
The increased responsibilities of the parish involved corporate labour for many purposes. A famous statute of
Philip and Mary charged the parish with the upkeep of its
roads ; and many of the beautiful bridges of Dorset—those
at Wool, Holme, Spettisbury, for instance—were either
built or restored in this period. The building activities
of the new men, setting up their comfortable houses, must
have provided a good deal of employment, as must also
their business enterprises, like Clavell's undertaking at
Kimmeridge. Their sports and pastimes were numerous.
Perhaps George Turberville, himself of the great Dorset
family, had the profiteer sportsman in mind when he wrote
his *Book of Falconry* (1575) and *Book of Venerie or Hunting* :
though after all many of them were country born, and could
feel sincerely, as he did, that " a good Spaniel is a great
jewel, and a good Spaniel maketh a good Hawk."

Turberville, indeed, is an interesting example of an
average Elizabethan of the better classes, not so rich or
so able as to be eminent, but versatile and eager in all he
did. It is hard to know whether he was a genuine outdoor
man or not. He went to Russia—apparently because he
was crossed in love—with the mission to Ivan Vasilivitch
(Ivan the Terrible), so vividly described in Hakluyt. But he
was only thirty-five or so when the Privy Council were told
that he " hath been always from his youth, and still is, given
to his book and study, and never exercised in matters of
war." He had an epitaph of his own. " Ding, dong, cease
now the bell—he loved a pot of strong ale well." Perhaps
it has some connection with his advice to the huntsman :
" When he is up and ready, let him drink a good draught.

. . . And let him not forget to fill his bottle with good wine."
These admirable sentiments are followed by a luscious
description of the most enormous cold luncheon of which
any human being could be capable.*

And here it may be convenient to insert, by way of contrast, a brief mention of another Dorset man—Arthur
Gregory of Lyme Regis. His gift to the Tudor polity was
a peculiar skill in opening even sealed letters, in such a
manner that the recipient could by no means detect the
interference. Walsingham, perhaps through the Dorset
connections already mentioned, heard of this attractive
artist, and conveyed him to London for suitable employment in the Civil Service.

The ordinary town life was likewise varied and vigorous.
A few extracts from the account books of the Mayors of
Weymouth (quoted by Mr. H. J. Moule in his excellent
survey of the Borough records) suggest more than any
description. These are expenses incurred :—

		£	s.	d.
(1596)	Conveying a mad man out of the Town .			3
	A shroud for a poor man that died in John-			
	son's porch, and to the woman that			
	shrouded him		3	4
(1597)	Wine bestowed upon the lieutenants and			
	the captains at times in their lodgings .	1	5	0
(1606)	Sending into Portland about the pirates .			3
(1611)	Paid H. Tuckey for whipping a sailor .			4
(1615)	Given the Queen's players for not playing			
	here, by order of the Aldermen . .	1	10	0
	9 dozen of lobsters Jno. Poop at Mr. Re-			
	corder and 2 dozen of crabs, which cost	8	16	0

* The legend of the Turberville coach is referred to in *Tess*. It is
said to drive out of an evening from the beautiful Jacobean manor-house
at Wool (an old Turberville dwelling), where the pictures on the walls—
still there—so frightened Tess. Only Turbervilles can see the coach. A
writer in the Dorset Field Club's *Proceedings* has this curious story :

" A gentleman whom I have the honour to know was passing near here
one evening of late years—going to dine with friends. On arriving he
asked which of their neighbours kept a four-in-hand. ' No one.' ' Yes,' he
said, ' someone must, for I've just seen a four-in-hand—a queer, old-
fashioned, but handsome affair, with outriders.' ' No,' they said, ' no
one here keeps such a turn-out, but—you've surely seen the Turberville
coach.' Now he is akin to the old Turberville race."

" Sending into Portland about the pirates "—the Privy Council sent into Weymouth itself often enough " about the pirates." The predatory instincts of the Dorset mariners were apt to get England into trouble with other nations. In 1546 " all the men of war adventurers " in the Dorset ports had to be ordered not to put out to sea ; and the same year an enquiry was held at Weymouth about a certificate for cargo landed :

" The captain of a pinnace called the *Mary Grace* of Saltash . . . did enter into Weymouth Haven, and discharged out of her goods to the value of sixty pounds ; forasmuch as in the said certificate no mention was made where the ship that the goods were taken out of is become, nor what was done with the mariners in her, which made the matter savour somewhat of a piracy. . . ."

The result of the enquiry is not given. It is clear that there was a thoroughly well-organized system of receiving and distributing the booty obtained by these means. The ransom of prisoners was a common transaction on ordinary hard business lines. There are constant complaints and enquiries about piracy all through the reign of Elizabeth and James. In 1582 a Weymouth man, newly turned pirate, landed at Studland with his companions, and there cut down the gallows on which men of his trade were hanged. But the luck was not all on one side. In that same year the Mayor of Weymouth was the accuser, not the accused : he wrote to the Privy Council that " four ships have been taken by the Turks and are sunk, to the value of more than £2000." In the later abortive attempts, in 1619–20, to suppress the Barbary corsairs, Weymouth was also keenly interested.

The great impetus to seafaring and oversea trade given by the discovery of America, especially after the destruction of the Armada, affected the Dorset ports. It was at this time that the country's close connection with Newfoundland was established. Poole boats were certainly going to the Newfoundland fisheries as early as 1583. Early in

1588, when a general embargo was laid on all foreign-going boats in view of the Spanish preparations, it was worth the while of certain " contemptuous persons " in the ship *Primrose* of Poole to risk breaking the embargo and sail for the Banks. In 1618, the Privy Council were informed that " the adventures of this town (Poole) are not in any staple, but in fishing voyages for the New Found Land, and so home." By 1628, according to the *Victoria County History*, Poole used to send twenty boats a year to the Banks ; in 1622, Weymouth, which had previously sent thirty-nine, sent eleven. They sailed in spring and returned late in the summer. The trade continued to grow for two centuries : it was at its highest in 1813 ; then it waned, and Poole sent only seventy vessels west in 1839—which is estimated at a fifth of the 1813 tonnage. The fishers had gradually taken to setting up huts to cure the fish on the spot ; and then huts for their own lodging : and so to complete settlement.*

It is in those daily events which go to the making of a livelihood that life continues. Three and a half centuries later we are apt to think of the climax of Elizabeth's reign as

---

* There were risks about the voyage. "And when the sixteen were in the boat, some had small remembrance, and some had none : for they did not make account to live, but to prolong their lives as long as it pleased God, and looked every moment of an hour when the sea would eat them up, the boat being so little and so many men in her, and so foul weather. . . . Thus while we remained two days and two nights . . . there was in our company one Master Hedly that put forth this question to me the Master. ' I do see that it doth please God that our boat liveth in the sea, and it may please God that some of us may come to the land if our boat were not overladen. Let us make sixteen lots, and those four that have the shortest lots we will cast overboard, preserving the Master among us all.' I replied unto him, saying, ' No, we will live and die together.' . . . Thus we continued the third and fourth day without any sustenance, save only the weeds that swam in the sea, and salt water to drink. The fifth day Hedly died and another moreover : then we desired all to die : for in all those five days and five nights we saw the sun but once and the stars but one night, it was so foul weather. Thus did we remain the sixth day." They reached land the seventh day. The narrative is by Richard Clarke of Weymouth, Master of the *Delight* : the date 1583.

It may be interesting here also to enter the name of another Newfound-land-Dorset man—Captain Robert Abram Bartlett, whom Peary left at the end of the last stage on his journey to the North Pole. Captain Bartlett's ancestors, of Poole, settled in Newfoundland three generations ago. He is proud of his Dorset lineage, and is an overseas member of the Society of Dorset Men in London.

the few years which produced Shakespeare and the defeat
of the Armada. I must deal with Shakespeare as Weymouth
dealt with him : the Queen's players shall not enter here.

I am inclined to think that except for a week or two
of excitement just before and after the battle with Spain,
local feeling was likely to be chiefly concerned with local
men, of whom there is evidence to indicate " a certain
liveliness." Of course, the defeat of the Armada—the main
encounter began off Lyme, and filled the Dorset ports with
prizes—was a national affair. But it was probably looked
upon locally through short-distance glasses, in which the
hero of Poole or Weymouth or Lyme would stand out as
through a stereoscope. Even so, he often had a wide
background. Consider the arrival at Poole in 1582, in the
ship *Landret*, of Miles Philips, after sixteen years in the
power of Spain. This is a little of the story he had to tell
Poole of his adventures after the Spanish treachery at San
Juan de Ulloa. When Drake and Hawkins escaped so nar-
rowly from the consequences of their filibustering, Philips
and others were perforce put ashore in Mexico, and duly
captured by the Spaniards, and taken to Mexico City and
tried by Inquisitors. " Then did they proceed to demand
of us on our oaths what we did believe of the Sacrament,
and . . . whether we did not believe that the host of
bread which the priest did hold up over his head, and the
wine that was in the chalice, was the very true and perfect
body and blood of our Saviour Christ, yea or no : to which
if we answered not yea, then there was no way but death.
. . . About the space of three months before they proceeded
to their severe judgment, we were all racked, and some
enforced to utter that against themselves, which afterwards cost them their lives." They were taken out publicly
for the delivery of sentence, " every man alone in his yellow
coat, and a rope about his neck, and a great green wax
candle in his hand unlighted. . . . The first man that was
called was one Roger the armourer of the *Jesus*, and he had
judgment to have three hundred stripes on horseback, and

after condemned as a slave to the galleys for ten years."
Others got less, but enough. Philips was awarded no
stripes, but " to serve in a monastery for five years, and to
wear a fool's coat, or San Benito, during all that time."
He made various escapes and attempts at escape : and at
last, after almost incredible hardships, reached Spain itself,
and so to Majorca, where " I found two English ships, the
one of London and the other of the West Country, which
were ready freighted and stayed but for a fair wind." That
little ship of the dear West Country which had ventured
so near to the Barbary coast carried him safely back to Poole.

But though the great event was at hand, and Dorset
knew it—for in 1586 two Liverpool men fresh from Bilboa
landed at Weymouth with news of 700 sail and 280,000 men
being prepared against England—when it arrived, there was
not overmuch eagerness to serve, or having served, to do it
again. Sir George Trenchard, of the Commission for the
county, was pressed to expedite the despatch of 1000
footmen, for the national forces, to " Stratford of the Bow,"
by July 29, 1588, and lancers and light horse a week later.
The county armour had to be looked up, men pricked and
mustered (Falstaff and Mr. Justice Shallow no doubt took
a hand), defences over which for two or three years there
had been argument hastily put into some sort of order,*
ships furnished—at the county's expense. Eventually,
though they did their best to get out of paying for it, Poole
provided one ship and one pinnace, Weymouth and Melcombe two ships and a pinnace, and Lyme (with Chard and
Axminster contributing) two ships and a pinnace. Even if
they had been able to evade the levy, they could not have
used the ships ; for on March 31, 1588, by order of the
Privy Council, a total embargo was laid on all shipping.

I am not to describe the great fight. The Dorset ships

---

* Sometimes at the enemy's expense. The Privy Council commanded
Trenchard " to deliver unto Carew Rawleigh, Esquire, [elder brother of
Walter] or his deputy, six port pieces of ordnance, being demi-culverins,
of those that were taken in the Spanish ship lately brought into Weymouth, for the provision of Portland Castle."

were there.   One was the *Revenge* of Lyme, which later under
Grenville was to engage a whole Spanish squadron without
assistance.   " The Spanish Fleet, came, went, and was
vanquished. . . . The magnificent, huge, and mighty fleet,
such as sailed not upon the Ocean Sea many hundred years
before, in the year 1588 vanished into smoke."

I have said those times were not altogether spacious ;
but that is unfair when one looks at the Armada fight from
a national point of view.   It is at close quarters at home that
the Elizabethan loses the grand air.   And yet a Dorset
leader and his companions gave the age a spaciousness that
will live for ever.   The " still-vexed Bermoothes," the
Bermudas, were in 1609 rediscovered—discovered, so far
as the New World matters—by Sir George Somers of Whitchurch Canonicorum, M.P. for Lyme Regis in 1603–4, and
Mayor in 1605.   And the account of that voyage, written
by another Dorset man, is as certainly as may be the
foundation of much of *The Tempest*.

By a queer coincidence of our English contradictions,
it was the austere Milton's secretary, Puritan of Puritans,
who translated into liquid golden verse the historian's
splendid catalogue of the wonders Somers found in the
remote Bermudas :—

> " Where He the huge sea-monsters wracks,
>   That lift the deep upon their backs. . . .
>   He gave us this eternal Spring,
>   Which here enamels everything ;
>   And send the fowls to us in care,
>   On daily visits through the air.
>   He hangs in shades the orange bright,
>   Like golden lamps in a green night,
>   And does in the pomegranate close
>   Jewels more rich than Ormus shows ;
>   He makes the figs our mouths to meet,
>   And throws the melons at our feet ;
>   But (with ?) apples, plants of such a price,
>   No tree could ever bear them twice ;
>   With cedars, chosen by His hand,
>   From Lebanon He stores the land ;
>   And makes the hollow seas that roar
>   Proclaim the ambergris on shore."

Andrew Marvell got his enthusiasm, doubtless, from his friend Oxenbridge, who visited the Bermudas after Somers : but he got his language—except the glorious couplet about the orange—direct from Somers' fellow-voyager, Sylvester Jourdan,* whose account of 1610 is dedicated to a Dorset Justice of the Peace. The Bermudas had been called " An Isle of Devils," " a most prodigious and enchanted place, affording nothing but gusts, storms, and foul winds " —watched by God Setebos, inhabited by Caliban and Sycorax ; maybe by Prospero also, for it was an isle of voices. Somers, in the *Sea Adventure*, bound for Virginia, was wrecked. " For three days and three nights together " he sat on the poop, guiding a ship whose crew, fearing no better fate than a " more joyful and happy meeting in a more blessed world," were as drunk as Trinculo and Stephano. They " fell in between two rocks " in the Bermudas, whence they could land, and built from their materials a new ship. The island, instead of being peopled by devils, was found to be a paradise. " Fish is there so abundant that if a man step into the water they will come round about him ; so that men were fain to get out for fear of biting." Somers with a hook took enough in half an hour to feed the whole company for a day. A thousand mullet could be taken at a draught with a seine ; and anyone who knows the subtlety of the netted mullet will appreciate that plenty. " Infinite store of pilchards . . . great abundance of hogs, as that there hath been taken by Sir George Somers to the number of two and thirty at one time " (by another odd coincidence Somers died there of a surfeit of pig the next year !) . . . " great store of tortoises (which some call turtles), and those so great that I have seen a bushel of eggs in one of their bellies . . . one of them will suffice fifty men a meal at the least. . . . Fowl in great number, that there hath been taken in two or three hours a thousand at the least. Great store and plenty of herons. . . . Prickled pears,

* Jourdan is a name constantly recurrent in the municipal records of Dorchester. Sylvester was a Lyme man.

great abundance, great plenty of mulberries white and red.
. . . And there is a tree called the Palmito tree, which hath
a very sweet berry upon which the hogs do most feed ;
but our men, finding the sweetness of them, did willingly
share with the hogs for them, they being very pleasant and
wholesome, which made them careless almost of any bread
with their meat. . . . An infinite number of cedar trees
(the fairest I think in the world). . . . No venomous
creature so much as a rat or mouse. . . . Great store of
pearl. . . . Some good quantity of ambergris . . . Great
plenty of whales."

The fortunate isles. . . . No wonder that

> " Thus sung they, in the English boat,
> An holy and a cheerful note,
> And all the way, to guide their chime,
> With falling oars they kept the time."

When they had rebuilt that happy boat—rebuilt ; and yet
people wonder that the Swiss Family Robinson could tame
ostriches, or Crusoe build a hut !—they went on to Virginia ;
and from there " being willing to do service unto his Prince
and Country, without any respect of his private gain, and
being of threescore years at the least, out of his worthy and
valiant mind," Somers undertook to go back to Bermuda
for the hogs Virginia needed ; and so died.

It is really in the villages and towns of to-day, as secluded
and forgotten as Somers' birthplace, that the historical
vestiges can give out the breath of life. Walk from Burton
Bradstock to Sherborne, and let the Tudor folk speak for
themselves of their own greatness and pride and cruelty and
ambition.

Start from Burton Bradstock, not only because it is a
good place, but because the church contains the old clock
of the only institution where the Elizabethan dress is to-day
in daily use—the clock from the old Newgate Street buildings of Christ's Hospital. Proceed thence along the Bride
valley. You will come near Bredy Farm to the disused
stone pillars of a gateway. It is the entry to the Bedford

L

Estate, for here at Berwick manor (now a farm) were founded the fortunes of the Duchy of Bedford. A little of the old house is left, and a small barn to the north-west looks as ancient as the Duchy.

The Russells were a Dorset family established at Kingston Russell—further east—two hundred and fifty years before John Russell of Berwick, a member of that house, saw and seized his opportunity of fame. The Archduke Philip and his wife Joan, daughter of the King of Castile, were driven by a storm in 1506 to land at Weymouth, and were entertained—not, perhaps without some neutral vigilance—by Sir Thomas Trenchard at his new-built manor-house, Wolverton, near Dorchester. They needed a man of "habylytie and standing" to make the commerce of hospitality smooth. John Russell had lately returned from travels abroad, and was summoned in aid : he spoke Spanish. He was so efficient and companionable that he accompanied the guests to London when Henry VII desired to be their host. He obtained a post at court and improved it under the eighth Henry. He fought brilliantly in France, held the position of ambassador at Rome, became a privy councillor and at length the first Baron Russell, Warden of the Stanneries, Knight of the Garter, Lord Privy Seal, and Earl of Bedford.

"He had a moving beauty that waited on his whole body, a comportment unaffected, and such comeliness in his mien as exacted a liking, if not a love, from all that saw him. . . . In dancing "—one of Henry VIII's delights—" he was not too exquisite, for that is vanity : but his dancing was a graceful exercise wherein he was carelessly easy, as if it were rather natural motion than curious and artificial practice which endeared his severer virtues. . . . Though Mr. Russell brought himself into court by what did humour, he kept himself in there by what obliged ; standing not so much upon his prince's pleasure as his interest, and adding to his more airy courtships the solidity of serviceable actions."

With Russell's marriage to Anne Sapcote of Chenies,
and his later grant from Henry VIII of the Cistercian Abbey
of Woburn, his illustrious family passes out of close connection with the county of Dorset, except in so far as the
holding of various high offices brought its members into
touch with local government.   They retained the greater
part of their Dorset estates till recently, however, and Lord
John Russell, when he accepted his earldom in 1861, took
the title of Earl Russell of Kingston Russell.

That is the foundation of one great family, though the
founder came of a good enough line originally.   Take the
footpath across country from Berwick to Swyre and see how
a deal in fish founded another.   In the plain little church
(now too often locked) is commemorated James Napier
(the name is also spelt Napper, as in Napper's Mite, the
Dorchester almshouses).   He was a capable Scot, who
" came into England in the reign of Henry VII, settled here,
and supplied the adjacent abbies with fish, from whom are
descended the Napiers of Dorset and Scotland."   It seems
a surprising origin : but the panegyrist is careful to
exclude the fish by mentioning that James was the brother
of Sir Alexander Napier, Knight, and that James I (his
kinsman) commanded Sir Robert Napier, " on creating him
Baronet, A.D. 1612, to send for his pedigree out of
Scotland."*

Hutchins' editors mention another remarkable inhabitant
of Swyre churchyard who died in 1613—a Bridport doctor,
Walter Gray.   He " was a little desperate doctor commonly
wearing a pistol about his neck."   He had a bodyguard of
the younger gentry, whom he called his " sons," and was
apparently always in debt.   He would prophesy with
accuracy the date of the death or recovery of his patients :
but it is not clear how he so far evaded the Sheriff's constant
attention as to have any patients.

I like better than James Napier that Sir Robert who is

* The trade in the huge mackerel catches of this part of the coast passed
under George V to another great merchant whose title is also new.

buried at Puncknowle, a mile away to the north-east, across the fields. His epitaph—he died in 1700—is simple :—

> " Σκιᾶς ὄναρ ἄνθρωπος
>   (Man is the dream of a shadow)
>   Non magna loquimur, sed vivimus.

Reader, when as thou hast done all thou canst, thou art but an unprofitable servant ; therefore this marble affords no room for fulsome flattery or vain praise. S^r. R.N."

The helmet and gauntlets of one of his ancestors rest above the slab. The carver of the inscription may have been nearer in spirit to James Napier of Swyre and Scotland. At any rate, he appears on the epitaph as prominently as Sir Robert : " Johannes Hamiltonus, Scoto-Britannus, fecit."*

The whole of this church is interesting. The key—to be obtained at the vicarage—is a massive and complex piece of Tudor work. The font seems to be Norman. The Bexington aisle or chapel forms a curious little domestic enclave to the south, and there is another large Napier tomb of the seventeenth century. The lychgate has a fine roof of Dorset stone tiles.

In the village (" William holds Puncknowle of the wife of Hugh, son of Grip : Alward held it in King Edward's time . . .") may be found a cosy inn where the landlady

---

* The Napiers or Nappers, like the Strangways, Digbys, and Shaftesburys, were great figures in Dorset for many generations, and sometimes in English life also. This modest Sir Robert sat in Parliament for Weymouth and Dorchester successively. He was son of an untitled Robert, who was Receiver-General, and brother to Sir Gerard, a comparatively temperate Royalist who sat for Melcombe Regis and won the favour of Charles II. A Sir Nathaniel begat Sir Gerard, and another Sir Robert begat Nathaniel, being in his lifetime M.P. successively for Dorchester, Bridport, and Wareham, and Chief Baron of the Exchequer in Ireland. The aforesaid Sir Gerard begat a Sir Nathaniel (" dilettante "—proh pudor !), and he yet another Nathaniel : from whom, collaterally, are descended the Sturt or Alington families of to-day. A miraculous draught of fishes. The first Lord Alington bequeathed a set of waistcoat buttons to King Edward VII : he was the owner of St. Blaize, Common, and much property in Hoxton and Dorset. I still like the self-concealing Sir Robert best. (The above statements are taken from the *Dictionary of National Biography* and G.E.C.'s *Complete Peerage*.)

sits weaving nets—a local industry—with a shuttle that flies so quickly in her skilful hands that you can hardly see it ; the remains of the stocks ; a pleasant drinking trough carefully shaded ; and behind the church stands the most compact and charming of all the Dorset manors, a tiny gabled Jacobean house of grey weathered stone, exquisitely proportioned.

From here there is a footpath directly across the water-meadows to Litton Cheney : but it is very difficult to trace at times, and if you miss it you will be lost in a maze of little brooks. There is a slightly longer path, through Look Farm (" William holds Lahoc of the Earl of Moreton. Aluric held it in King Edward's time ") ; and this is worth following, for the early eighteenth-century house has a demure comfortable beauty not soon forgotten. (The track lies through the farm barton and then to the left, not past the front of the house.)

A former tenant of Look had an epitaph (at Litton Cheney) which is in keeping with the gracious house :—

> " Beneath this stone in a darke dusty bed,
> lamented much a virgin rests her head ;
> And such an one who (dying) hath bereft
> the world of that worth as scarce in it is left.
> Of a sweet face, but of a sweeter minde,
> and a sweet fame (dying) shee left behinde.
> Smitten by death even in her blooming age,
> and height of beauty, shee went off ye stage
> Of this frail world ; this with grief wee see
> that such rare creatures seldome aged bee.
> For why, the Angels want such company
> to joyne with them in heavenly melody.
> With whom in Heaven she doth now possess
> the fruit of vertue's lasting happiness."

Litton Cheney (save for an episode to be recorded later) is remarkable only for loveliness. Down each side of the street runs a silver stream between the road and the golden houses ; and argosies of silver ducks float garrulous upon their waters, or stand, dibbling snakily with their long necks, on the massive stones that serve as footbridges for each house. Right at the top of the village, on its own knoll, rises the church, a plain building with a handsome tower and an oldish painting of David playing the harp in a theatrical ecstasy.

A byroad leads from Litton, past a comely eighteenth-century house, to Long Bredy, a pleasant hamlet of no great interest. Here once more you are in the kingdoms of the dead. There is a long barrow just above the village and tumuli all around. The stone circle called the Grey Mare and her Colts is in the parish, and other Neolithic remains. The ruins of Kingston Russell House (where Admiral Hardy lived and J. L. Motley died) are also in the parish.

The way lies now across country utterly desolate. Take the footpath past the church over the hill, cross the main road, and go by other faint tracks straight to Compton Valence, three miles away. In the valley leading down to that hamlet, traces of the Roman water supply for Dorchester have been found. The little village takes its second name from the Earls of Pembroke, but they did not succeed in giving it any history. It must have slept among its trees undisturbed since Hugo de Porth received the manor from the Conqueror, in lieu of Bundi the Saxon.

Another winding track, also in places undiscoverable, leads to Grimstone, in the cool spacious Frome valley. There is nothing of note here. But it is necessary now to choose between two routes to the next objective—Batcombe, on the edge of Blackmore Vale. You can get on to a pretty byroad by Grimstone station and go along past Sydling Water to Sydling St. Nicholas, and through Up-Sydling to the hills. Or you can follow the Roman road. The first four miles are utterly deserted and very beautiful; then it becomes the main Dorchester-Yeovil road, and there is more traffic. A little before the fourth milestone (fourth from Maiden Newton, twelfth from Dorchester) turn to the right, and you will come to the same point as by the Sydling route.

Or by adding an extra mile or so to your walk you can combine the best of both routes ; go three miles or more along the Roman road and then take the track already mentioned* down to Sydling.

Certainly Up-Sydling (a form of name similar to that seen in Up-Cerne, Up-Lyme, Up-Wey) should not be over-looked. It has a charming little farm-manor-house, and the way to it lies alongside streams at many points. Behind it rise the great hills, and the path climbs through a glorious wooded valley to the summit, nearly 800 feet up.

This is the best approach to almost the best view in the south of England ; for you come to it quite unexpectedly. But I shall speak of that later. For the present, do not wait, but go down the steep track to Batcombe Church. As you stand on the top of the hill, you look right on to the building, and its seems almost as if you could leap over it with a little effort. Indeed, a less desirable person than the reader of this book is said to have done so. It was anciently a custom of the devil to exercise his horse in this manner. A former vicar of Batcombe (the living goes with that of Frome Vauchurch, five steep miles away) told me that when he first went to the place, a generation ago, one of the pinnacles of the tower had fallen and was lying in the churchyard. He had great difficulty in replacing it ; for the villagers insisted that the devil's horse had knocked it off with his hoof as he leapt in derision over the holy building, and to restore it would be to their hurt.

The devil was not the only wizard in Batcombe There are strange tales of one Conjuring Minterne, who lived in the seventeenth century—John Minterne, of a well-known local family. Sir Frederick Treves recalls these stories. Formerly, according to Hutchins, half his gravestone lay in Batcombe churchyard. Like another Dorset man of the same century, he would be buried neither in nor outside the church, and had his tomb placed in the wall.

The church itself has a simple slab recording his death.

* Pages 115, 116.

It has also that rare thing, a stone screen, of plain good design. It is a little unpretentious place of worship, suitable, somehow, to this village lost between the great hills and the great valley.

Lost ? No : not entirely. Batcombe was the town of the Little Commonwealth ; a penal settlement for children, on advanced and successful lines. Hither came little delinquents from the London Police Courts, and learnt by experience the duties of freedom. They were their own governors, held their own law courts, under wisely veiled supervision. There were incorrigibles among them, run-aways, idlers, of course, but on the whole the place made for a real reform of the spirit, a genuine application of the theory of social punishment which does not try to penalize but to change the soul. It was closed during the war, for reasons unconnected with its ideals. And then it had another ideal ; it became a farm settlement for ex-service men. But that too has perished.

So down into the Vale of Blackmore, a great weald formerly closely wooded, and once called, according to Coker of Mappowder in the Vale, the Forest of White Hart; for a gentleman of that district killed, at King's Stag Bridge over the Stour (the name still stands), a white hart which Henry III, hunting there, had spared ; "but he soon found how dangerous it was to be twitching a lion by the ears," for the King imprisoned him and exacted a yearly fine called White Hart Silver.

Except in May, this weald country is not of great beauty or interest as compared with the hills or the heath. The road runs quietly to Leigh. Here there is a miz-maze or curiously wrought earthwork, the meaning of which is not certainly known : formerly in spring the young folk used to scour it every few years, with mirth and cheerful ritual. There is another at " Troy," not far from Dorchester, to the east, and there used to be one at Pimperne.

Hence, still by road, either to Lillington or Long Burton, and so at last to Sherborne, the old seat of the bishopric, the capital of Western Wessex, "the most frequented town in the county " in Elizabeth's day.

I have spoken of Sherborne Abbey and its glorious fan tracery, and of Aldhelm its great first bishop. I will not now dwell on the school, with its splendid buildings, new and old, its library, its high traditions ; nor upon the conduit in mid-town, nor the " hospital " whose residents are so anxiously eager to show its treasures ; nor upon the many old houses, nor upon the unseemly architecture and solid comfort of the chief inn : nor even at any length upon the Castle, except to mention that its central portion was built by Sir Walter Raleigh, who here, it is said, first performed the miracle of smoking, and caused his servant to try to extinquish him with a bucket of water.*

It is in the fate of Sherborne Castle as Raleigh's possession that the Tudor spirit seems to me to stand out most vividly. " Great Raleigh," he was called : a man of imagination and high courage, a writer of noble English, a sanguine discoverer : I wonder if he was great.

He desired the manor of Sherborne exceedingly. It belonged to the bishopric of Sarum. His biographer says that " his eagerness to improve his own position came into happy conjunction with a strong opinion, which he shared with a large body of contemporaries, that Bishops and Church dignitaries ought not to be too heavily weighted with secular wealth." The bishopric opportunely fell vacant. It was a more than hinted condition of the appointment of a successor to it that he would convey the Castle estate to the Queen—for Raleigh. " I gave the Queen a jewel, worth £250, to make the Bishop." She made the Bishop. Raleigh got Sherborne.

His life there was simple. He liked the place. He was concerned chiefly with domestic affairs. One Meeres, bailiff of Sherborne, was always plaguing him with writs—

* In testimony whereof it may be observed that forty years after Raleigh's death Sherborne possessed a presumably well-to-do tobacco-cutter, Robert Wyer.

and Meeres had married a kinswoman of Lady Essex, " a poor man's wife of this country, but too good for such a knave." He hawked. He looked after Cecil's son. He had the inconvenience of learning that his wife and son had (in his absence) to flee in different directions because " the plague is in the town very hot." He could easily get to the coast to look after his shipping monopoly. He met with annoyance once at Weymouth in that connection ; one Gilbert had landed a cargo of sassafras wood : " I have a patent that all ships and goods are confiscate that shall trade there without my leave, but whereas sassafras was worth 10s., 12s., and 20s. a pound before Gilbert returned, his cloying of the market will overthrow all mine, and his own also."

From these little things he went to the Tower and lay under sentence of the grim and clumsy block for alleged treachery, never proved. He wrote distractedly to his wife at Sherborne, when he could no longer endure the suspense, and believed his doom certain : he had resolved on suicide. But even then he cared for the Dorset and Devon men who had trusted him : he asked his wife to sell his possessions, " and let the poor men's wages be paid with the goods, for the Lord's sake. Oh, what will my poor servants think, at their return, when they hear I am accused to be Spanish who sent them—at my great charge—to plant and discover upon his [the King of Spain's] territory."

A little later he was in a greater mood, and would fain leave the world as a gentleman, and lie last of all in the place he loved : " You shall receive, dear wife, my last words in these my last lines. My love I send you, that you may keep it when I am dead ; and my counsel, that you may remember it when I am no more. I would not, with my last will, present you with sorrows, dear Bess. Let them go to the grave with me, and be buried in the dust. And, seeing it is not the will of God that ever I shall see you in this life, bear my destruction gently, and with a heart like yourself. . . . Beg my dead body, which living was denied you ;

and either lay it at Sherborne, if the land continue, or in Exeter church, by my father and mother. I can write no more. Time and death call me away. . . . My true wife, farewell. Bless my poor boy ; pray for me. My true God hold you both in His arms.

" Written with the dying hand of sometime thy husband, but now (alas) overthrown.

" Yours that was ; but now not my own,

" W. RALEIGH."

But there remained the last reprieve for the unhappy expedition to Guiana : James I was ready to pardon one who might make him rich. Raleigh's letters to Sherborne on that voyage are uneven ; as a rule he is uncertain and despondent, but occasionally he says a word which must have sounded exotic to quiet Dorset. " To tell you I might be here King of the Indians were a vanity ; but my name doth still live among them. Here they feed me with fresh meat, and all that the country yields ; all offer to obey me."

His son died while he was on the voyage : " I shall sorrow the less, because I have not long to sorrow, because not long to live. . . . My brains are broken, and it is a torment for me to write, and especially of misery."

He failed ; Eldorado was not to be discovered by him, and he came back to pay the penalty of failure. He knew how to die : " He was the most fearless of death that ever was known ; and the most resolute and confident, yet with reverence and conscience. . . . He gave God thanks that he never feared death, and much less then, for it was but an opinion and imagination." . . . " He was very cheerful that morning he died, ate his breakfast heartily, and took tobacco, and made no more of his death than if he had been to take a journey."

" At Sherborne, if the land continue . . ." As soon as Raleigh was dead, King James clutched at the estate for his favourite Robert Carr : " I mun ha' it for Robbie." Carew Raleigh, the son, remonstrated in vain : " they called the conveyance of Sherborne in question, in the

Exchequer," he wrote to the House of Commons, " and for want of one word (which word was found notwithstanding in the paper-book, and was the oversight of a clerk) they pronounced the conveyance invalid, and Sherborne forfeited to the Crown : a judgment easily to be foreseen without witchcraft ; since his chiefest judge was his greatest enemy, and the case between a poor friendless prisoner and a King of England."

IX

" . . . for the deliverance of King James I, the Queen, the Prince, and
all the Royal Branches, with the Nobility, Clergy, and Commons of
England, by Popish treachery appointed as sheep to the slaughter,
in a most barbarous and savage manner, beyond the examples of
former ages."

The Book of Common Prayer.

" During the time men live without a common Power to keep them all
in awe, they are in that condition which is called War ; and such a
war as is of every man against every man. . . . The nature of War
consisteth not in actual fighting ; but in the known disposition
thereto during all the time there is no assurance to the contrary.   All
other time is Peace.

" Whatsoever therefore is consequent to a time of War, where every man
is enemy to every man, the same is consequent to the time wherein
men live without other security than what their own strength and
their own invention shall furnish them withal.   In such conditions,
there is no place for Industry, because the fruit thereof is uncertain ;
and consequently no Culture of the Earth ; no Navigation, nor use
of the commodities that may be imported by sea ; no commodious
Building ; no Instruments of moving and removing such things as
require much force ; no Knowledge of the face of the Earth ; no
account of Time ; no Arts ; no Letters ; no Society ; and which is
worst of all, continual fear, and danger of violent death ; and the
life of man, solitary, poor, nasty, brutish, and short."

THOMAS HOBBES,
Leviathan.

" The sons of Belial had a glorious time."

JOHN DRYDEN,
Absalom and Achitophel.

PRINCES IN FLIGHT

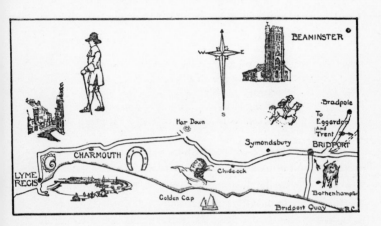

I HAVE said more about economic and social changes than political, hitherto, because, on the whole, political ideas were hardly so diffused as to be the property of more than a limited class of Englishmen. The people in general felt the incidence of the policy informed by such ideas ; but except for the brief outburst of the Peasants' Revolt, their concern with the state of society was material rather than reflective. In the seventeenth century, however, they tampered actively with the State machine. All classes were, at least potentially, property owners ; all paid national taxes, received national justice or injustice, did national service through their local agency, the parish. Newspapers were started. A king was beheaded, his elder son chased, his younger son, also a king, exiled, his bastard grandson beheaded.

159

There is a famous passage in the first Lord Shaftesbury's autobiography which gives a lively picture of one side of Dorset life in that century. The gentry used to meet once a week (usually at Handley, on the edge of Cranborne Chase) to play bowls. There were notable men among them : Lord Bristol (Charles I's Secretary of State), for instance, and the Denzil Holles, who in 1629 held the Speaker in the Chair to prevent the House from adjourning at the King's command.* They were not to be all on the same side in the Civil War ; and the most brilliant of them all, Shaftesbury himself, was the least stable in principle and in fact :—

> " A fiery soul, which, working out its way,
> Fretted the pigmy body to decay, . . .
> Bankrupt of life, yet prodigal of ease,
> In friendship false, implacable in hate,
> Resolved to ruin or to rule the state."

It is impossible, nevertheless, for all his " close designs and crooked counsels," not to be fascinated by Shaftesbury's restless, versatile, indomitable spirit and fine mind. Frail of body, in constant pain, he showed high courage all his life, from the day when, as a freshman at Oxford, he put down the barbarous custom of " tucking," to the time when, dying a refugee in Holland, he was brought back for burial in the county of which he had been so great a part.

But not all the people of Dorset were occupied in the manner of the Handley company. At the very time of Shaftesbury's account, the Rev. John White (an Oxfordshire man) " held a strong sway " in Dorchester. " A grave

---

* " God's wounds ! " cried Holles, " you shall sit till we please to rise ! " It is interesting to find so lively a figure commemorated at Dorchester in a panegyric exceptional in an epoch of complacent epitaphs : I may quote a sentence or two : it is very long :

" All that Denzil's wit or courage, probity or industry, presaged in his youth, he made good and exceeded when grown a man, for, as excellent endowments and abilities made him early known to his prince and country, so he could, by his eloquence and valour, intrepidly defend the liberty of the last without refusing the obedience that was due to the former." Two of the chubbiest possible cherubs shed frozen marble tears before the effigy of Denzil posed very uncomfortably in the costume of a Roman senator.

man, without moroseness, as who would willingly contribute his shot of facetiousness on any just occasion. A constant preacher. . . . A good governor, by whose wisdom the town of Dorchester (notwithstanding a casual merciless fire) was much enriched ; knowledge causing piety, piety breed-ing industry, and industry procuring plenty unto it. A beggar was not then to be seen in the town, all able poor being set on work, and impotent maintained by the profit of a public brewhouse, and other collections. He absolutely commanded his own passions, and the purses of his parishioners, whom he could wind up to what height he pleased on important occasions. He was free from covetous-ness, if not trespassing on the contrary ; and had a patriarchal influence both in Old and New England." Thomas Fuller, from whose *Worthies* the quotation comes, possibly knew White personally, for from 1634 to 1641 (and perhaps again at the end of his life) he held the Dorset living of Broadwindsor, where his pulpit is still in use.

White, however, was more than the parson of the county town. He was a leader of the West country Puritans, and it was largely due to him that the non-conforming party formed the Massachusetts Company (often called the Dor-chester Company), and in 1628 founded (or rather, organized) a settlement in that colony. A monument to John Endicott or Endecott, the first governor, was unveiled at Weymouth in 1914 by Endicott's descendant, the wife of Joseph Chamberlain. Endicott is said to have been a Dorchester man. The first colonists sailed from Weymouth in the *Abigail* on June 20, 1628.

It seems probable that the idea of this settlement arose out of the Dorset fishing " adventures " oversea. The boats in that trade sailed with double crews, to expedite the catch and packing. " It was conceived," says an authoritative pamphlet on the New England traffic, almost certainly written by White himself, " that, the fishing being ended, the spare men that were above their necessary sailors might be left behind with provisions for a year ;

M

and when that ship returned next year, they might assist them in fishing, as they had done the former year ; and in the meantime, might employ themselves in building, and planting corn, which, with the provisions of fish, fowl, and venison that the land yielded, would afford them the chief of their food." They raised " a stock of more than £3000, intended to be paid in five years, but afterwards disbursed in a shorter time." But it was found (" which experienced fishermen could easily have foreseen beforehand ") that good fishermen do not necessarily make good land settlers, nor a fishing ground an earthly paradise. They wanted shoe-makers, vineplanters, " men skilful in making of pitch, of salt," a barber-surgeon, mining experts, and so on. It needed Endicott's arrival with new settlers not bound to the fisheries, but akin in their desire for religious liberty, and amenable to the governor's genuine powers of organiza-tion, to set up the new colony on a sound footing ; though even so the sort of practical difficulty that had to be faced can be gathered from a letter to White, of 1632, about a Dorset man : " I have much difficulty to keep John Galloppe (Gollop ?) here by reason his wife will not come. I marvel at her woman's weakness, that she will live miserably with her children there, when she might live comfortably with her husband here. I pray you persuade and further her coming by all means ; if she will come let her have the remainder of his wages, if not let it be bestowed to bring over his children, for so he desires. It would be about £40 loss to him to come for her."

Moreover, in addition to this vigorous undertaking of White's, the Puritan movement had long had a strong support in Dorset in the increasingly numerous non-con-forming churches. Poole, possibly, was the earliest Dorset centre of dissatisfaction with either the Roman Catholic or the Protestant organization. One Thomas Hancock of that place was in the first year of King Edward VI " called to be minister of God's word at the town of Poole, which town was at the time wealthy, for they embraced God's word,

they were in favours with the rulers and governors of the
realm, they were the first that in that part of England were
called Protestants : they did love one another ; and every
one glad of the company of the others ; and so God poured
His blessing plentifully upon them."

The domestic life of the period was largely a matter of
small beer laced with spite. Individualists of to-day are
rather apt to call upon the past to support their cries for
liberty. They would find it hard to appreciate a condition
of things in which the community as a whole had so much
power as it had in Stuart times. A genuine conservative
might indeed feel sympathy with the examiners of Roger
Honiborne of Dorchester, who in 1630 affirmed that Robert
Hoskins and Thomas Waite " were in Mr. Angell Greyes
grounds of Kingston and fished in his waters and tooke
fishe there," and wouldn't put them back again when
Honiborne (who seems to have been a keeper of an early
type) " willed " them to do so. But some of the more
socialistic interferences with the liberty of the subject might
prove displeasing. You were liable to be examined by the
magistrates or " presented " to the parish or the justice
for any trivial offence—and that before the Puritans held
the reins : and your examiners, the authorities of the
community, had full power to do justice upon you. " Mary
Tuxbury, for scolding at the sergeants . . . is ordered to be
plounced when the weather is warmer." Justice, but mercy
. . . plouncing is ducking—in the Frome. " Hugh Baker,
carrier of this Borough, was complayned of to Mr. Maior that
he went out of church yesterday at Morning Prayer before
prayers were ended, and confesseth to the same, and is
censured to sit in the stocks two houres for his misdemeanor "
(1629). John Gape was summoned for playing " at the
ball " in the prison court : Anthony Wood for saying to
Matthew Swaffield " that his heart was so hollow that the
Divell might dance in it." In 1630 the Justices had to hear
this terrible story : " John Graunt upon oath. Yesterday
coming from Weymouth, [Robert] George demanded of

Pouncy where he beloed like a calfe ; he said he was a man, and George said he was a puppy ; then Pouncy alighted from his horse and after divers speeches George strake Pouncy with a Cudgell." No wonder that in 1632 the sons of Roger and Thomas Pouncy (" greate boyes ") were fined 12d. apiece, with others, for being absent from church and playing " at Nine Holes for money, a farthing a game." Yet one of them was put in the stocks for doing it again a few months later ; and Thampson Pouncy, " the wife of Thomas Pouncy the elder," shortly afterwards was plounced " three several times " as a common scold : and Thomas Pouncy the younger was charged in 1637 with being at the bull-baiting and " breaking the bullkeeper's head with his cudgell." A spirited family.

And while I am dealing with names so well known still in Dorset and Dorchester, here is yet another of 1632. " William Hardy, gent, dwelling everywhere (as he said), charged with swearing eight oathes, and abused the constables, saying : ' that he durst say they weare all a company of dampned creatures and the divell would have them all, and called them cod's heads and sheepe's heads.' " It cost him eight shillings and a day in gaol, from which he was released on " plenary confession."*

I do not propose to dwell in detail on the historical events of this period. The county was fairly evenly divided in the Civil War. Like other counties, it had its grievances, particularly the extraction of shipmoney, the administration of the forest and highway laws, and the billeting of soldiers. No great battle was fought within its borders, but it was in a constant state of warfare. Corfe and Sherborne castles were duly besieged and " slighted."

* The quotations are from the *Dorchester Municipal Records*, edited with loving care by Charles Herbert Mayo and Arthur William Gould (Exeter, 1908). That great Dorset antiquary, Mr. H. J. Moule, aided the project of publication. But it is clear from Mr. Gould's modest preface that most of the cost (apart from all the toil) of production fell on the Editors. This is a most valuable social document. When will the greatest country in the world be able, or feel able, to do for its local records what it has done for its State Papers ?
A strange picture of the equally squalid party strife of this period is contained in the annotated edition of James Strong's *Joanereidos*.

Lyme withstood a memorable siege. It was of high importance to Charles to win it ; Blake, who afterwards defeated Van Tromp off Portland, was one of the defenders. It is difficult to understand to-day how a town so situated —at the very bottom of a steep cup—could not be taken with some ease. But the defence was determined. The great historian of Lyme, Roberts, from whom Macaulay drew, without excessive acknowledgment or accuracy, his picturesque information, says that " the resistance of the townsmen was most obstinate : their courage was increased by the vehement harangues and violent rhapsodies of twenty-five puritanical preachers, who confidently assured eternal salvation to those who should fall in the contest." The women joined valiantly in the struggle. One lost a hand in conflict. All she said was " Truly, I am glad with all my heart I had a hand to lose for Jesus Christ, for whose cause I am willing to lose, not only my other hand, but my life also."

Fairfax on the one side and Goring on the other encamped often within the county borders ; and Wareham and Poole —Roundhead, in spite of an offer by the Marquis of Hertford to spend £200 a week there if it would change sides—had their usual full share of any available fighting. William Wake, rector of Holy Trinity, Wareham (grandfather of a Dorset Archbishop of Canterbury), suffered exceptionally. He was first shot by a Parliamentary agent ; then cut over the head and left for dead : then sent prisoner to Dorchester, where he caught the plague. Meanwhile his family were turned out of doors and his goods seized. He was set free, joined the Royalists, was captured at Sherborne, stripped and paraded naked through the town, and sent prisoner, first to Poole, where plague was raging, and then to Corfe. When the main fighting was over, he retired to Blandford, but the Parliament men " kept him, a very infirm man, on their guards, and daily moved him with them as they were commanded from place to place." " He was nineteen times a prisoner in the time of the rebellion, and all that time under sequestration."

The Bridport records contain a valuable document on the realities of the taxation Charles I found it desirable to impose. It requires Dorset to provide a man-of-war of four hundred tons, one hundred and sixty men, guns and equipment, and victuals for twenty-six weeks : six or eight assessors were to supervise the levy. The alleged cause was " that certain pirates and sea robbers, both Mohametans, detesters of the Christian name, and others," had " collected together, robbing and spoiling the ships and goods not only of our own subjects but of the subjects of our allies upon the sea, which had been formerly accustomed to be guarded by the English nation." The order in which the municipal authorities of Dorset were addressed in this writ is curious, and perhaps significant : the towns run thus—Poole, Dorchester, Weymouth and Melcombe Regis, Bridport, Lyme Regis, Corfe Castle, Shaftesbury, Blandford, " the good men of Poole and of the Isle of Purbeck, of the Vills of Portland, Burton, Sherborne, Cranborne, and Stoborough, and all other places " : no Wareham, no Wimborne.

There was, however, one feature of the war in Dorset which deserves special notice : the rising of the Clubmen. This is sometimes spoken of as though it were the work of a rabble of irritated peasants, who simply desired to live and let live, and to keep their fields free of bloodshed. It was at least serious enough to cause both Fairfax and Goring to pay attention to it. It occurred in 1645. In that year, on May 25, a meeting of men from Dorset and Wilts was held at Badbury Rings ; neither the first nor the least resolute gathering in that ancient fortress. There were present " near 4000 armed with Clubs, Swords, Bills, Pitchforks, and other several weapons, etc." The meeting declared, in resolutions read by one Thomas Young, that " our ancient laws and liberties . . . are altogether swallowed up in the arbitrary power of the sword," and covenanted, among other things, " to join with and assist one another in the mutual defence of our Liberties and Properties against all Plunderers, and all other unlawful violence whatsoever." Their immediate concern was to prevent violence. In every parish there was to be a committee of three, " for assistance and direction," with two constables to raise the alarm at any sign of tumult ; and all were to " furnish themselves with as much, and good, arms, weapons, and ammunition as they can procure."

A few weeks later the inhabitants of Dorset petitioned the King himself ; " the petitioners, since these unhappy Civil Wars, having in a deeper measure than other subjects of this kingdom, suffered by means of the many garrisons within this little county (they being ten in number) and the armies partly drawn into these parts by reason thereof." Charles, in a statesmanlike reply filling several pages of print, said that the matter was receiving attention. So did Fairfax, when a deputation waited upon him also, and asked " that all laws not repealed be in force, and executed by the ordinary officers : that all men who desire it may lay down arms : and others, who have absented themselves from their homes, may have free liberty to return and live at home." Fairfax knew what civil war meant : he found at Dorchester, for instance (" a town famous for piety and good affection " —to his cause), that " divers of the best inhabitants being forced from it, the beauty of the town is much impaired, and many houses empty." But how could he maintain an army, he asked in his reply, and so attain his just aims, if everyone went home ? Necessity . . .

The deputation to him was led by men of good name. It contained a Trenchard and a Holles : John St. Loe, Peter Hoskins, Esquire, Master Robert Paulet, gent ; and " Master Thomas Young, an attorney, more eloquent than honest." I should like to know more of Master Thomas Young, the orator of Badbury : but history is silent.

The chief recorded motto of the Clubmen was on one of their banners :—

> " If you offer to plunder our cattle,
>   Be assured we will give you battle."

The London news-sheets of the time regarded them as both partisan and dangerous ; but the alleged partisanship depended on the journal. " The Clubmen speak altogether the royal language, however they may seem to be neuter," says the *True Informer*. " The most eminent gentlemen, and others, for the King in those parts, are their leaders : neither are they without some from Oxford, the most notoriously profane and noted wicked persons in that county and Wiltshire are among them, and but few either of seeming civility or religion." " There are Knights among them," cried the *Moderate Intelligencer ;* " they are armed very well." But the *Scottish Dove* said that " these men (as they first resolved, hold perfect neutrals) oppose free quarter by both sides, and yet accommodate either with provisions for money . . . which assures me their affections stand right to the Parliament."

The elementary Soviet system did not live up to the hopes or fears formed of it. Cromwell himself arrived in August, 1645, and persuaded one section to go quickly home. The rest encamped on Hambledon Hill, above the Stour. Cromwell demanded surrender, which was refused. Major Desborough was ordered to approach and prepare to charge. The Clubmen fired, whereupon Desborough " got in the rear of them, beat them from the work, and did some small execution upon them ; I believe killed not twelve of them, but cut very many, and we have taken about 300 ; many of which are poor silly creatures, whom if you please to let me send home, they promise to be very dutiful for time to come, and will be hanged before they come out again."

Cromwell, who wrote this, was made for larger wars and greater policies. It is suggestive to notice how intimate and petty and personal all the Dorset connection with the Civil War is. The county seems only to touch larger issues in a venture like White's, or in the supreme tragedy of " King Monmouth " ; though by a curious chance it may have had a vision of what was to come in the great world. It is recorded that " a very learned pious man," Mr. John

Sadler of Warmwell, in 1661 prophesied to his Rector :
he said a " Someone " in the room in which he lay ill told
him "that there would die in the city of London so many
thousands, mentioning the number, which I have forgotten,
and the time that the city would be burnt down. . . . That
we should have three sea-fights with the Dutch. . . . That
afterwards there would come three small ships to land in
the west of Weymouth, that would put all England in a
uproar, but it would come to nothing. That in the year
1688 there would come to pass such a thing in this kingdom
that all the world would take notice of it." It was, as the
gentleman in *Martin Chuzzlewit* says, " a prediction cruel
smart."

But for one strange alarm Dorset had little to do with
great events between the Restoration and the coming of
Monmouth. That alarm was experienced at the time of
the Oates affair. One Capt. John Laurence of Grange, in
1678, reported that he had seen " a vast number of armed
men, several thousands, marching from Flowers Barrow
over Grange Hill ; and a great noise and clashing of arms
was supposed to have been heard." People on the hills
and the heath fled hastily to Wareham, which was barricaded.
The militia were called out. And nothing was ever seen of
the phantom army, to whose existence Laurence and his
brother subsequently swore on oath before the Privy Council.
Hutchins ascribes it to the effect of mist on the Purbeck
rocks.

It is not difficult to follow on foot the path of the two
princes, father and son, who made Dorset notable in this
seventeenth century. Charles II tried to leave England by
way of the county in 1651. Monmouth entered England
through it in 1685 and was captured within its borders a
few weeks afterwards.

The flight of Charles II through Dorset is adorned with
many picturesque details. It was from Boscobel that he
came to Col. Wyndham's house at Trent, a village near
Yeovil, now part of Dorset. Mrs. Wyndham wrote the

fullest of the accounts of his stay " in that Ark in which God shutt him up, when the Floods of Rebellion had covered the face of his Dominions." He arrived on September 17, and a secret chamber was kept in readiness for any emergency. His purpose was to take a boat from some western port to France. Apparently he was unaware that the western ports were full of Parliamentary troops preparing for an expedition to Jersey. He knew, of course, that there was a hue and cry after himself ; and at Lyme, there had just been set up a proclamation, dated September 10, in which " a heavy penalty was thundered out against all that should conceal the King or any of his party," and a price of £1000 set upon Charles's person.

At Trent, however, he seemed to be reasonably safe, and it was within easy distance both of the Dorset ports and of the Bristol Channel. His adventures in Dorset begin with a visit which Col. Wyndham paid to William Ellesdon of Lyme, one of a family long of repute in that town. Ellesdon was a known Royalist, and, as he himself says, " would with the utmost hazard of my person and whatsoever else was dear to me strenuously endeavour " to serve the King. Wyndham asked him to find a vessel for France, telling him the truth about the proposed passengers (Lord Wilmot was with Charles). Ellesdon had a sea captain, Stephen Limbry, as tenant of a house of his at Charmouth, and they rode over to see him. Limbry agreed to do the business for sixty pounds, payable on completion of the undertaking. He was master of " a small vessel of about thirty tons."

Here there is some room for geographical conjecture. The arrangements made provided for embarking for Charmouth " by the seaside." " Indeed," says Ellesdon, " a more commodious place for such a design could hardly be found, it lying upon the shore a quarter of a mile from any house, or footpath." Charmouth village was and is a quarter of a mile from the sea—a peculiarity of distance shared in various degrees also by Abbotsbury, Swyre, Burton Bradstock, Bridport town, and Chideock, along this coast. On

the other hand Limbry's boat was moored off Lyme Regis
Cobb, from two to three miles away. A little before the time
appointed for departure, Limbry took the boat out " to
the Cobb's mouth for fear of being beneaped." The September neap tides are usually the lowest of the year, as the
spring tides of the same month are the highest ; and at a
neap tide all along that coast from Axmouth to Burton the
moorings can hardly be reached or quitted because of the
low water.

Further, Ellesdon, riding back with Wyndham to Lyme,
" chose the land road . . . that upon the top of a hill
situate in our way betwixt these two towns, upon a second
view he might be more perfectly acquainted with the way
that leads from Charmouth to the place appointed for His
Majesty's taking boat." The whole coast has altered since
then : it has altered even so recently as 1921 ! The cliffs
have fallen. The land where twenty-four years after Charles's
flight Monmouth enrolled his poor peasants at Lyme is now
beneath the sea. The road now known as the Devil's
Bellows was not in existence in 1651. Charmouth stream,
maybe, ran openly to the sea instead of burying itself in the
shingle bank.

I think that Charles was meant to be rowed from Charmouth beach to Cobb's mouth, a stiff pull ; and that Ellesdon
took Wyndham up to the still existing old high road, an
inflexible steep track from which not only Charmouth but
Lewsdon and Pilsdon and Marshwood Vale, and far more
distant hills, and the most glorious curve of coast in England,
are seen spread out in a magnificent pageant. There
(among the bracken and blackberries which would conceal
him as well as any Boscobel oak) well might the King of
England look out over his realm with pride and love.

The course of English history was very near deflection
in the next few hours. Wyndham rode back to Trent. He
sent a servant, Henry Peters, to the *Queen's Arms* at
Charmouth to bespeak rooms for the fugitive while he waited
for the boat. He was to represent Charles as a runaway

lover eloping with his lady (who was to be played by Juliana
Coningsby, Wyndham's niece). This was satisfactorily
arranged over a glass of wine with the hostess.

They set out in due course, Miss Coningsby riding pillion,
Wyndham in front as guide, Wilmot and Peters a little
way behind, " that they might not seem to be all of one
company." Ellesdon met them, and took them to his
brother's house at Monkton Wyld, a village to-day very
beautifully placed among trees, just off the road from Charmouth to Hunter's Lodge. (The brother is said in one account
to have been " a violent Oliverian.") It is impossible to
tell, among the many lanes of Marshwood Vale, what roads
were then in existence for them to follow, in the days before
the main highways of the present time were even thought of.
They may have gone along something like the present
main road round the top of the vale, or even through
Axminster.

The king gave Ellesdon, for remembrance, a gold coin,
" which in his solitary hours he made a hole to put a ribbin
in." There were more solitary hours to come, but some
of them full of fears lest the solitude be broken. At dusk
they moved to Charmouth. The *Queen's Arms* is now
a private house, marked by a commemorative tablet.
Ellesdon had told Limbry, for the benefit of the crew, that
his friend " Mr. Payne," a merchant—Lord Wilmot—and his
servant (the King) wanted to sail by night because, " Lyme
being a Town Corporate," " Payne " feared an arrest in his
sudden voyage to St. Malo to recover property from a dis-
honest factor. Limbry seems to have swallowed this tale.
Unfortunately for the King, however, he did not warn his
wife of his intended voyage till the last moment, when he
went home to get some linen. Now she had been at Lyme
Fair that day, and had read the proclamation of September
10th : and she was not minded to lose her husband. She
suspected his alleged cargo to be refugees from Worcester,
to say the least ; and she locked her Stephen in, and " by
the help of her two daughters kept him in by force."

Limbry seems to have done his best. He "showed his wisdom," Ellesdon said, "by his peaceable behaviour, for had he striven in the least it is more than probable that His Majesty and his attendents had been suddenly seized upon in the inn." But later on, apparently, he got some mitigation of his duress; for Wyndham, watching, in the moonlight, on Charmouth beach, for the boat that was to save his King, "discovers a man coming, dogged at a small distance by two or three women. This indeed was the master of the vessel, who by this time had obtained liberty (yet still under the eyes of his over-zealous keepers) to walk towards the seaside with an intention to make known to those that waited for him the sad tidings of this disappointment together with the causes." Wyndham thought the figure was Limbry's, but was not certain, and dared not question him because of the women.

It was one of many curiously suspicious mischances in Charles's flight. Half a dozen incidents seem to hint that everyone knew who he was, and many would help towards his capture, but none would commit the direct act of betrayal.

One or other of the party waited on the beach all night for the boat which never came. Their horses were kept saddled, their gear not unpacked. In the morning Peters, Wyndham's servant, was sent to Ellesdon at Lyme to enquire what had happened. Charles and Wyndham and Miss Coningsby set off towards Bridport : Lord Wilmot was to follow them and meet them at the *George* in that town (now the frequented and pleasant shop of Mr. Beach) as soon as Peters came back with news.

The news might well have been even more disturbing than, in the end, it was. The hostess of the *Queen's Arms* had lately taken on as an ostler an ex-service man (as we should say to-day)—"a notorious knave," who, "perhaps inspired and prompted by the devil," called her attention to the strange behaviour of her guests. Ellesdon, in his narrative, half hints that she herself had some know-

ledge of their identity. But she would not listen to Henry
Hull the ostler. Henry, however, had to take Lord Wilmot's
horse to be shod that morning ; and when Hammet the
smith saw the hoofs, he exclaimed, " I am confident these
shoes were made and set in the north." Thereupon Hull
goes " to one Wesley, the puny parson of the place, and a
most devoted friend of the parricides, to ask his advice."*
Wesley was praying and could at first take no heed. But
when his " long-breathed devotions " were over, he went at
once to the host of the inn and " with most eager blattera-
tions catechiseth him " ; and from him to Robert Butler, a
justice, and a member of the Dorset Standing Committee,
for a warrant to set people on to apprehending the King.
Butler, it is said, refused. But Captain Massey or Macey,
in charge of troops at Lyme, to whom Wesley then repaired,
set off posthaste along the Bridport road with as many men
as he could get together.

I said " the host " was interrogated by Wesley. That
is one account. Another is that the parson went to the
hostess and said, " Why, how now, Margaret, you are a
maid of honour now ! " She asked what he meant. " Why,
Charles Stuart lay the last night at your house and kissed
you at his departure, so that now you can't but be a maid
of honour." Whatever Charles did or said, the hostess,
according to this story, was on his side : " if I thought it
was the King, I would think the better of my lips all days
of my life ; and so, Mr. Parson, get you out of my house,
or else I'll get those shall kick you out."

Something of all these suspicions—how much is not
evident—must have come to Wilmot's ears, for he and
Peters set off in haste after Charles. The Charmouth-
Bridport road in its present state was not constructed till

---

* Bartholomew Wesley or Westley, John Wesley's great grandfather.
"This Westley," says the author of *Miraculum-Basilicon* (1664) " is
since a Nonconformist, and lives by the practice of physic in the same
place. He told a good gentlewoman that he was confident, if ever the King
did come in again, he would love long prayers ; for had he not been longer
than ordinary at his devotions, he had surely snapped him."

over a century later, but doubtless followed much the same natural lines—up the long slow hill to Morecombelake, round the curve of Har Down (most unexpected and lovable of the sudden shaggy Dorset hills), down to little Chideock, up again, and down over the bridge past Allington into Bridport town, where the then *George* is almost at the main cross roads.

In the paved yard which is still behind Mr. Beach's shop, Charles in his character of servant was tending his mistress's horse. The place was full of soldiers preparing for the Jersey expedition. To him one Horton the ostler, " Ho, friend ! I am glad to see thee here. I know you well ! " Charles did not accept the recognition. Horton explained that he had met him at Exeter, where he had been at an inn eleven years with one Mr. Porter. " And I likewise," said the prince, readily, " did serve Mr. Porter. I am glad that I have met with my old acquaintance ; but I see now thou art full of business, that thou canst not possibly drink with me ; but when I shall chance to return from London, we will talk more freely concerning our old affairs."

Fortunately Lord Wilmot arrived with Peters just afterwards, and, spurred by his alarming news, the fugitives set forth again at once, taking the Dorchester road. They met many travellers, and among them one who was formerly a servant of Charles I. One account puts this meeting between Charmouth and Bridport. But at any rate the risk of recognition was becoming menacingly real, and they resolved to take the next turning off the main road, " which might probably lead towards Yeovil or Sherborne," and so back to Trent.

Mr. A. M. Broadley was instrumental in placing a stone slab to commemorate this " miraculous divergence." I cannot feel sure that his choice of the lane or of the quotation on the stone is correct. He cites Fuller's doggerel :—

> " At Worcester great God's goodness to the Nation
> It was a Conquest Your bare Preservation.
> When midst Your fiercest foes on every side
> For your escape God did a LANE provide."

It is quite true that Fuller, as rector of Broadwindsor, might know the more intimate details of Charles's adventures in Dorset. But it seems to me more likely that the " Lane " is not a road but a person—Jane Lane, by whose aid he got safely away immediately after Worcester fight.

Mr. Broadley insisted that the Lane is Lee Lane, a by-road running down to his own house at Bradpole. But that would not take the fugitives to Yeovil or Sherborne, except very indirectly—even if the road then existed. It would take them into marshy ground north of Bridport. What looks like an older track, however, diverges from the main road at the same place, in a much more promising direction —a disused broad path between hedges, which may well have been an ancient bridle track, pointing (and in fact leading) direct to the great land-mark of Eggardon—which *is* on the way to Yeovil and Sherborne.*

What is more, had they taken Lee Lane they would have found themselves almost immediately in Bradpole village ; whereas Mrs. Wyndham's account says they reached a village " after many hours' travel." The village was Broad-windsor. By following the track I have mentioned they would have come out on higher ground near Powerstock, and might easily have wandered through the desolate wooded country near Hooke and Wraxall, as certain eminent

* Ogilby's *Traveller's Guide*, a " description of England undertaken by the express command of King Charles II," describes (I quote the 1699 edition) the road from Exeter to Dorchester. " At the end of Bridport an indifferent straight way by Walditch and Lytton Churches on the right, Long Lother and Askatham on the left." Long Lother is Loders ; and Lee Lane can only reach Loders deviously, whereas the deserted track I have mentioned goes close by Loders almost in a straight line. It is true that Denzil Holles in 1651 held the manor of Loders ; but he was not necessarily there, and Charles was not necessarily to know it if he was. Bradpole is not mentioned by Ogilby. Askatham I take to be Askerswell. The turning for Loders is given as at three furlongs from the bridge at Bridport ; that for Askerswell at two miles three furlongs. A hundred and more years later, the turnpike roads that still endure began to be constructed, and the mean byroads of to-day lost their then importance. It is much more likely that a track disused to-day is an old road of the pre-turnpike era than that a better engineered one now in use is of continuous ancestry. The present stretch of main road from the top of Chilcombe Down to Axminster was built in 1754.

gipsies did later, without meeting a soul or seeing a house till they fetched up at Broadwindsor inn.

At any rate, they found the inn in safety. If they had kept to the Dorchester road, Captain Macey would have caught them up. He was close upon their heels ; but he followed the main road, up over Askerswell Hill and on all the way to Dorchester, where, " with the utmost haste and diligence, he searched all the inns and alehouses "—in vain.

It chanced that the host of the *George* at Broadwindsor was an old servant of Wyndham's, one Rhys Jones. He gave them a private room. But they were not wholly out of danger. Many houses round Charmouth were being searched ; apparently it was common knowledge that Charles was somewhere in the neighbourhood. One party of soldiers came as near to Broadwindsor as Pilsdon Manor (owned by Wyndham's uncle), where they offered much indignity to the daughter of the house, believing that she was the prince in disguise. Gregory Alford (of whom more shortly) says that Ellesdon himself was in charge of this party, and was eager for the £1000 reward ; the assertion is hardly consistent with Ellesdon's own account, for he says that he knew from the first who the fugitives were ; and if so, he need not have postponed the betrayal. Alford hints at a possible reason for disloyalty : " Ellesdon was newly married to a very rich but rigid Presbyterian." Alford himself was vigorous against Dissenters.

But there was danger even nearer than Pilsdon. They had not been in the *George* long when the village constable arrived with forty soldiers for the Jersey expedition, whom he billeted on the inn. With them was a " leaguer-wench," a camp-follower so far gone towards motherhood that she bore a child in the inn that night. This " made the inhabitants very ill at ease, fearing the whole parish should become the reputed father, and be enforced to keep the child." Their uneasiness was fortunate, because it led to a hot argument between the parish and the troops, and allowed the royal party to relax their vigilance and consider their

N

position. They thought it "very hazardous to attempt
anything more in Dorsetshire " ; and after resting, left the
house quietly at dawn and returned without mishap to
Trent. Charles remained there undisturbed—save for one
alarm about some mysterious troops at Sherborne—till
October 6th, when he set out for the coast again : this time
more successfully, for he sailed from Brighton for France
on October 15th.

I have mentioned Gregory Alford. He is a Dorset link
between this flight of Charles II and the adventures in the
county of his wretched son, James Scott, Duke of Monmouth, at this time only a year-old baby. When the
Dorset plan was first mooted, Col. Wyndham rode off
to Giles Strangways at Melbury Sampford,—thinking him
a knowledgeable person who could find a boat, and also
a financial supporter. But Col. Strangways' father was
still living.* "He had no great command of money."
Moreover, most of his seafaring acquaintances were "for
their loyalty banished." He managed, however, to furnish
£100 for the King's use, and he advised Wyndham to try
either Gregory Alford or William Ellesdon, both of Lyme.
But Alford was in Portugal, "forced," he says, "to be
abroad by reason of his loyalty."

Now Alford had married the daughter of one George
Potter of Exeter ; and the Bridport ostler Horton had been
in George Potter's service. It was in that service, Horton
said to Charles in the yard of the *George* inn, that they had
formerly met !

Gregory Alford prospered, it seems : and he was able to
show his loyalty to the Stuart dynasty later, for it was he
who, as the zealous mayor of Lyme, did so much to frustrate

---

* John Strangways, buried with others of his notable family in the
little church at Melbury Sampford, close to the great house. His Latin
epitaph records that he was "faithful to the King for whom he stood up,
boldly and continuously, throughout the severest hardships, while the
internecine conspiracy was at its height ; suffering the loss of his private
possessions, imprisonment, and every indignity, with the greatest fortitude,
and now "—at the date of his death, at the age of eighty-two, on December
30, 1666—" beholding the restoration of King Charles II."

Monmouth's rebellion by sending early word of his landing to London.

It was on June 11 (June 21, "N.S."), 1685, that "a ten-oared boat landed three gentlemen [from three ships off Lyme] at daybreak at Seatown [under Golden Cap]. They asked some fishermen, while they treated them with bottles of Canary and neats' tongues, what news there was; who said they knew none, but they had heard there was a rebellion in Scotland by the Earl of Argyle." Two went towards Taunton, and the third—Colonel Venner, who appears at Bridport a few days later—re-embarked.

The local surveyor of customs heard of it, and became suspicious. He told the mayor of Lyme, Alford. The surveyor of Lyme had already put off to examine the vessels, and had not returned. Later in the day, towards evening, a newsletter from London arrived with the intelligence that three boats well armed had sailed from Holland, ostensibly for the Indies, but probably in reality for England, bearing the Duke of Monmouth.

Gregory Alford and his friends were uneasy. They would have summoned the boats to salute—if there had been any powder for the town guns; but there was not. Suddenly they saw seven boatloads of men fully armed rowing ashore. The town drums were beaten, and the deputy-surveyor with a few seamen ran to the Cobb, procuring a little powder on the way from a West India merchant, and handing it over to a magistrate. He was too late for any resistance. The Duke's men were ashore, escorted by townsmen crying, "A Monmouth! a Monmouth—the Protestant religion!"

They proceeded to enlist men in a field on the Church Cliffs. "The Duke was in purple, with a star on his breast, wearing only a sword." He said he had arms enough for twenty or thirty thousand men. A long and wordy Declaration was read, calling King James "a murderer and an assassin of innocent men; a Popish usurper of the Crown; Traitor to the Nation, and Tyrant over the People."

The Duke's welcome was of a mixed character. A good number of peasants joined him at once ; by June 12 he had 1000 foot and 150 horse. He does not seem to have had arms for more than twice that number at most (he had to turn hundreds away), and he was not well provided with money. Nor did the gentry join him as he hoped ; James had been vigilant : some were arrested, some fled. In the meantime the mayor of Lyme also fled : Lyme was now hardly safe for him. But before he fled he despatched the active deputy-surveyor of customs to London with a letter to the King, reporting the invasion.

The next day men still flocked in—Daniel Defoe was one of them—and there were soon sufficient for the formation of four regiments, the Blue, the Yellow, the White, the Green.*

Then came a futile reconnoitring visit to Bridport, and " Edward Coker, Gent, second son of Captain Robert Coker of Mapowder, was slain at the Bull Inn, by one Venner," as the brass in the parish church and a rubbing of it at the *Bull* testify. The fighting is said to have been very hot while it lasted, but it seems to have been purposeless and indiscriminate. Local tradition says that the invaders pushed James's men up the steep Bothenhampton Hill (above the present village, to the north and east of it), and fought so fiercely that the lane up which they struggled—a narrow path between hedges now—ran with blood. It is called Bloody Lane to this day. But after a short time both sides, according to the written accounts, seem to have lost their heads. Lord Grey and his horsemen " ran and never turned till they came to Lyme." Venner, being left in command, was wounded, and rode after Grey. But Wade continued an intermittent attack, gradually retreating, while, on the other hand, " the militia remained contented with having reoccupied the centre of the town, and shouting, out of musket shot, at Monmouth's men."

---

* Their memory lived long. Roberts, the historian of the rebellion, writes : " the generation has passed from us, whose countenances glowed at any mention of the Blue and the Yellow regiments, in which their fathers and grandfathers served with their darling Monmouth."

On June 15th the little army left Lyme and Dorset ; many
to return only to the justice of Lord Jeffreys. The inept
manœuvres and fighting which ended miserably at Sedgemoor need not be described here. It is estimated that
3200 men were in Monmouth's force on the dark morning of
July 6, 1685, " many half drunk."

The Duke came back to Dorset after the battle, in which
he does not seem to have borne himself well. He re-entered
the county, a fugitive, near Shaftesbury, and at Woodyates
inn disguised himself as a shepherd. He was soon traced :
the country was being beaten for him ; and there was a
price of £5000 on his head. They found him " in a ditch
covered with fern and brambles, under an ash tree . . . in
the last extremity of hunger and fatigue." (The remains of
the alleged tree stood till recent times.) He could not even
run away competently. He was taken first before Anthony
Ettricke, of Holt Lodge, the magistrate whose curious
coffin lies half inside, half outside Wimborne Minster ; and
thence he was sent to Ringwood, and so to London.

He was beheaded on Tower Hill less than a fortnight
later. On the scaffold he bore himself with dignity and
courage. He had need of all his courage. " The executioner
had five blows at him ; after the first he looked up, and
after the third he put his legs across, and the hangman flung
away his axe, but being chid took it again, and severed not
his head from his body till he cut it off with his knife."

The executioner was John Ketch, immortal through his
immediate passage into the newly introduced Punch and
Judy show, and so into proverbial speech. He had already
been accused, in 1683, of unnecessary brutality in the case
of one of the Russells' (William Lord Russell), who had
certainly been connected with Monmouth and Shaftesbury
before they both fled from England, but was perhaps
hardly guilty of the treason for which he was executed.
Ketch, according to an " apologie " or defence alleged to be
by himself, was drunk on that occasion, and did not hit
straight. Russell, Ketch says, had given him ten guineas

to make a quick job of it, and then would move about and not lie in the right position. Other accounts say that the executioner severed the head with two blows, a common necessity : Burnet, who was an eye-witness but could not bear to keep his gaze fixed on the sight, hints that he put the axe lightly against Russell's head as if to take aim, and may have touched him then, but took only one blow afterwards.

Burnet also speaks in moving terms of Russell's fortitude. Monmouth's own fine demeanour at the last moment was at last equalled by that of his followers. They " nothing common did, nor mean." They made the usual simple protestation of innocence or guilt, bared their necks, pulled a cap over their eyes, and laid their heads " down, as upon a bed "—" rather to die like men than live like slaves."

I give these and later gruesome details partly because an age which has invented high explosive and poison gas, and still uses capital punishment and shrapnel and the bayonet, has no right to be shocked at slightly less efficient methods of taking life ; but mainly because they illustrate the complete acceptance of those methods by the people then chiefly concerned. The proceedings were common form. The British Museum has recently acquired a fine drawing by Visscher, and his subsequent engraving, which show how well the routine was observed even many years earlier. It is of the execution in 1606 of the Gunpowder Plot conspirators. Two or three prisoners, pinioned, on their back on flat wattle hurdles, are being drawn rapidly over the cobbles by horses, urged on by mounted grooms. A few halberdiers keep back a curious crowd—men, women, and children, some jeering, some cheering ; from the windows grave persons in large hats look down ; the inevitable dog intrudes. One prisoner is already dangling from the gallows —he must die by suffocation, not dislocation, so short is the rope. Another, hanged, is on a table just beyond, a man with a knife busy " drawing " him, while one with an axe is about to sever a limb. Beyond again is a huge cauldron,

from which an attendant is taking a tarred leg. There are
bundles of faggots ready to feed the roaring fire under the
cauldron, and a bent figure is hurrying up with a fresh
bundle.

" Decently and in order." . . . It was only indecent disorder that made Ketch pass instantly into a figure of
ridicule and ill-fame. And Jeffreys has also passed into
that grisly immortality. But it was probably not so much
the punishments he ordained, in themselves, that made the
Bloody Assize burn so long in Western hearts, as their
number and the blind, deaf rage with which they were
reached and delivered.

Immediately after Sedgemoor the survivors of Monmouth's unhappy rabble had scattered and fled. Summary
justice, more or less in accordance with the civil law—if
they had been duly tried—was done upon those whom
Kirke caught soon after the battle. They were hanged till
they were almost dead, then cut down—still living—and
disembowelled (" drawn," as in Visscher's picture), the
entrails being burnt before their faces, and then quartered—
" the four parts to be disposed of at the pleasure of the King ;
and the Lord have mercy on your souls."

That may be considered merely as military fury. When
Jeffreys came on to Dorchester after the ghastly execution
of Alice Lisle at Winchester, the forms of law were more
fully employed. The terrible judge—he was really one of
five—attended Divine service in the parish church on
Friday, September 4th, 1685, and immediately afterwards,
in a court hung with red cloth, began his Assize. Two
hundred and ninety-two prisoners were sentenced within a
week at Dorchester—thirteen hanged by Monday the 7th ;
the roll for the whole Western Assize containing 2611
names. Three hundred and forty-five in all were Dorset
men, and of these 74 were executed, 177 transported,
9 whipped ; shopkeepers, tailors, mariners, weavers, shoe-
makers, poor common men and lads and even boys.

Jeffreys bullied witnesses and counsel alike ; guilt was

predetermined. Often he foamed at the mouth in his frenzy. The very pleas for mercy were turned into cruel jests, as Macaulay records. John Bennett, whom he mentions, was a Lyme man ; John Tutchin, who had some connection with Bridport, and a Weymouth boy of fourteen, both noticed by Macaulay, were sentenced to be whipped at every market town in the county every year for seven years : a parson rebuked the gaoler for not whipping the boy hard.

As I have suggested, care was taken to organize the functions properly. The authorities of Bath were ordered beforehand, by the high sheriff, to prepare gallows and halters, " with a sufficient number of faggots to burn the bowels, and a furnace or cauldron to boil their heads and quarters, and salt to boil them with, and tar to tar them with. You are also to provide an axe and a cleaver for quartering the said rebels." The quarters were distributed for widespread exhibition, even in places which the rebellion had not touched directly. Piddletown, for instance, got four quarters and a head : Winfrith the same : Weymouth (the Weymouth barber's apprentice mentioned above was whipped for reading Monmouth's proclamation, but the town was not itself implicated) sixteen quarters and six heads : the new post for two of the quarters cost 1s. 6d.

There can have been few villages in Dorset and Somerset, west of a line drawn from Bath to Wareham, which did not contain folk who had seen their friends' flesh displayed in public, or heard of the price paid for a kinsman's living body for toil in the plantations, or for a girl sold to a Court lady for a servant. Jeffreys' chair and a spike on which a rebel's head was set are still preserved at Dorchester in the museum opposite his house : it can hardly have been accident that has distinguished and kept them. Local memories show how deep and intimate was the touch of his work. One man (" Burn-guts ") sold furze to the authorities for burning rebel entrails: his horses one by one pined and died. A woman said it did her eyes good to see a very old man called Larke hanged. She lost her sight within a short time.

One man of Wareham, Thomas Delacourt, was present at the final stage in this horrible drama. Quarters of some of the victims were exposed on Bloody Bank at Wareham—the place gets its name therefrom. Delacourt and some friends stole the remains and buried them. Delacourt was one of the first to join William of Orange, and went to London in his train : and it fell to him to be made sentry over Jeffreys when the judge, in the year of that more successful Revolution, was cast into the Tower, where he died.

" Your Majesty may think it is the misfortune I now lie under makes me make this application to you, but I do assure your Majesty it is the remorse I now have in me of the wrong I have done you in several things, and now in taking up arms against you ; for my taking up arms, it was never in my thoughts since the King died ; the Prince and Princess of Orange will be witness for me of the assurance I gave them, that I would never stir against you, but my misfortune was such as to meet with some horrid people that made me believe things of your Majesty, and gave me so many false arguments, that I was fully led away to believe that it was a shame and a sin before God not to do it."*

James II, it has been argued, never received that miserable letter, written by Monmouth at Ringwood soon after his capture : certainly the poor folk of the West who treasured his unhappy memory never heard of it.

* From the *Camden Society's Papers,* 1879.

X

" An objection may perhaps be apprehended from the more delicate, that this dish is too common and vulgar ; for what else is the subject of all the romances, novels, plays, and poems, with which the stalls abound ? Many exquisite viands might be rejected by the epicure, if it was a sufficient cause for his contemning of them as common and vulgar, that something was to be found in the most paltry alleys under the same name. In reality, true nature is as difficult to be met with in authors, as the Bayonne ham, or Bologna sausage, is to be found in the shops."

HENRY FIELDING,
Tom Jones.

X

THE AGE OF ELEGANCE

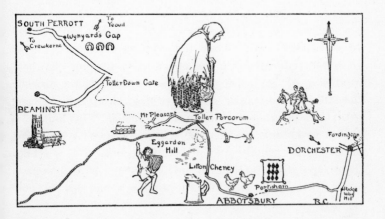

THE eighteenth century, whose slim, elegant, dry hands still clutch our social order secretly and often, is a disease like the measles. Sooner or later all who are interested in the more humane letters catch it. My own long-past attack I can still regard with affection, and I like to see others succumbing to the infection, and exhibiting the symptoms in print. But I feel a little unhappy when I come, cured, and, I hope, immune from fresh attacks, to eighteenth-century Dorset. I see the ruffles, the grace, the domestic pomp, the complacency, the emergence of the bourgeois into a certain social autonomy, and, at the end, the legions thundering past, going decorously to death. I should once have liked to make that story either an epic or a triolet : it would have had to be one or the other, while the disease was still contagious : and now I can achieve neither.

There is, it is true, an element of epic in the period, and that I have cut off bodily and made into a separate chapter, in defiance of chronological order. The seamen of the Dorset littoral have always been heroic venturers. In what remains after the mariners have been detached, there are, between 1688 and about 1831, three important threads in Dorset life, all woven together, but making a pattern which is more easily understood in the separate threads than in the complete design. There is the social side of life, lived by the gentry and middle classes ; there is the agricultural interest, developing, from the capitalist point of view, almost incredibly during this epoch—and altering the whole condition of rural life in England ; and there are the cheerful semi-domestic scenes which close the century with the appearance of Farmer George at Weymouth. I cannot make any one of these spheres of activity (the cant phrase) either wholly epic or wholly elegant. But if I take them separately—and again independently of chronological order—it may be possible to provide some sort of perspective view of the whole.

There are indeed plenty of eminent social figures in the county's life under Anne and the Georges. But I will begin with one of the less fashionable of them—one whose labours make possible the knowledge of all the rest.

The life and work of John Hutchins, the historian of Dorset, are a genuine monument of the most liberal side of the eighteenth-century spirit. The very self-satisfaction of the period itself became a virtue for his benefit. Once a proposal was approved in the correct quarters, the Nobility and Gentry could not but exhaust the resources of polite learning in forwarding the cause. This son of " an honest parochial priest, a character esteemed by all good men, and reverenced even by the profane," accomplished a great work, modestly, sincerely, and finally, in no small measure because social conditions allowed him leisure and encouraged his activities.

He was born in 1698, and educated at the excellent

grammar school at Dorchester. He had the unusual experience of being at two colleges at Oxford and at two universities—at Hart Hall and Balliol, Oxford ; he took his B.A. degree there, and his M.A. degree at Cambridge. He was admitted to Holy Orders about 1723, and became " curate and usher " to the pluralist who was at that time vicar of Milton Abbas and master of the ancient grammar school there : a school subsequently transferred to Wimborne and of high repute all through the West in later years.

It was through the liberality and help of two friends, Jacob Bancks and Browne Willis, that he undertook what even the austere *Dictionary of National Biography* calls " this noble history." He seems to have been ill-fitted for the duties of a parish priest. " He deserved the character of a sound Divine rather than of an eminent preacher. His delivery was no ways engaging ; and his discourses were not generally adapted to the capacity of his hearers." Later in life he suffered from gout, bad sight, deafness, and failing voice. He seems to have incurred the disapproval of his parishioners at Wareham, which living he held, in the common eighteenth-century way, together with that of Swyre. He was also for a time rector of Melcombe Horsey. He died in 1773. " The profit arising from his history was the chief provision he made for his family. Whether the benefit already received, or hereafter expected from hence, be sufficient to encourage others to engage in a like laborious undertaking, is a question much to be doubted."*

Two incidents in his life at Wareham are as typical of his period as his historical labours. Almost the entire town was burnt to ashes in 1762. The Dorset towns and villages of to-day owe much of their architectural charm to those otherwise unhappy fires : Blandford, Beaminster, much of Bridport and Dorchester, the best of Wareham, rose from their ashes.

The fire, incidentally, almost cut short the History.

* The quotations are from the biographical notice in the standard and last edition of the *History*.

The rectory was burnt, and only " the care and presence of mind of Mrs. Hutchins, not without hazard to herself "— the historian himself being absent, presumably on one of his many necessary journeys to collections of books and archives elsewhere—saved the MS.

The other event of note was his engagement of a curate to take his duty during absence in London and Oxford. " He was mistaken in his man. His friends informed him he had engaged a Methodist, but he proved to be a madman. Yet his noise procured him admirers, and in so high a degree, that, had he been dismissed absolutely on the return of the rector, there had been an open rupture between the minister and many of his parishioners, who entered into a voluntary subscription to support their favourite lecturer. He [Hutchins] judged so well of the temper of his people that he appeased the storm by not resisting it ; and in a little time the poor man was confined in a madhouse, and Mr. Hutchins at ease by the good offices of a more regular assistant."

This distrust of "enthusiasm " . . . I am reminded of one of the inimitable Browne and Sheridan epitaphs in Frampton Church. The family even in the nineteenth century kept up the eighteenth-century mode in their obituaries, and it is recorded of one of them that she was " polite without flattery, generous without ostentation, pious without enthusiasm."

I shall deal briefly later with the Dorset activities of the greatest of all " enthusiasts," John Wesley, the descendant of the Charmouth parson. Vigour not less notable than his, but of quite another kind, was displayed by two of the more eminent social figures in the county's history. In writing of Shaftesbury I have mentioned the behaviour of two "nabobs " who devoted their wealth to politics. The perfect nabob of all time was a Dorset man.

From about the year 1675 onwards to that of the glorious Revolution, the Honourable East India Company showed an increasing anxiety about the activities of a certain " interloper " in Bengal. He was trading there—and trading successfully—in spite of their exclusive charter. "Send him home," they instructed their local Councils. The Councils conveyed this wish to the interloper, and he promised to go home. But he was " a fellow of a haughty, huffing, daring temper," and he didn't go. On the contrary, he visited certain towns " in great state, with four or five files of soldiers in red coats, well armed, and great attendance of native soldiers, with trumpeters, and taking up his quarters with the Dutch, by the name of the New Company's Agent, bespattering the Old Company."

The enterprising competitor was at length apprehended and fined £1000. But the Company for some obscure reason remitted £600 of this, and in November, 1688, admitted him into their freedom gratis. This seems to have been a futile proceeding (unless the records themselves err in regard to dates) ; for intermittently during the next six years the same complaints of interloping were made, and the same successful competition carried on. In the intervals of making money, the ingenious gentleman returned to his native place, Blandford St. Mary's, in Dorset, and among other proceedings, got himself elected Member of Parliament for Old Sarum, a political unit with a somewhat lurid history. His epitaph in the parish church suggests that his efforts in church restoration carried him to a heavenly mansion : there is no housing or population problem in heaven if his actual achievements suffice to get him a mansion.

Finally, Thomas Pitt (for that was his name) was appointed —by the Company itself !—President of Fort St. George, which now we know better as Madras : to the scandal of the shareholders, who at the next election turned out eighteen of the Committee which appointed him. By a delightful irony, one of the Nabob's chief troubles while in office was the activity of another interloper—his own cousin, John Pitt. His orders to Cousin John come well from the former " New Company's Agent " : " If you

o

pass by here you must behave yourself very civilly, no
drums, flags nor trumpets within our bounds, for here shall
be but one Governor whilst I am here."*

It was while he was Governor that he acquired the
famous Pitt Diamond, whose curious adventures are a
solace to the superstitious. He paid £20,400 for it : it was
sold to the Duke of Orleans, Regent of France, in 1717,
for about £135,000 (2,000,000 livres).† It cost £5000 to cut,
and the chips alone yielded £8000. Pitt was suspected of
having obtained it by crooked means, but was able to dis-
prove the charge. He collected many other stones, and by
his indubitable commercial genius amassed a large fortune,
which he invested in many estates in England, among
others that of Woodyates in Cranborne Chase. The rest of
his life, for all practical purposes, was spent in politics. He
died in 1726. He begat Thomas Pitt, Baron Londonderry,
governor of the Leeward Islands ; John Pitt, governor
of the Bermudas ; a daughter who married the first Earl
Stanhope ; and (his eldest son) Robert Pitt. Robert Pitt
begat William Pitt, Secretary of State, first Earl of Chatham
(" My Lord, I am sure I can save this country, and no one
else can "). William Pitt begat William Pitt, First Lord of
the Treasury (" England has saved herself by her courage :
she will save Europe by her example "). Government was
inherent in the family, like writing in that of the Sheridans,
who also, resident aliens till they became acclimatized,
dwelt in Dorset.

There had been Pitts in Dorset for at least a hundred
years. One, born at Blandford in the same year as Thomas
Pitt, but apparently only distantly related, was an extremely
competent physician and writer. He upheld—and it needed
support in his day—the professional point of view. His
work on *The Craft and Frauds of Physic Exposed* was a
vigorous assault on quackery, and what we should call patent

* The quotations and most of the information are from the Hakluyt
Society's edition of the *Diary of William Hedges*, edited by Col. Yule.

† Napoleon, Thomas Pitt's great-grandson's mortal enemy, had it set
in the hilt of his sword.

medicines, and ill-equipped compounding of prescriptions. Another of the name and family was Christopher Pitt, a none too exciting poet, rector of Pimperne 1722–68 : " he lived innocent and died beloved." Of yet another I speak later.

But Dorset did not produce Pitts alone. It gave England another illustrious family of administrators. John Churchill, first Duke of Marlborough, was the son of Sir Winston Churchill of Dorset and of St. John's College, Oxford. This Winston Churchill (by marriage and circumstances later transplanted across the border a few miles into Devon) was a prominent Royalist in Dorset during the Civil War, and afterwards M.P. for Weymouth and Lyme in turn. The name of Churchill in those days had some variety of connotation. Marlborough's sister was a mistress of James II ; Churchill the bookseller, Dunton's friend, was the son of a Churchill of Dorchester, for which he was afterwards M.P. ; Charles Churchill's respectable fame as a general was to be overshadowed by his great brother's ; and yet another son of Sir Winston, George, the admiral, " governed the navy as his brother governed the army."

Neither the prototypical Nabob nor the nabobs of Shaftesbury, however, were the finest fruit of political life in that century. The most swollen figure of a diseased political age was the man Dodington. George Bubb Dodington— is it a possible name ? He himself eventually improved upon it, at any rate, for he concealed it under the title of Lord Melcombe. It began originally as George Bubb, *tout court*, for his father was said to be Jeremias Bubb, an apothecary of Weymouth : alleged also in other quarters to have been by race Irish, which might account for his son's singular gift for devious politics. An uncle died and left to George, when he was about twenty-nine, the estate of Eastbury in Dorset, and a large fortune, whereupon, being already M.P. for Winchelsea, he commenced wire-puller in a more advanced degree.

I do not propose to go into the obscure and disingenuous

policies Dodington pursued, first in Walpole's behalf, and
afterwards against him, and from time to time on whatever
side suited his love of secret importance. But some account
of his activities, fortified by quotations, may be of use in
illuminating the political aspect of country life.

The main part of his celebrated but very dull Diary
begins, for all practical purposes, with the offer in 1749 of a
peerage by Frederick, Prince of Wales—when he came to
the crown : " and I give you leave to kiss my hand upon it
now, by way of acceptance ; which I did accordingly." He
was appointed " treasurer of the chamber," in which
capacity he afterwards was present, with at least fourteen
other persons, at the birth of Prince Frederick William,
whose mother, he says, gave him to the world " without once
complaining or groaning the whole time."

The Prince also promised to provide for Dodington's
friends : which promise he duly conveyed to at least one
of them at Eastbury, a Mr. Bance, who " received my
narrative with great pleasure." Dodington gave Bance
the alternative of " the reversion of the Remittances, or
of the Board of Trade." The wise Bance said " he should
choose the Remittances, and to have the secret and government of the bank, as what he thought would render him most
useful to his friends ; to which I agreed, and promised to
undertake the affair with the prince." And so *ad infinitum.*

Unfortunately for these patriotic enterprises, Prince
Frederick, to Dodington's mortification, had the same
experience as Captain Blifil. In 1751, " while he was
buried in deep contemplations of this kind, one of the most
unlucky as well as unseasonable accidents happened to
him." He died. Dodington attended the funeral in an
official capacity, on a very wet day in a very wet season,
the neglect of formality in the treatment of the mourners
being such that " there was not the attention to order the
Green-cloth to provide them a bit of bread ; and these gentlemen, of the first rank and distinction, in discharge of their
last sad duty to a loved and loving master, were forced to

bespeak a great cold dinner from a common tavern in the neighbourhood." It is a grievous picture.

> " Here lies Fred,
>   Who was alive and is dead ; "

and round " the corpse and bowels " (I am not sufficiently expert in the details of interment to say why Dodington separates them thus) were gathered all the wire-pullers, all the flunkeys, all the place-hunters, with not a crumb to eat, getting wet through in their fine raiment.

I wish the diarist had identified the tavern : it was somewhere near Westminster Abbey and the House of Lords ; and I wish it, not because I want to picture the persons of quality in draggled finery sitting at mean tables in a sanded parlour, but because the Board of Green Cloth at the last moment, at three o'clock, " vouchsafed to think of a dinner, and ordered one—but the disgrace was complete, the tavern dinner was paid for, and given to the poor." I should like to hear the conversation of the poor on that occasion : it would be real history.

But though he lost, for the time, that hope of elevation, Dodington commanded votes. The borough of Weymouth was in his pocket, and he had much influence in all the Dorset seats. He arranged, at the *Antelope* in Dorchester, with " Lord Milton, Messrs. Drax, Trenchard, and most of the Whig party," for the election of Knights of the Shire in 1753. " There could be no doubt of the Whigs carrying the election if they resolved upon it, because, to my knowledge, two-thirds of the property of the county were in their hands, and because I had carried it for Mr. Pitt's father (who was scarcely capable) when our property was considerably less." He had pledged his interest to Lord Digby against Mr. Pitt.

A little later, to secure the favour of the Duke of Newcastle, he was offering to pay (" and not bring him a bill ") " those who would take money " at Bridgewater and Weymouth : and he specially recommended " my two parsons " of those places. The Duke " entered into it very cordially, and assured me that they should have the first Crown livings that should be vacant in their parts." Dodington held Weymouth successfully for the Duke, but not Bridgewater. The effort cost him £2500. A few months later he writes of " the insufficiency, falseness, and meanness " of the Duke's administration. He changed sides several times thereafter.

His intrigues bore the usual fruit. He got his peerage in 1761, and died childless the next year. His monstrous house in Dorset, built by the ponderous Vanbrugh, and decorated by Sir James Thornhill of Weymouth, was pulled down in great part by his heir. It had " an enormous portico of Doric columns ascended by a stately flight of steps." It was " gilt and finished with a profusion of finery, that kept no terms with simplicity, and not always with elegance or harmony of style." Dodington was of vulgar taste in such matters ; " his bulk and corpulency gave full display to a vast expanse and profusion of brocade and embroidery." He had " a passion for magnificence and display." " Of pictures, he seemed to take his estimate only by their cost." But " he made more display at less cost than any man in the Kingdom." At any rate, he did not waste his money on mere pictures. He had none on his walls. Instead, " he had stuck up immense patches of gilt leather shaped into bugle horns upon hangings of rich crimson velvet, and round his state bed he displayed a carpeting of gold and silver embroidery, which too glaringly betrayed its derivation from coat, waistcoat and breeches by the testimony of pockets, button-holes and, loops, with other equally incontrovertible witnesses, subpœna'd from the tailor's shopboard. When he paid his court at St. James' to the present queen upon her nuptials, he approached to kiss her hand in an embroidered suit of silk with lilac waistcoat and breeches, the latter of which in the act of kneeling forgot their duty, and broke loose from their moorings in a very indecorous and uncourtly manner." " Being a man of humble birth, he seemed to have an innate respect for titles, and none bowed with more devotion to the robes and fasces of high rank and office."

The criticisms are by the irascible Sir Fretful Plagiary— Richard Cumberland. Even if they are exaggerated, they can hardly do much injustice to the author of that astonishing Diary. But it must not be forgotten that he was an active and not wholly tasteless patron of literature, by no means negligible as a writer, widely read, versatile in manner (now, according to Cumberland, " snoring in his lethargic way," and at the next moment " setting the table in a roar " by his wit), subtle but clear-headed.

An election account of 1784 may serve to show how a politician of that century commanded success. Mr. John Bond and Mr. Henry Bankes were in that year elected members for Corfe Castle (whose later loss of all Parliamentary representation roused the anger of the gentry), and returned, among other items, the following expenses :—

	£	s.	d.
To 5 Half Hogsheads of Beer on the Election Day	10	0	0
To the Poor	10	10	0
To 45 Voters at 13s. each	29	5	0
Dinners on the Election Day . £10 16 10 ⎱	11	7	4
To Servants at the *Ship* . £0 10 6 ⎰			
Musick		2	0
To Two persons to protect the Beer		2	6

The association of another historical figure with Dorset is not quite so definite, though I believe it to be certain. Matthew Prior is said to have been born near Wimborne, the son of a carpenter.* His own connection with the county is slight. His uncle Arthur and his cousin Catherine were brought into nearer and unhappy relation with it. Arthur kept the *Rummer* tavern in London, a " great resort of wits " : he often visited Wimborne for a holiday. His daughter was too attractive to be safe in London. So " to

* The story that he fell asleep over a chained book in Wimborne Minster Library, and let his candle burn a hole in the page (still exhibited) has been proved untrue.

secure her virtue " he sent her to Wimborne, " where she was a blazing star for some time." " But it proved too late ; one Grey of Yorkshire," says Conyers Place, " called then, I remember, the Great Grey, followed her, and attended her here with his coach and six, whence he carried her off."

I wonder if the report of that " blazing star " had anything to do with the wretched career of Mary Channing. Her parents took the opposite course to Arthur Prior's, at any rate. They bred her at Dorchester in the usual way as regards education, and had her taught to read and write with " a proficiency suitable enough to one of her sex " ; but they added the accomplishment of dancing, and sent her to London and Exeter to see the world. When she came back she went to many jovial parties with her neighbours, and at one of them met an unnamed gallant, on whom she speedily " doated," giving him presents, entertaining him to wine at inns, even contriving to hold a ball in his honour : she robbed her parents for the money for this happiness. They took action at length, and tried to make her marry Thomas Channing, a respectable young man of Maiden Newton. She refused. But she found that her lover would not marry her, and at last she yielded and married Channing. She spent thirteen weeks of more or less riotous living as his wife, and then poisoned him. She was tried and found guilty : h r execution was deferred to let her give birth to a child. In 1706 came the end, which can best be given from the placid contemporary record. " After the under-sheriff had taken some refreshment, she was brought out of prison, and dragged by her Father's and her Husband's Houses, to the Place of Execution [Maumbury Rings.] She manifested nothing of Alteration when fixed to the Stake, but justified her Innocence to the very last, and left the World with a Courage seldom found in her Sex. She being first strangled, the Fire was kindled about five in the Afternoon, and in the sight of many thousands of Spectators she was consumed to Ashes."

A pleasanter picture of the county is given by Defoe, who

traversed it in his journey to Land's End. He entered it,
in 1705, from the New Forest, by way of Wimborne, thence
to Poole, notable for " the best and biggest oysters in all
this part of England," and so on to Weymouth. From
Weymouth he went to Dorchester, which pleased him, in
spite of his being summoned before the Mayor as a " dis-
affected person." He found men of all religions dwelling
together in unity, " drinking tea together, and conversing
with civility and good neighbourhood. There is good
company, and a good deal of it ; and a man that coveted a
retreat in this world might as agreeably spend his time as
well in Dorchester as in any town I know in England." An
old resident has told me that precisely the same amiable
intercourse existed there in the mid-Victorian era.

He was immensely struck by the richness of the down
soil and the admirable sheep. " The grass or herbage of
these downs is full of the sweetest and most aromatic plants,
such as nourish the sheep to a strange degree." They " are
all fine carpet-ground, soft as velvet, and the herbage sweet
as garden herbs, which makes their sheep be the best in
England, if not in the world, and their wool fine to an
extreme." He was told that within six miles every way of
Dorchester there were 600,000 sheep ; and he was fain to
believe it. (Fielding, in his last journey, touched at Portland and wanted to buy a whole sheep, so sweet was the
mutton. Portland had and has its own breed of sheep—a
small, very perfect species.*)

Defoe visited also Portland and Abbotsbury (" a town
anciently famous for a great monastery, and eminent for
nothing but its ruins ") and went on to Bridport—" a pretty
large corporation town on the seashore, though without a

* Macready, who had a house at Sherborne for many years, and conducted an evening school there, found the Portland mutton expensive
at one time. " We dined," he writes in 1815, " at the Royal Hotel—a
dinner which, from the impudent extravagance of its charge, would cause
us to remember Weymouth, if all else were to be forgotten. In a dull
dingy room, looking out on the back of the premises, with ordinary table
service, for a haddock, leg of Portland mutton, apple tart, bottle of Madeira
(charged 8s.), bottle of port (6s.), a bill was presented me of £2 10s." But
the same meal (wine apart) only cost him 5s. in 1850 !

harbour." He describes the method of mackerel fishing : it is still in use. Mackerel were bought and sold on the shore "a hundred for a penny." Something like that price still prevails at rare intervals. And thence he passed out of the county by way of Lyme, whose Cobb impressed him mightily. He notes that pilchard fishing began there— the first stage on the western grounds for that fish.

What struck him most forcibly, however, was the behaviour of the gentry in Dorset—" some of the most polite and well-bred people in the isle of Britain." "They seem to have a mutual confidence in and friendship with one another, as if they were all relations." (Coker put it a little more strongly in 1732 ; he said they *were* all relations, through countless intermarriages ; and the pedigrees given in Hutchins bear this out.) As for the ladies of Dorset, they " do not seem to stick on hand "—they " are equal in beauty and may be superior in reputation " to all the ladies who go to the play or the assembly elsewhere.

He noticed also the great local industry of knitting stockings, and the fine bone lace of Blandford (he apparently went on expeditions from time to time off his main route), and cloth-making at Shaftesbury and Sherborne. But the stocking trade was " much decayed by the increase of the knitting-stocking engine or frame, which has destroyed the hand-knitting trade for fine stockings through the whole Kingdom."

A somewhat similar picture of an established and complacent gentry is given in the unpublished diaries of John Richards of Warmwell, which are quoted in the *Proceedings* of the Dorset Field Club. They cover the years from 1697 to 1701. Richards coursed with greyhounds—he had a great match with Mr. Gundry in Fordington Field—bred fighting-cocks, and betted at the *Antelope* in Dorchester on the races. He kept ferrets, grew corn, bred sheep, drank punch, visited his neighbours, had the gout ; and on one occasion he warned a huntsman with a pack of hounds off his wheat land, " asking him by what authority he presumed to enter upon my ground, disturbing my sheep, and break down my fences. . . . I scolded him very passionately, whipped off his dogs and forbade him coming any more in that circuit on pain of having all his dogs killed, and himself soundly banged."

Richards was indeed rather an irascible person. The *Retrospective Review* for 1852 gives other extracts which make him a little more than a touchy landlord. He quarrelled bitterly with his wife, and his brief diaries—the more personal entries in Italian, not English—hint at a good reason. On June 29, 1701, " I kissed Mary Lillington for the first time." His wife was frequently " mad." On a day in December, 1700, " she was mad all the afternoon, and roared all the while all night when I shut her up in the dining-room." He may or may not have been a good " housekeeper " ; he was not above operating on his wife if need be—" I cut ye flesh from her gum with my pen-knife."

For a domestic contrast read this simple inscription on a woven ring : " Betty Porter of Henstridge this and the giver is yours for ever and so pray God bless us both to-gether. I am your humble servant, James Huson, 1721."

Dorset certainly enjoyed its sports. Blandford Races, on the downs, were a great county event : they go back to Elizabeth's reign. Thomas Fownes, of Winterbourne Steepleton, set up a pack of foxhounds as early as 1730, and the great Peter Beckford was his successor. There was even falconry in Cranborne Chase, where the deer-stealers were only a little more obnoxious to its owner than his neighbours. Dodington had a rather absurd quarrel over the deer. Like other owners of land in or adjoining the outer walks of the Chase, he was in a quandary—whether to kill trespassing deer or to fence them out. Finally he appointed a game-keeper on his estate—a novelty. Such a thing had never been done. It so happened that the head ranger, Mr. Chafin—last of his office—met this keeper in Bussey Stool Walk, and warned him off. He met him again a few days later, and this time took the law into his own hands : he " shot three dogs at one shot." " This of course caused a serious rupture between Mr. Dodington and the Ranger " ; and Dodington issued a challenge, which Chafin accepted. Chafin " was at the expense of buying a sword, which was never made use of, but is still [1818] in being, and of blood guiltless "—for Jacob Bancks of Milton—Hutchins' bene-factor—intervened, and " found Mr. Dodington peaceably inclined." " He acknowledged his error, and instead of fighting, invited both gentlemen to dine with him ; and they spent a very jovial day together."

It makes a curiously diverse yet familiar picture : a picture, really, in which, on the whole, the figures differ from those in earlier pageants only because they have changed their clothes. Things go on much as usual. The well-to-do enjoy themselves in much the same way ; the middle-classes remain well in the middle : the underlying English brutality, which Fielding " contemplated with concern," and from which he suffered, seems to be neither mitigated nor even concealed. You have only to glance at Swift's more obscene poems to realize how utterly nasty elegant society could be and was. I suggest an excursion into low life as an antidote to the *contes des fées* of an artificial age. The most famous trial of the eighteenth century had Dorset for one of its scenes. The wits and fine ladies of London were all excitement over a parcel of gipsies wandering through Dorset villages.

The case is that of Elizabeth Canning. There is only one really certain fact in it, and that is that she disappeared on New Year's Day, 1752. She was a servant girl in Alderman-bury in the City of London, and she set out that morning to visit an uncle at Moorfields. She returned late at night on January 29th, dishevelled and completely worn out ; very near death, in fact.

I am not much concerned with the London end of the tale ; but I believe I have solved in Dorset a mystery which has baffled, among others, Andrew Lang. Canning said she had been kidnapped and imprisoned in a house near Enfield, kept by one Mother Wells, and inhabited also by certain gipsies, especially an old woman called Mary Squires, who was preternaturally ugly ; tall and dark, with a stoop, of a complexion remarkably swarthy, she had also an underlip " of a prodigious size "—" as big almost as a little child's arm."

The gipsy and Susannah Wells were arrested on Canning's information, and tried for assault and putting in bodily fear. Mary Squires' defence, produced immediately she was accused, and maintained consistently for fifteen months, was that at the time of the alleged assault she, with her son George and her daughter Lucy, were tramping in Dorset and Hampshire and Wiltshire ; two witnesses from Abbotsbury, in Dorset, one from Coombe Bissett, in Wiltshire, supported this alibi at her trial.

Before their trial, however, Canning swore a fuller information—to no less a person than Henry Fielding, who published a famous pamphlet about her. The splendid quack, John Hill, answered it. Essays and flyleaves began to fly to and fro. Subscription lists for Canning were opened at the coffee houses. She and Wells and the formidable gipsy were the talk of the town.

In due course Wells and Squires were tried, found guilty, and sentenced : the former to branding, which was carried out at once, the latter to death. Happily for Squires, a public-spirited Lord Mayor, Sir Crisp Gascoyne (who was mobbed for his pains), was uneasy about the verdict, scoured Dorset for further evidence, petitioned the King, and finally got Canning herself tried—for perjury : of which she in turn was found guilty, and for which she was sentenced to seven years' transportation—$\ddot{o}\pi\epsilon\rho$ $\kappa\alpha\grave{\iota}$ $\dot{\epsilon}\gamma\acute{\epsilon}\nu\epsilon\tau o$. Mary Squires was first respited, and then received a free pardon. They could not unbrand Susannah Wells ; and anyhow she was an undesirable person.

After the conviction of Squires the three country witnesses were indicted for perjury : but when they came up for trial, opinion had flowed against Canning, and, no evidence being offered against them, they were acquitted. It is curious that when they gave evidence at Squires' trial, a member of a well-known Dorset family was one of the judges —Mr. Justice Gundry. He took their part in a vigorous cross-examination, and did not believe they were perjured. But it did not occur to him to ask, from his own local knowledge, certain questions about the gipsy's alleged movements which have not been asked to this day.

At Canning's trial thirty-seven witnesses swore to seeing the gipsies in the West during the disputed period. Of these thirty-seven, eleven came from Abbotsbury, and only three of the eleven had not seen the Squires before : the three comprised a temporary exciseman (afterwards discharged for neglect of duty), a schoolmaster, and a carpenter whose attitude towards life appears later. " Abbotsbury evidence " became a temporary proverb. Four other witnesses (pre-Abbotsbury) were from places farther north and had not seen the Squires before : one was a little doubtful in her evidence. Four witnesses out of five from places near Abbotsbury knew the gipsies well ; the fifth was apparently quite young. The witnesses from places outside the Abbotsbury district, with three exceptions, had positively not seen previously the singular figure of Mary Squires. These details are important.

Twenty-seven witnesses, on the other hand, swore to the presence of Mary Squires at or near Mother Wells' house at Enfield during the same period. The majority, however, prevailed with the jury against Canning, as I have said, and the alibi was believed.

That Dorset alibi has never yet been scrutinized closely with reference to local conditions. The general opinion of all who have written on the strange case tends definitely to one side or the other—to the belief that one of the two parties told practically the whole truth, and the other lied like troopers. I believe they both lied and both told the truth.

Follow now their singular trail in Dorset. Mary Squires, her son George, and her daughter Lucy emerge into legal history first at South Perrott near Crewkerne on the Somerset border. But how they got to South Perrott they did not know themselves. George said that before going West they had been into " the wild " of Kent or Sussex— he was not sure which county—to leave another daughter, Mary, to help a sick relative, Mrs. Squires' sister. He could remember little of the journey to Dorset. He thought he went to Shaftesbury, but he did not even know whether he stayed a night at Shaftesbury. He was ignorant of the name of any place between Yeovil and South Perrott, though he admitted there were several villages. In fact, the arrival of the party at South Perrott resembled nothing so much as that of the Apostle Philip at Azotus on a celebrated occasion : they simply were " found " there.

They were identified by two witnesses, previously un- acquainted with them, as having been at the *Red Lion*, South Perrott, on the night of Friday, December 29th, 1751. The next morning, " between eight and nine o'clock," they were at the *Three Horseshoes* at Wynyard's Gap, a mile and a half away on the Dorchester road—a steep ascent rising from two hundred and twenty-one feet to eight hundred and twenty-six feet a few hundred yards past the Gap. At that inn, according to Alice Farnham, the hostess's daughter, they had a quart of beer and some bread and cheese and " stayed about an hour." They said they would come back at " Old Christmas " (January 6th).

The old woman, Alice thought, " was very unhealthy, seemingly, coming up against the hill." Mary Squires was seventy years old. She was clad in a drab-coloured cloak and serge gown. Lucy was a personable figure, " a very clean sort of a body, and of a black complexion, not like a traveller or gipsy by her dress," neat in appearance, wearing a white gown and a red cloak. George, five feet ten in height, wore a greatcoat with glass-black buttons, over a blue coat and red waistcoat, and a dark brown bobwig, and carried " a little fardle "—a bundle containing, according to Alice, hardware, but according to George, " aprons, worked gowns, nankeens, white waistcoats, and hollands and such things."

They were next seen at Litton Cheney, in the Bride Valley. The Dorchester road, followed throughout, would not take them thither, save deviously : and they certainly were on the Dorchester road—if they were in Dorset at all—till between nine and ten that morning, and set forth from Wynyard's Gap along that same road, up the hill. Two other roads run nearly parallel to it, to the south-east ; the nearer, the "Roman" road over Eggardon Hill; the farther, the present Bridport-Dorchester road. All three converge on Dorchester. And if the gipsies were going straight to Litton Cheney, they must abandon the first road not far from Wynyard's Gap, follow the second for a little distance, and cross the third.

The road-books of the period are not helpful as to cross-country routes. But there is an excellent map of 1765 which indicates how they could have reached their destination most quickly, if they were acquainted with the country —and, as an old man in the neighbourhood said to me not long ago, " the gippos do know the lie of the land."

From the standpoint of the cartographer this map and its slightly later Wiltshire companion are very interesting. They show the curious persistence of the most venerable trackways. Between the first two roads to Dorchester there were in 1763 very few links : the byroads running from either towards the other are nearly all blind alleys. They are precisely the same blind alleys to-day. The reason lies in the nature of the country, which contains very high downs alternating sharply with damp wooded valleys. And the main through roads, at this and a later stage in the gipsies' journey, often ran, not on the turnpike routes just then in process of construction, but upon the still-existing but now virtually deserted Celtic trackways.

This first stage in the Egyptian Hegira is important :

to anyone who knows the country, it is the first stage of
doubt of their veracity. By their own account, they walked
as if in a hurry : the figure of one William Clarke, now
looming near, may be a clue to their haste. They *must*
have chosen the quickest route, because of their time-table.
They must, however, have followed roads, not mere footpaths ; because not only was George Squires taken later
over their route five times in a coach—his own counsel's
statement—but the season was exceptionally bad. Compare
1751 with that odious year 1920, for rainy days : 1920's
rainy days are in brackets : May, 1751, 15 (12) ; June,
10 (11) ; July, 20 (16) ; August, 17 (8) ; September, 12
(13) ; October, 9 (9) ; November, 11 (16) ; December,
10 (25) ; in January, 1752, it snowed, and, as will be seen,
the floods were out.

Give the travellers the benefit of the doubt, and assume
that they went the shortest way *by road ;* not the easiest
way, but the shortest. If they *did* know the lie of the land,
they went along the main road to Toller Down Gate (called
Fair Down in 1763 : Fair Field to-day is close by)—three
miles (from Wynyard's Gap) at about the 800-feet level.
At the cross-roads by the milestone, they turned to the
right, went a quarter of a mile uphill (possibly a mile,
to a perhaps easier road) along the Beaminster road, and
took either a footpath or a byroad through Toller Whelme
to Warren Hill and Mount Pleasant. On their way they
would have to cross two streams, descend to 500 feet through
wooded country, and climb again to 674 feet.

Mount Pleasant, by this route, is eight and a quarter
miles from South Perrott, six and three-quarters from
Wynyard's Gap. From there onwards to the summit of
Eggardon they would need all their knowledge of the " lie,"
for it is even now a bewildering region, in which the streams
and sudden small valleys make short cuts dangerous.
They would follow the present road towards Toller Porcorum
for about 550 yards, downhill, and then bear south-south-
east, along a parish boundary (and that was an important

P

thing to know in 1752), still downhill, to cross another
stream at 411 feet, just where the railway runs to-day :
thence up to the 700 contour, and higher, to 828 feet on
Eggardon Hill. Here they would follow the very old track
eastwards for about a mile, past tumuli and cromlechs,
and then turn more nearly due south and go downhill,
over the ghostly earthen circle close to the third diagonal
track, the Dorchester-Bridport road—down, down, at last,
to Litton Cheney, with its two streams and the green
water-meadows beyond. And that adds another six miles
to their journey : fourteen and a quarter from South
Perrott, twelve and three-quarters from Wynyard's Gap.

The interesting thing about this route is that it tallies
with George Squires' statement that the only "town"
between South Perrott and Litton was Wynyard's Gap.
By any other route, longer or shorter, they must have come
upon hamlets or villages more impressive than the Gap.
The route, moreover, is not at all far from a crow-flight
between the two places. George underestimated the total
distance by two miles or so in his evidence.

They left the Gap between 9 and 10 ; say, 9.30. They
reached the inn at Litton, twelve and three-quarter miles
away over bad country, in bad weather, at 2 o'clock, on the
testimony of the innkeeper ; four and a half hours—a very
old woman, "unhealthy, seemingly," a young girl nicely
dressed, and a man in an overcoat with a bundle of wares.
As the visitor to the Zoological Gardens said about the
giraffe, " I don't believe it." However, go with them all the
way.

A plasterer of Litton Cheney, John Fry, who had known
" the old gipsy " for thirty years, and had often seen her
there, testifies that on that Saturday evening, December 30th,
1752, the party were sitting in the inn, in a new room. They
stayed there that night. The next day, Sunday, December
31st, George went to the house of Francis Gladman, a
gardener, and got shaved, and in the forenoon went on to
Abbotsbury to see one William Clarke.

Now William Clarke, one of the three witnesses called at the first trial, and discharged of perjury afterwards, is an outstanding figure in this strange affair. He was a shoemaker or cordwainer of Abbotsbury. By his own account, he had met the gipsies before : four years before. In 1751–2 he " was dear to " Lucy Squires, as his association with her and her family from this point would suggest. When and how he first became dear to her is an interesting mystery. He had not met any of the gipsies—again by his own account—between that encounter " four years before " and the present occasion. His affection lasted well. Yet his feelings for Lucy, as he himself described them, were hardly tumultuous : " We were upon civil terms ; I never saw anything by her but civil terms ; she is as honest a girl as any in the world for what I know." Is a romance of that nebulous character sufficient ground for this strange cross-country sprint—sufficient to set the family running, like mating badgers, over hills and dales which lovesick Lucy was too stupid to be trusted to identify, and which her brother, who found Clarke unerringly, had to revisit five times for certainty ?

And George did not at once fetch William to his Lucy, but lodged that night at Abbotsbury ; thereby missing some good cheer at Litton, for the villagers were wont to ring in the New Year on the church's peal of six bells at daybreak, and thereafter to resort to the public-house, " with our jug of cider, that was given us, to have something put in it." The horticultural barber, Gladman—it is a good name—in his exhilaration tried to get the old woman to tell his fortune, or to talk Spanish or Portuguese or Dutch or French to him ; but she would not. " Then I said, ' You are one of the family of the scamps ' ; she said, ' No, I am no scamp.' "

James Angel of Litton also noticed her : he had repaired to the inn " after evening prayer " on the Sunday. But the cheerful party, after two hours of cider—doubtless with " something put into it " (gin, " says I, knowing the

language ")—adjourned to go fox-hunting with " the
minister's kinsman." (This may have been Mr. William
Chafin Grove, of Friar Waddon, a few miles away, one of the
earliest recorded keepers of a pack.) They were hunting
all Monday till about three o'clock—just as the Cattistock
hunt there every January now ; and then Angel came back
to the inn : for why ? " The minister's kinsman gave the
people some money."

On the Monday George Squires walked back to Litton
with William Clarke, and William met his Lucy " about three
or four o'clock—it might be three o'clock . . . I know it
was some time before it was dark." He *should* know, as a
lover. But the other witnesses gave conflicting evidence.
It is at least agreed that the three gipsies and Clarke ate
two fowls (boiled) at the Litton inn that afternoon. George
had bought—not stolen—the fowls from Dance Turner of
Litton, for sixpence apiece, making " a cludation " for the
feathers, which Mrs. Turner was to have. This struck the
London lawyers as curiously luxurious ; but " we don't
eat roast meat in the country but very little," said the innkeeper, and George stated that he often ate fowls, because
they could be purchased in that district " cheaper than beef
or mutton."

After the meal they set out for Abbotsbury. According
to Clarke (who was pressed on the point) the old woman
could not do more than two miles an hour. The actual
distance from Litton to Abbotsbury, for a crow, is three
and a half miles ; but by either of the two old farm-tracks
across country to-day it is at least four and a half ; the first
mile through flooded water-meadows, and the last over
Abbotsbury Hill (691 feet)—a hill at which even Ford cars
boggle to-day.

At Abbotsbury the vagrants—vagabonds in the eyes of
the law, and in point of fact provided with very little money,
as will be seen—became at once part of the minor society of
the place. On that very first evening there was dancing
at the inn, country dances, up to midnight. Melchisedech

Arnold, the blacksmith, " played on the music." He was
a fiddler and a cider-seller as well as a smith, and he played
for them again the next Saturday (January 6th) : three times
at least they danced that week—for they had reached
Lucy's promised land, and need no longer haste away.
Lucy danced with her William, and George with the host's
sister, Mary Gibbons.

And there came to the dancing many folk. Andrew
Wake was there, a temporary exciseman lodging in the house,
who slept in the same room as George Squires, and borrowed
his coat to go his round in, and was afterwards discharged
His Majesty's service for neglect of duty : Hugh Bond the
schoolmaster, who according to George had given the boys
a holiday and " got fuddled that night," but by his own
account was not at the *Old Ship* at all till January 8th :
John Ford (the innkeeper's uncle), a carpenter and baker,
who kissed Lucy and drank with George, and was said to be
intoxicated when giving evidence a year later ;* a merry
fellow. These are the only three of the Abbotsbury
witnesses who did not claim previous acquaintance with
the gipsies.

There were present also many other villagers. There
was Daniel Wallace, a mercer, who " generally drank
cider "—as who would not in that hamlet of admirable
cider ? George bought sugar of him, and Mrs. Squires
asked him to dinner on Sunday ; but he refused, for the
ungallant but intelligible reason that he " had something
particular to dine on "—a roast shoulder of mutton. Also
John Hawkins, a weaver, John Bailey, a carpenter and
barber, and George Clements, who dined with the gipsies
on January 7th, and drank with them on two other days,
and had, he said, seen Mary Squires fifteen or sixteen years
before.

---

* His evidence has a cheerful tone of inebriety. One of the pamphleteers
states that at Canning's trial " he was so intolerably drunk that he was
bid to go about his business." Canning's prosecutor, to whom Ford was a
friendly witness, did not keep him long : " You are drunk now, and ought
to be ashamed of yourself."

Thus in mirth and solace they abode at the *Old Ship* till January 9th, a Tuesday. Where did the money come from ? The inn was " the most public house in the town," according to the vicar, who afterwards upheld the good faith of his corybantic parishioners : it was the excise-office of the place, and the dancers evidently were not of the lowest labouring class. George Squires said he had set out originally from " Kent " with about twenty pounds' worth of goods. The whole journey from London to Dorset and back, by his evidence, lasted at least ten weeks. By the time he reached Abbotsbury, he stated, he had disposed of all his wares, except a piece of " check," and two waist-coats : he still kept, however, as will be seen, a small piece of nankeen (not " check," he himself explained), worth two shillings a yard. Clarke said he sold two aprons at the *Old Ship*. Gibbons the innkeeper, at the first trial—that of Squires and Wells—asserted that the gipsies " came with handkerchiefs, lawns, muslins, and checks "—not a mere penultimate nankeen or apron. George paid all expenses, and at Abbotsbury, or a little later, remitted payment for a debt to a London friend. He subsequently borrowed six shillings from William Clarke, and evidently was hard up for ready money. Their expenses were probably not high : the tavern bill at Litton was three shillings and sixpence, apart from the cost of the fowls. But even if they kept down to that level, a seventy days' pilgrimage, with a week's cheerful holiday thrown in, demands money. I shall come to a possible explanation later.

If their sojourn at Abbotsbury was fantastic, their departure is equally hard to understand. Somewhere they received a letter from the invisible Mary Squires *fille*—Polly, she was called by George Clements. Polly was ill, and they must hasten to her. George Squires said this was their reason for leaving Abbotsbury : but he could not decide when he had received this letter, and his sister had been given no address to which to write, nor did he remember to what address the missive was directed. Moreover, Polly could not write. I am informed by the learned historian of the post office that there was no official mail from London to Abbotsbury in 1751-2 : letters had to be sent on by private effort from Dorchester, which was on the Exeter mail route. The same authority tells me that the postboys travelled about five miles an hour. It seems safe to assume that a letter from London to Dorchester would take at least two days in transit. It would then have to await local facilities. The gipsies *may* just have been able to write to " Kent " (but Polly was actually in London, as George said at this point in his evidence : how did he know ?) and get an answer, during their stay at Abbotsbury ; but it seems unlikely. Here, too, an explanation may be possible on the general facts of the case.

At any rate, they, who were now in haste, who ten days before, with less reason for speed, had accomplished at least thirteen difficult miles in about five hours, set out from Abbotsbury on January 9th (William Clarke accompanying Lucy as faithfully as the dog of Tobias, Tobit's son), and struggled as far as—Portisham. It is from one and a half to two miles from Abbotsbury, according to the route taken : two by the present-day drier road.

In that village a tailor, William Haines, who had seen Mrs. Squires before, and known her " thirty years and upwards," saw them at the *Chequers* inn. Haines subsequently said that George Squires was not with the party at first, but that on his way to Abbotsbury, where he rented a shop, he met George " in the fields " : there is still a field-path, a short cut through marshy ground, between the two places. Haines' son also saw them.

They remained there the rest of the day and night. " It was terrible bad weather the next day " (January 10th), but they made a slightly better journey, nevertheless, and attained Ridgeway, four and a half miles east, on the Dorchester-Weymouth road. They arrived between nine and eleven in the morning, according to Francis Bewley, the landlord of the *Sloop Aground* public-house, where they

had at first " some roll and cheese," and about one o'clock
" some beef-steaks for dinner."

It is here that the financial crisis occurred. George not
only borrowed from Clarke, as has been said, but he was too
short of cash to pay his tavern bill. Early in the morning
of January 11th he repaired to the bedroom of Bewley with
a nankeen " waistcoat " (a piece suitable for a waistcoat),
and woke Bewley and offered it as payment in kind. Bewley
demurred : he had never had a waistcoat like that. To
them, Mary Squires : by whose suave arts the innkeeper
was persuaded to accept the cloth. He marked it there and
then. It was produced in court at Canning's trial, and
identified beyond doubt. The Squires, *or some of them*,
were certainly at the *Sloop Aground* somewhere about
that time.

And here Clarke must leave his Lucy and romance, and
return to his last at Abbotsbury. Fortunately for him, a
man with two horses turned up, one Thomas Mockeridge,
a turnip-seller of Abbotsbury, on his homeward way. He,
like Clarke, shared the Squires' beef-steaks : he had seen
Mary Squires three years before, as also had the landlord.
They left early the next day, and went off along the Dorchester road to Fordington, which joins the county town
at its south-eastern corner. If the *Sloop Aground* was
at Ridgeway Hill Gate—none of the inns mentioned now
exist under the names quoted—the distance is three miles :
it is four if the tavern was at Ridgeway hamlet. John
Taylor, of the *Coach and Horses*, close by the mill at
Fordington, who had known the gipsies " some years,"
saw them between 8 and 11 a.m. on Thursday, January 11th.
He made the curious statement that " they were not in my
house, they were in my stable *on the 10th*." The discrepancy
in the date may be a reporter's error. But it must be
remembered, for later suggestion, that Taylor knew the
Squires.

There is another discrepancy in the evidence here. Taylor
said the road was almost impassable through rain. " The

waters were so high, they (the gipsies) went through a
neighbour's house and my stable the back way." To get
them through "the water" a fortuitous miller's boy
appeared with a horse. He carried Lucy behind him over
the floods—for "a pint of beer " : but the human, humane
young man "could not stay " to give the old woman a lift
too. According to Taylor, who agreed as to Lucy's cavalier,
"the old woman took up her coats and went along through
it." He saw her cross two of the three bridges at this point.
"Nobody carried her, she went on foot." According to
George, "I took my mother, and carried her on my back
through the water." When Taylor last saw them, they were
on the Blandford road, the great highway through the
middle of Dorset.

That small conflict of evidence raises two other points.
George Squires does not say quite clearly that he got Polly's
letter at Abbotsbury : he may have got it at Dorchester.
In that case the gipsies either went out of their way to the
centre of the town before or after crossing the streams, or
never went to Fordington at all. And why did they go to
Fordington ? It so happens that their visit coincided with
a recent piece of road development. In 1746 the main road
from Dorchester eastwards *did* run through Fordington, in
a great curve. In 1747–8 the present road over Grey's
Bridge, a beautiful straight causeway, was built over two
new bridges, rendering the Fordington curve south unnecessary. It might be a strong point in support of the
a priori truth of the gipsies' evidence that, not having
visited Dorset for three or four years before 1751, they went
by the old way. On the other hand, why did they not find
and use the new road ?

But they were really in a hurry now. They did not stop
at Dorchester, but, says George, "went forward almost all
night." It is not disclosed where they lay that night
(Thursday, January 11th), but "the next day we got to a
place called Tawney Down, and we went into a little alehouse on the road, and had some bread and cheese and a

pint of beer. We lay at Chettle that night, which was the
Friday." "We went through Blandford."

I cannot identify Tawney Down, unless it is a strange
version of Tarrant Hinton. Blandford is sixteen miles, by
the present fairly straight road, from Dorchester : Chettle—
to the left of the main road—at least another six and a half ;
making twenty-five and a half in all from Ridgeway Hill
Gate. No wonder "my mother was very weary," after
travelling a day and a half without a proper night's rest.

There was no alehouse at Chettle. They lay in a barn
shown them by Thomas Hunt, a thresher of that place ; he
saw them at about four in the afternoon, and said they set
off again the next day, which was very wet, about ten or
eleven o'clock, "or it may be something more." He had
never met them before, but in evidence he swore to knowing
George "as I know my right hand from my left." He was
less certain of Lucy "because she was covered over " ; he
was "very sure" of Mary Squires.

From Chettle next day they went to Martin ; there was
no alehouse here either, "so a gentleman let us lie in his
barn." There is some obscurity here. Their next place of
call was Coombe Bissett, near Salisbury. But, as George
admitted, Martin is "not in the direct way from Chettle to
London : it is the bottom way ; we came there because it
was night." That *should* only mean that they followed
either the present road—or the very old track which con-
verges with the Ackling Dyke near Bottlebush Down—up
to somewhere near Pentridge village, under the wild and
desolate Celtic camp on Pentridge Hill, and across the
Bokerly Dyke by Martin Down to Martin itself : nine and
a half miles by the shortest line of older tracks.

Perhaps nine and a half miles was a long enough walk.
There was no lover awaiting Lucy as at the setting-forth
from South Perrott. They reached Martin at about 4 p.m.
on Saturday, January 13th. Three witnesses who had
never seen them before swore positively to their appearance.
One was a carter who found them shelter, by leave of his

master, Farmer Thane, in an outhouse or barn : he testified
that they "got up" about 8 a.m. the next day (Sunday).
Another was a servant of Thane, who spoke to their sleeping
in the same outhouse, and also to the fact that he " saw the
old woman in master's house by the fire, and her daughter
was joining china for them " ; and the third was a blacksmith who lived at Farmer Thane's. Farmer Thane was to
have given evidence, but was taken ill on the way to London.
From the presence of the visitors in his house, it would seem
almost as if he *had* previous acquaintance with them. The
question of foreknowledge is important. I should like
Farmer Thane to have been cross-examined.

Their journey through Wiltshire from here onwards is
full of small mysteries. I will not pursue it in detail. From
Martin, " on the Sunday night," though they got up so early,
they marched only five miles, to Coombe Bissett. Witnesses
who had not seen them before identified them. They left
Coombe on the Monday (January 15th) apparently about
seven in the morning. They next appeared at Basingstoke,
forty miles away, on Thursday, January 18th. They put up
at the *Spread Eagle*, kept by Mary Morris. Their movements
between these points are totally obscure.

Here a second letter episode comes in. Lucy had not
forgotten her William ; and thus she indicated her feelings,
by the hand of Mary Morris, whose little boy took it to the
post office, urged to the appropriate speed by a present of a
halfpenny from George :

" Sir : This with my kind love and service to you, and all
your family, hoping you are all in good health, as I be at
present. This is to acquaint you that I am very uneasy for
your troublesome journey, hoping you received no illness
after your journey ; so no more at present from your most
obedient and humble servant,

                                        Lucy Squires.

" I desire to hear from you as soon as possible. Direct
for Lucy Squires at Brentford, near London. George and
mother give their compliments to you, and all your family."

A reasonably warm message, as eighteenth-century love-letters go. But why Brentford, when the sick sister was in London ? The tale told by George was that they arrived in Brentford on a Saturday. On the Sunday he went to White Hart Yard at Tottenham " to look after Sister Mary," and on the Monday he took Sister Mary to Brentford. On the Tuesday they all—Lucy, George and Mary *mère et fille*— went back to Tottenham. All this prodigious haste along neolithic byways for a girl whose good- or ill-health was never even questioned in evidence, although she could run to and fro between Brentford and Tottenham a fortnight after her mother's alarmed departure from Abbotsbury.

I will leave them at Basingstoke. They were on the clear high road to London, over Bagshot Heath (but doubtless in no fear of highwaymen) to Brentford, and so to Mother Wells' den, where it was admitted they lay for some days before their arrest.

That is the story. Neither at the time nor since has any-one hitherto thought it worth while to go closely over the ground of this alleged journey. And there was another strange omission of enquiry. Counsel for her prosecution suggested that Canning really was at the Enfield house, and that she went there to be delivered of a child. The wit-nesses called in reference to her medical condition were curiously chosen and very casually examined. A City apothecary testified that she was completely exhausted when she returned home. So did a City doctor. No one doubted that fact. These witnesses said nothing of possible childbirth. Dr. Daniel Cox, of the Middlesex Hospital, whom one of the pamphleteers treated as a standing joke, did not give evidence, but published a pamphlet himself, describing how he had chanced to be near when she returned to Aldermanbury, and had called in two midwives and an old friend of the family to examine her. (The midwives gave evidence in a language oddly like Mrs. Gamp's.) Their examination of her was cursory, to say the least. It was adequate, if believed, to show that she had not borne a child during that month of absence : it was entirely inadequate to show (indeed, it ignored the possibility) that she had not undergone what would now be an illegal operation, or procured abortion by medicinal treatment.

But can Mary Squires, that deformed witch, have been at Enfield, in view of the numerous witnesses from the West ? Consider two other features in the case—both brought out by the anti-Canning counsel. When William Clarke, the steadfast lover, was brought to London for the first trial, Canning's attorney, " with several persons well armed," accompanied him—in fact, carried him to London forcibly. They beset him perpetually on the journey to town, trying to make him admit that Mary Squires " was not the same woman he knew at Abbotsbury ; at the same time assuring him that his compliance should not hurt him, and that he might do it very safely, seeing there were two sisters so much resembling each other that they could not be distinguished." Mary admittedly had a sister—who was not called in evidence, though she could have borne out the story about Polly's illness and strengthened the alibi if it were true. Was this sister something like a double of Mary ?

The second point is that the gipsies avowedly travelled in smuggled goods, and Abbotsbury was a smuggling centre. It is in this connection that the question of previous acquaintance is important. The country witnesses, if they gave evidence at all, must hang together—in more than one sense. They had no wish to dance on air. There was enough money behind the gipsies to take George Squires five times over his alleged route, in a coach. The smuggling trade was enormously powerful. Its chief problem—distribution—was solved by means of a network of regular secret routes and storage centres far inland. And there was enough feeling in this case to cause some of the Enfield witnesses to be intimidated. London society, at any rate, guessed what was behind the gipsies' defence : " all the people at Abbotsbury, including even the Vicar, are Thieves, Smugglers, and Plunderers of Shipwrecks."

The evidence as to the gipsies' journey all points to one thing—the fabrication of an elaborate tale based on a few genuine facts, and so concocted as to keep in the background all the elements dangerous to the great Free Trade industry. George Squires learnt his itinerary by heart. He would not give away a single place of call outside that prescribed route : " Really, sir, I hope you will excuse me, be pleased to excuse me : I cannot tell indeed : please to excuse me." The smugglers' lines of communication must be kept secret, except for the few stages needed for the alibi, and on most of those stages friendly witnesses were ready to swear anything.

At the same time, the evidence as to the presence of George, Lucy and an ugly old gipsy in Dorset and Wiltshire during that January is too strong to be dismissed altogether —just as the Enfield evidence is. The details may be false : knowing the country, I simply cannot believe the alleged rate of progress. But I can believe that the places mentioned were visited *approximately* as stated—by George, Lucy, and the unproduced duplicate sister. As for Canning, she may have been detained as she stated—Andrew Lang's warning against disbelieving the incredible is a good one ; or she may have gone to Enfield voluntarily for the purpose suggested. The two explanations together at least meet in some degree the preposterous facts—which appear even more preposterous after a close geographical survey.

XI

" He is the wisest and ablest of all politicians who, by promoting the glory
of God, interests the Divine Providence in extending the power of
any nation. We know in how wonderful a manner the gospel was
propagated ; and we may confidently expect, that when this is
sincerely the aim of any government, the same assistance will not be
wanting : for whatever men may do, the great Author of all things
never alters His maxims, and to follow them is the most infallible
method of securing, might we not say commanding, success."

DR. BROCKLESBY, quoted by John Brownlow in
The History and Design of the Foundling Hospital.

" It was always considered as a piece of impertinence in England, if a
man of less than £2000 or £3000 a year had any opinion at all upon important subjects ; and in addition, he was sure at that time to be
assailed with all the Billingsgate of the French Revolution—Jacobin,
Leveller, Atheist, Deist, Socinian, Incendiary, Regicide, were the
gentlest appellations used ; and the man who breathed a syllable
against the senseless bigotry of the two Georges, or hinted at the
abominable tyranny and persecution exercised upon Catholic Ireland,
was shunned as unfit for the relations of social life."

The REV. SYDNEY SMITH,
Preface to *Collected Essays.*

XI

THE BEST OF BOTH WORLDS

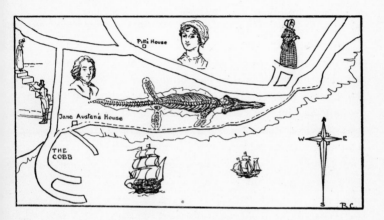

I CANNOT but continue the records of elegance immediately, before I descend to the seamen, and to the clod upon whose rheumatic shoulders the superstructure of fine living rested. In due course it pleased Almighty God to call to the throne of Britain not the nugatory Frederick, but his son, the homely sovereign often called Farmer George. I cannot feel so certain as his subjects were of Almighty God's affectionate admiration for George III. But at least he made the fortunes of Weymouth, whose inhabitants constantly invoked his Creator in his behalf, not only by means of the terrific effigy still dominating the motor buses on the Parade, but by other and less solemn methods.

Nothing, in the long and engaging history of monarchy, has surpassed in delightful absurdity the welcome given to the good king at Weymouth in 1789. He had just recovered

Q

225

from one of his more severe indispositions, and the sea air and bathing of Weymouth were recommended, and were indeed beneficial. Happily Fanny Burney was with the Court. She tells of the triumphal progress of the popular sovereign through Hampshire and Wiltshire : the huge crowds everywhere, the festooned arches, the green bowmen who accompanied the royal carriage, the incessant strains of " God Save the King." " The King's late dreadful illness," Madame d'Arblay exclaims, " has rendered this song quite melting to me." Dorchester surprised her by " the amazing quantity of indigenous residers " who crowded every window as they passed. The indigenous residers were noticeably less numerous on a later occasion : they were not wholly indigenous on this first visit.

But *the* surprise was the sea bathing at Weymouth, whose passionate devotion to the national anthem knew no bounds. Comment on Miss Burney's account would be impertinent.

" Not a child could we meet that had not a bandeau round its head, cap, or hat, of ' God Save the King.' All the bargemen wore it in cockades ; and even the bathing-women had it in large coarse girdles round their waists. It is printed in golden letters upon most of the bathing-machines. . . . Those bathers that belong to the royal dippers wear it in bandeaus on their bonnets, to go into the sea ; and have it again, in large letters, round their waists, to encounter the waves. Flannel dresses, tucked up, and no shoes nor stockings, with bandeaus and girdles, have a most singular appearance ; and when I first surveyed these loyal nymphs it was with some difficulty I kept my features in order.

" Nor is this all. Think but of the surprise of His Majesty when, the first time of his bathing, he had no sooner popped his royal head under the water than a band of music, concealed in a neighbouring machine,* struck up ' God Save great George our King.' "

* " A machine follows the royal one into the sea, filled with fiddlers "— Fanny Burney's Diary : the rest of the quotation is from a famous letter to her father.

"The three princesses," Hutchins tells us, "also bathed frequently and were much delighted with these ablutions."

In the course of this first visit to Dorset the royal party were entertained at Lulworth Castle by the then head of the Weld family : his elder brother, deceased, had been the first husband of the lady who was at that time Mrs. Fitz-herbert, and afterwards wife of George IV.

Sherborne, Milton, and Cerne were also visited, and then, after about eleven weeks' stay, during which Mr. Pitt ("his appearance is his least recommendation ; it is neither noble nor expressive ") waited on the King, the royal party went on through Bridport and Axminster to Exeter. "About the beginning of August," Hutchins says, "the Duke of Gloucester made a short visit, which afforded no inconsiderable addition to the happiness of the inhabitants."

Gloucester Terrace and the other beautiful Georgian houses on the parade sufficiently testify to one of the real virtues of that complacent age. Weymouth and its spacious bay, still, in spite of piers and pierrots, a great stretch of loveliness at all times and in all seasons, did benefit the good King, who returned thither many times, to the sustained joy of its citizens.

It is worth while to record, to set against the gloom which the contemporary history of the labouring classes inspires, the cheerful orgies at Dorchester at the time of one of these later visits—in 1798. Sports were organized at Maiden Castle ; and the ancient ramparts saw contests for the following, among other, rewards :—

"To be played for at cricket, a round of beef ; each man of the winning set to have a ribband. . . .

"A pound of tobacco to be grinned for.

"A handsome hat for the boy most expert in catching a roll dipped in treacle, and suspended by a string. . . .

"A pig ; prize to whoever catches him by the tail."

Another delight in the sovereign's honour was a monstrous hollow pie filled with canaries : " When the pie was opened the birds began to sing "—probably the National Anthem.

Weymouth certainly benefited by the royal favour, apart from its immediate establishment as a watering-place. It became customary, for instance, for the chief actors of the day to appear there. Kean obtained his first chance of popularity by a performance which caught the chance eye of a "London Manager" more effectively than the efforts of Mr. Crummles and his company at Portsmouth. Grimaldi senior trod the Weymouth stage and wrote some verses in its honour. Elliston was another passing visitor. He had the joyous experience of dropping casually into the theatre one day, and finding his sovereign fast asleep in the royal box. George had been caught in a shower of rain and had taken shelter there. Elliston did not like to wake him crudely. He retired, and obtaining some musical instrument, played " God Save the King." The King woke.

One of the more memorable desires expressed by King George was to the effect that he wished every child in his dominions to be taught to read the Bible. It was as a result of a Dorset resident's efforts that he came to this decision. The age extended its care to morals unceasingly, and the West was a strong centre of morality. Hannah More was not far away, engaged in her devastating controversy with the incumbent of Blagdon. The celebrated Madras System, over which Joseph Lancaster, Mrs. Trimmer, Sidney Smith, and Andrew Bell generated so much heat, and out of which arose the National Society for Promoting the Education of the Children of the Poor in the Principles of the Established Church (I love its almost unknown full title) and the British and Foreign School Society—that celebrated system was adopted at Dorchester in 1812, after a meeting of the Grand Jury of the County of Dorset assembled at the Lent Assizes, and a subsequent meeting of the " Nobility, Gentry, Clergy, and Inhabitants " (in due order). The inventor of the System, the virtual founder of the National Society, Bell

THE WEYMOUTH OF GEORGE III
From an engraving of 1789

himself, the inspirer of the monarch's hope, was rector of
Swanage from 1801 onwards.

It need hardly be said that the Committee formed in
1812 laboured to advance the then policy of the Society—
to educate the poor, but not to educate them too much, nor
so as to render them discontented with their station ; and
to teach them useful arts, but not to withdraw them from
economic occupations. " No Girl," said the Dorset regula-
tions, " to be permitted to learn to write or cypher, till she
has completed her ninth year, nor then, unless she can read
the Bible fluently, repeat the Catechism, Prayers, etc.,
knit stockings, and do all sorts of common plain work. . . .
It has been found that in many of the smaller parishes,
it is not practicable to introduce Day Schools, as the children
from a very early age are called out to employment in
husbandry, and other industrious pursuits." I wonder what
Mr. H. A. L. Fisher considers " practicable " in popular
education to-day.

And I wonder also, for I fear after all it is now as impossible
to get into theirs as into the mediæval mind, in spite of
still existing survivals—I wonder what the less advanced
clergy really thought ; or for the matter of that what any
decent Tory thought. Read Moritz or Arthur Young about
the squalor of peasant life (still squalid) : read Fielding,
keep reading Fielding, who though he might choose to label
people Allworthy and Square and Thwackum, was not
deluded by his own sentimentality as regards the real state
of the countryside. They at least thought. But though they
knew better they *did* little. On the whole they accepted.
How much more easily would lesser men accept a millennium
to be won by the least humiliating form of boot-licking—un-
questioning acquiescence in the policy of the good and great ?

I asked how the clergy accepted it : in mid-century
by marrying, almost at command, the lord of the manor's
housekeeper ; unless they happened to be younger sons,
when the rich living was nursed and the rich bride provided
if she were available. There was a place between the grades

(Mr. Collins is a later product of the system) and there was under Wesley and Simeon a place outside them. The real indictment of the clergy, as of the better type of Tory squire, is on the charge of blindness, not of lack of sympathy.

But that indictment comes from the post-Darwin era, in which historical perspective is a schoolboy's commonplace. What decent gentry and parsons saw was that there was a lot of discomfort, a good deal of give-and-take, a certain habit of piggishness in the lower orders, a little discontent among those who usually turned out to be bad characters (bad—like Tom Jones, by what standard ?), and a reasonable amount of care for them by those set, by God and the British constitution, over them. From the evolutionary point of view, this was not a bad stage in progressive opinion to have reached.

(It is almost a piece of historical irony that Crabbe, the creator of that antidote to rural sentiment, " The Village " was a Dorset vicar in this reign—and an absentee. He held the living of Evershot from 1783 to 1786, but never resided there. For him the female amenities of Trowbridge.)

George's long reign was in many ways an age of personal and even aggressive philanthropy. Perhaps the stoutest-hearted of all its Dorset benefactors was a certain Benjamin Jesty, of Worth Matravers. He is an ornament to the local history of medicine—a history which includes not only the odd characters already mentioned, but the great name of Sydenham, and lesser lights like Case and Sagittary. Mr. Jesty discovered, many years before Jenner, the art of inoculating for small-pox ; and his epitaph records his " fortitude." He made the first test of his discovery—on his wife.

Amid all the absurdities, all the complacent and all the really sincere effort, deeper fires were burning. John Wesley, grandson of the Charmouth parson, included the county in some of his itineraries. He was at Corfe in 1774 :

"When we came to Corfe Castle, the evening being quite calm and mild, I preached in a meadow near the town, to a deeply attentive congregation gathered from all parts of the island. I afterwards met the society, artless and teachable, and full of good desires. But few of them yet have got any farther than to ' see men as trees walking.' "

Two days later he visited the ruins of Corfe Castle, which impressed him greatly : especially one small detail. "Some time since the proprietor fitted up some rooms on the south-west side, and laid out a little garden, commanding a large prospect, pleasant beyond description. For a while he was greatly delighted with it ; but the eye was not satisfied with seeing. It grew familiar, it pleased no more, and is now all run to ruin. No wonder ; what can delight always but the knowledge and love of God ? "

He went on to Langton Matravers, but "did not find any among them " (" a large and deeply serious congregation ") "who knew in whom they believed." And to Swanage, where three or four persons (" and all of one family ") "seemed really to enjoy the faith of the gospel. Few others . . . appeared to be convinced of sin. I fear the preachers have been more studious to please than to awaken, or there would have been a deeper work."

Perhaps the best summary of the epoch's self-satisfaction is in an epitaph of a slightly earlier period—that on the monument in Sherborne Abbey to the fourth Lord Digby, who died in 1696. It records his dignities—"titles to which the merits of his grandfather first gave lustre, and which he himself laid down unsullyd. He was naturally enclined to avoid the hurry of a publick Life, yet careful to keep up the port of his Quality, was willing to be at ease but scorned obscurity ; and therefore never made his Refinement a pretence to draw himself within a narrower compass, or to shun such expense as Charity, Hospitality and his Honour called for. His Religion was that which by Law is established, and the Conduct of his Life showed the power of it in his Heart. His distinction from others never made him

forget himself or them. He was kind and obliging to his
neighbours, generous and condescending to his inferiors,
and just to all Mankind. Nor had the temptations of honour
and pleasure in this world strength enough to withdraw
his Eyes from that great Object of his hope, which we
reasonably assure ourselves he now enjoys."

The walk which will cover this admirable epoch of our
history is a very short one. It begins at the very bottom
of the cup in which Lyme Regis lies—near the River
Buddle, just where, within my own memory, Mary Anning's
gabled house blocked what is still about the narrowest and
most dangerous corner on any main road in Britain. Go
through the posts towards the glimpse of sea, and behold
all the sea anyone needs: all the sea from Start Port to
Portland Bill, and the cliffs thereof. There is a curved
walk right round the " front " (by the way, who invented
the words Esplanade and Parade ? But Lyme is not so
sordid as to need them). You will find a raised wall and
promenade past some of the smallest and most decent
houses in the world. Here, in Jane Austen's words, several
past occupants have " thrown out a bow " : curved bows
of the proper Bertram type, facing a sea which must often
threaten them : graceful absurdities whispering the enchantments of a lost domesticity.

You will reach eventually a bathing beach. For those
used to more robust efforts, the bathing at Lyme is about the
worst known : equalled in my experience only by that at
Swanage and Studland in Dorset, and at places like Little-
hampton in Sussex. It seems that you could almost walk to
France with no water higher than your knees, if it were not
(at Lyme) for the silly sharp rocks (laminated, not rugose),
which try to prevent your having any legs at all below the
knees. (It is only fair to say that the Cobb provides aquatics
of quite a different sort.)

You will also come along the marine walk to strange
concrete erections, monuments of the Eternal Mind of Man.
The earth has here a tendency to slide into the sea, and so

its parasites desired to keep it above water. Rediscovering Rome's craft of concrete building, they fortified the sloping cliff with arches. It would seem that they originally intended some civic adornment of Lyme, for the arches resemble the beginning of those ignoble arcades, pleasaunces, promenades—I know not what to call them—which defile every few miles of the coast of Sussex : the beginnings, in fact, of a Front or even a Winter Garden. But they are fortunately rudiments only, and you may pass them in moral and physical safety—moral, because there is no bandstand; physical, because, through their presence, you need not beware the awful avalanche.

I cannot avoid that last quotation. All the mellowness of Longfellow must descend upon one at Lyme. A few score yards past the ferro-concrete you come to the very house where Jane Austen lodged. So suitable a house : smiling silently, like La Gioconda, with no change of expression in any weather, upon the ancient Cobb and the delicious promenade and the huge cliffs alike. " Golden Cap : yes, a very striking eminence. Gun Cliff—the Assembly Rooms are there, are they not ? The Cobb—a very fine undertaking, but a little boisterous and rude for elegant females." Nevertheless, the eternal fires are there, behind the bow-windows and the twinkling lights, and lovers looked out then as now over the far-stretched cliffs. This demure little walk was the only thing upon which Jane Austen let herself go, the only place she ever described with enthusiasm.

Tennyson, according to a famous anecdote, arrived at Lyme over the hills from Bridport on a visit to the discreet Palgrave, and demanded at once to be taken to the spot where Louisa Musgrove " fell to the pavement and was taken up lifeless." It was the right spirit. Controversy has raged upon the point of where Louisa lapsed. My own opinion is that " Granny's Teeth " are too terrible for an elegant young lady of the time, but that any other set of steps will do for her arch proceedings. At any rate the Cobb is as beautiful now as then. It is the only pier of its length

I know in England which remains unspoilt by trains, docks, entertainments, automatic machines, turnstiles or officials.

You can see something like what the old prints of the Cobb depict, in the curving breakwater where the few steamers touch. On the seaward side are the big more roughly shaped stones of the Elizabethan or even earlier breakwater. I can conceive no more contented isolation than to sit idly upon the wall of this pier, looking at empty space, or the antics of modern life, or the gracefulness of modern Lyme, or the bracken and blackberries on the happy hills.

Now go up the hill past the few needful offices and some not good later buildings, to the main street of Lyme. By this road you come upon it at its most lovely stage—where the roads fork for Axmouth and Uplyme. The street that drops away at your feet eastwards—" almost hurrying into the sea," as Miss Austen wrote—is to me far more beautiful than those of Clovelly or Robin Hood's Bay or Whitby. It is the most complete late eighteenth-century street in England, in spite of one or two vile molestations. And through and beyond the gracious houses you look over the incomparable bay : Stonebarrow Hill, Golden Cap, Thorncombe Beacon, even the little sheer cliffs by Burton, right across the curve of foam to Portland.

Close to you, as you enter by this road, is an elaborate modern chapel set up by a local rich. Avoid it, and also the public gardens, except as a short cut. Look rather inwards at the serene building nearly opposite, with conventional flower-pots crowning its decent façade : even though the excisions made by commerce hurt the proportions, it is still desirable. And then there is the smithy and its old cottage, and then the Retreat. Mary Russell Mitford once lived at the Retreat, a wholly delightful house whose late tenant was an impressive survival of the dignity of a little town's life. In the sloping garden beyond the well-proportioned rooms—rooms that Fanny and Edward Bertram could well have made their home, with never the need to achieve a single improvement—you will find the very stone arbour and the nut trees and the river by whose side Miss Mitford maintained that insatiable father of hers.

The house stands on the site of the stables of the Great House, to which the first William Pitt (Chatham) was a frequent visitor. The chemist's shop next door represents the Great House. Opposite is a place of business to which I am fain to pay tribute, for it belongs to one of the last of the provincial bookselling houses to do what all local publishers should do—produce their local histories. The firm of Dunster gave to the historians of England the works of Roberts of Lyme Regis : the man who made Macaulay's chapter on Monmouth's rising possible, and who chronicled his native town and the social life of the south-west with the widest knowledge and accuracy. He was mayor of Lyme in 1848. The same firm, still, I am glad to say, aware of a traditional pride in bookselling, tried, within my own generation, to produce a local literary magazine of high standing. They obtained, among others, Palgrave as a contributor : but Lyme did not live up to the ideal, and *The Grove* died in 1892.

A little lower down, on the same side, was born Francis Bickley, the author of an admirable book on *Where Dorset meets Devon*, and of a sound *Life of Prior*, and of much good criticism in the contemporary Press.

The street is marred by certain new buildings which affront the eye just below this stage. But within a few yards it regains its sedate beauty, and nothing could be better than the confrontation of the two chief hotels, the *Royal Lion* and the *Three Cups*. The *Cups* is the older house, and seems to go back to at least Stuart times in name and site. But they are both models of what a country inn of the better sort should appear to be.

And that brings me to an experience which makes one think about the practical details of civilization in a world to which I hope we may one day return : a world in which the simpler conveniences of life can be procured by travellers upon reasonable terms.

I went for lunch to the *Royal Lion** one Sunday
nearly a quarter of a century ago, with four or five friends,
on a Sunday in spring ; we had walked, like Tennyson, over
the cliffs from Bridport, and were hungry and a little tired.
We found an excellent coffee room ; and for 2s. 6d. each we
ate (i) dressed crab, lots and lots of it ; (ii) Easter lamb, the
real Dorset lamb ; (iii) a fruit tart of surpassing excellence ;
(iv) Blue Vinney in good condition and in its proper state—
a whole cheese. Cider was not absent. We were waited
on by a civil maid. After what I can only call a heavy lunch,
we were not disposed to set forth at once on our walk back
to Bridport (by road, not over the mountains). So we went
to what was then a cosy panelled bar-parlour, across the
hall-entrance, and found the comfortable landlord, and had
some excellent liqueur brandy. We talked to our host freely
of our adventures on the hills. Presently he said, " Well,
gentlemen, it's closing time now, and I'm going to have a
nap. I daresay you're not wanting to start back yet. Of
course this is Sunday. But the billiard-room is at the back
of the house "—it was in the present dining-room—" and
if you like to go up there and rest and have a game, well,
I've got no objection and no one'll know. And now I hope
you'll have another little drop with me."

His advice was followed in all respects. We stayed and
had tea and walked back in the twilight, feeling that the
world was a good friendly place, and swearing by the old
dark hotel, with its rambling staircases, its fine collection
of old sporting prints, its noble food, its wholly adequate
host.

I still swore by it a few years later when I did the same
walk with a friend who unhappily lives only on grass and
herbs, which for the moment I had forgotten when I told
him of the good inn. Still, I promised him cheese and fruit
and salad, having faith. We got there on a hot day in a

---

* Nothing I say here bears upon the present management or facilities.
The house has changed hands more than once since what I describe.
In one or two casual visits recently (1921) I found the accommodation
excellent, and the pretences to which I take exception do not exist.

temper demanding a soothing reception. The first thing I noticed was that the bar-parlour was gone. It was now an open "lounge," full of plush and bamboo and wicker and full-bosomed ladies. The coffee room still stood, however, and in it waiters in "jimmy little Tuxedos." It appeared that cold beef could be obtained. But the pickles therewith were of an abhorrent type, and the only salad was a cucumber. My vegetarian friend was a little dismayed by this gourd. He asked what sweets there were. "Prunes and rice or stewed plums," said the polite Austrian waiter. It was midsummer. "What cheese is there? Have you any Blue Vinney?" The politeness of the alien faded, and a look of surprise came over his face; he goggled. Some attempts to explain what was meant by Blue Vinney followed, and then the manager or proprietor—likewise Central European—was summoned. "No, sir, we haf no Blue Finney, but we haf some very goot Cheddar." "Do you get it direct from Cheddar?" (Most of the towns and villages in the district do or did.) "Oh no, sir. We get it fresh every week from Harrod's."

Now there are at this day several hotels in Dorset which live up to what you might call a good county or country standard. The *Royal Lion* is one. The *Greyhound* at Bridport, the *King's Arms* and *Antelope* at Dorchester, the *Grosvenor Arms* at Shaftesbury, are others; and there are yet more. There are also quite a number; which live up to what you might call a good village standard; places where you can get a clean bed, eggs and bacon, and a chop or cold meat and decent cheese and civility.* (By the

---

* Sometimes more than bare civility. At one little inn on the edge of Marshwood Vale, I went in and asked for bread and cheese. I was told I could have some cold beef and pickles and potatoes as well, and I assented greedily: I had walked fifteen miles. The landlord waited on me himself: he apologized for it, but explained that his wife was having a baby upstairs. I had lashings of really good food and three pints of home brewed cider (it was July). At the end I asked the reckoning. "Well, sir, I don't rightly know: I'd better leave it to you." I said I simply couldn't guess, and asked what it cost him, if he really did mean to leave it to me. "Well, shall we say a shilling?" he replied. That, I fear, was in 1903. But I said even then something more than a shilling.

way, how many chops are there in one sheep ? Why is there
never a chop famine even in the lowliest village ?) But
why should hotel keepers trying to be progressive merely
succeed, as a rule, in getting near an average and usually
dull uniformity—a uniformity either in pretentious failure
or in monotonous achievement ?

Cheddar from Harrod's : excellent Cheddar, excellent
Harrod : but why ? Dorset produces so much food as to
be nearly self-supporting in all but cereals : and it is good
food. Eat it. Don't send to London for substitutes.

The fault, I think, lies in the guests, not in the hosts.
Of course, at the present time many of the guests in country
inns are apt to be more stupid, more hoggish and more
exacting than before the war : they have only just made
their money and adopted the hotel habit. (The good
country hotel, not the big London restaurant, is the place
to see the real profiteer expatiating, family and car and all.)
But apart from and before that slight change, the guest was
always, I think, prone to expect too much, and as a result
to induce the production of too little. People who complain
of English hotels usually speak as if they had a right to a
pretty good French dinner in them at a minute's notice,
or no notice at all. They demand at Lyme Regis, if they
prefer English food, their Cheddar from Harrod's, their
oysters from Scott's, their home-killed beef from Smithfield,
instead of the Dorset horn lamb and the Blue Vinney of
Marshwood Vale. They make odious comparisons, as if the
bad cooking of poor food were confined to England. I have
sometimes pulled a cosmopolitan leg by telling of that shilling
meal of mine as one obtained in a fictitious Spanish village ;
and the comment has almost always been " How unlike
what you would get in England " : to my great joy.

The result of that false standard is that the innkeeper
becomes more ambitious than his knowledge and ability
warrant. He tries to do things in style (a great phrase,
that) : but he does not really know the style.

And that is the end of this walk. We do not possess

to-day the style which covers Lyme Regis with such conspicuous perfection : the style of an age which at least knew when to leave off. If you yourself do not wish to leave off so soon, go up through the fields, over the Devil's Bellows and the bracken-lined cliffs, to Charmouth, and back along the shore. You will only gain fresh visions of the perfect discretion, the enduring and not-to-be contaminated beauty of Lyme of the King.

XII

" We had bell-ringing and beer-drinking the night that we received the
list of the killed and wounded and likewise when we received your
letter. The colours were hoisted on the tower. Mother had hard
work to keep the beer barrell a-running. Our family is increased very
much for we have had no less than thirteen puppies ; Blossom seven
and Clara six. . . . All the Bridport Volunteers went to Church on
Thanksgiving Day. . . ."

> W. H. ROBERTS to his brother R. F. Roberts,
> aboard H.M.S. *Victory*, 1805; from *Nelson's
> Hardy*, by A. M. Broadley and R. G. Bartelot.

' There is no London merchant telling over gold in his counting-house, no
man-of-war's man standing his watch at sea, who does not owe his
gold or his rights to the men who lived wretched days long ago aboard
old wooden battleships under martinets. . . . In order that our days
might be pleasant, those thousands of long-dead sailors had to live
and suffer. They passed rough days—living hard, working hard, and
dying hard. In order that we might live in peace at home they were
dragged, with blows and curses, from their homes. In order that we
might walk erect among men they cringed before tyrants, and lost
their manhood at the gangway. . . . They passed, these mighty
ones, in the blackness of the cockpit, in the roaring hell of the gun-
deck, that we might hear no noise of battle. They were well pleased
to live among thieves and infamous folk, that our conversation might
be virtuous and our ways right ways. . . . Let us think that
patriotism, in its true form, is of the kind they gave. It is not a song
in the street, and a wreath on a column, and a flag flying from a
window, and a pro-Boer under a pump. It is a thing very holy, and
very terrible, like life itself. It is a burden to be borne ; a thing to
labour for and to suffer for and to die for ; a thing which gives no
happiness and no pleasantness—but a hard life, an unknown grave,
and the respect and bared heads of those who follow."

> JOHN MASEFIELD,
> *Sea Life in Nelson's Time.*

" For what design these extraordinary events have been brought to pass,
or for what purpose the present Atheistical Usurper is permitted to
keep so large a part of the civilized world in subjection, remains
concealed in the inscrutable councils (*sic*) of the Almighty."

> PEREGRINE BINGHAM, B.C.L., in the intro-
> duction to *Dissertations by the Rev. George
> Bingham*, 1804.

R

MARINERS OF ENGLAND

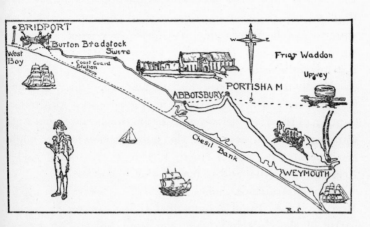

NOT long ago I spent a day of great happiness at and near Mosterton, a tiny village in a north-western projection of Dorset, near the Somerset border, in the Crewkerne district. Towards the end of the day, natural appetite and curiosity together led me into the *New* inn, a house dated 1751, but in architecture probably older. As I drank my beer, I asked the landlady about the building. She very kindly showed me over it, not without pride. It was the ancient manor-house of the Hood family, with timbers and stone floor, and staircases as old as they.

The Dorset admirals are a remarkable group. I am not sure that they do not surpass those of Devon. The Hoods alone would give lustre to any county. The earliest noted family of the name seems to have lived in Charles II's reign at Little Windsor in Marshwood Vale—Alexander

Hood. His collaterals and descendants were at Kingsland, near Bridport, at Mosterton, and in Somerset. The various branches of the family hover, so to speak, on the Somerset and Dorset border, and I am not going to claim them all as wholly Dorset men ; but they had Dorset in their blood, in one of their titles, and often for their home.

The most notable of the race was Samuel, afterwards Viscount Hood—" the best officer, take him altogether, that England has to boast of ; great in all situations which an admiral can be placed in," was Nelson's verdict. He was born in Somerset : his mother was a Beaminster woman. But his younger brother Alexander, first Viscount Bridport, was hardly less illustrious : his title was won at his " glorious first of June." His cousin of the next generation, Alexander, Captain of the *Mars*, served with distinction in the Napoleonic wars and died in action at the moment of victory, while *his* brother, Sir Samuel Hood, Vice-Admiral, fought under Nelson at the Nile, and in many other engagements.

And the tradition holds good still. Rear-Admiral the Hon. H. L. A. Hood commanded H.M.S. *Invincible* at the battle of the Falkland Isles, and went down with her at the battle of Jutland.

The Hoods are only the better known stars in the Dorset galaxy—better known, that is, outside Dorset. Admiral Marriott Arbuthnot, born at Weymouth, served at Quiberon Bay and elsewhere, and under Lord Hood's colleague, Rodney. I am afraid that his record, though he was not wholly unsuccessful as a seaman, leads to the *Dictionary of National Biography's* conclusion—he was " a late survival of the class of officer described under the name of Flip or Trunnion . . . a coarse, blustering, foul-mouthed bully." He was conservative in tactics. Of a different type was Admiral Sir William Domett of Hawkchurch, an officer under both Lord Hood and Lord Bridport (with whom he was on the First of June) and also under Nelson. He futhermore held office on land, at the Admiralty.

Yet another Dorset family produced admirals—the Ryves'

of Damory Court, Blandford : a family which also gave to England in the seventeenth century a Dean of Windsor, a Warden of New College, an Attorney-General for Ireland, and a judge. The more notable of their two admirals was Rear-Admiral George Frederick Ryves. He too served under Arbuthnot and Nelson. His eldest son likewise became a rear-admiral, and four others served in the navy.

It may be worth while here, in view of a later reference, to mention also two sailors of yet another family—two sons of Lord Dorchester of Milton Abbas, who in 1788 were borne on the books of H.M.S. *Thistle* without having been aboard her at all.

On the civil side there may be interpolated here two other figures. The first bears the later Dorset name of Nepean of Loders. Sir Evan Nepean, Secretary of the Admiralty throughout the period of the victories of Jervis and Nelson, bought the manor of Loders six years before Trafalgar : but he was a Cornishman by birth. And the great and good George Bubb Dodington's public services were rewarded by his holding the office of Treasurer of the Navy in 1744, 1755, and 1757.

Many letters were addressed to Nepean by Nelson and by the seaman whose name in Dorset is best loved and remembered of them all ; " Nelson's Hardy." Sir Thomas Masterman Hardy, as I have said, was born at Kingston Russell ; but not long after his birth in 1769 his parents moved to Portisham, to which delicious village his memory turned throughout his long and varied life. He was sent in due course to Crewkerne grammar school. He first went to sea in 1781, under a Dorset captain, Francis Roberts, whose descendants still inhabit his home at Burton Bradstock. Hardy seems to have returned after a time for more school-ing, and to have been sent to the famous grammar school at Milton Abbas. There is some doubt about these years, but it is certain that in 1790 he was a midshipman under yet another Dorset captain, Alexander Hood of Nether-bury. He made his way by 1793 to a lieutenancy, and in that rank won in 1796 Nelson's warm commendation. It was about that time, perhaps, or a year or two before, that their close friendship (so valuable to the mercurial admiral) commenced. The action for which Hardy was praised was a curious one. He was in charge of *La Sabina*, a prize, with Lieut. Culverhouse, when his own ship, the *Minerve*, was attacked by a superior Spanish force. The two lieutenants hoisted the English colours above the Spanish, " evidently," says Nelson, " with the intention of attracting the attention of the (Spanish) Admiral," and drawing him off from *Minerve*. *Minerve* got away ; *La Sabina* was recaptured, and the two officers with her. " This is, Sir, an unpleasant tale," wrote Nelson to Jervis, " but the merits of every officer and man were conspicious through the whole of this arduous day." Hardy and his brave companion were taken, but exchanged almost immediately. " By God, I'll not lose Hardy," Nelson said a little later, when Hardy, trying to save a comrade's life, was in danger.

Hardy took part in the Battle of Cape St. Vincent (1797) and not long afterwards got his captaincy (at the age of twenty-eight) from Jervis himself. It is unnecessary here to go into the full details of his life. He returned whenever he could to his beloved " Possum " (Portisham), whose ale and mutton he never wearied of praising. He became in due course Admiral, First Sea Lord, and Governor of Greenwich Hospital. At no time in his career, it seems safe to assert, did he fail to win affection and esteem from his companions, or to display complete efficiency in his profession. Everyone knows of the scene at Nelson's death. The late Mr. A. M. Broadley gives a homely version of it from an interlude inserted after Trafalgar in the traditional Dorset mummers' play : it is the shortest tragedy on record. Nelson and Hardy enter :

" *Nelson :* Hardy, I be wownded.
    Hardy : Not mortually I hopes, my lord.
    Nelson : Mortually I be afeard. Kiss me, Hardy, thank
       God I've done my duty.''

There was another Dorset man at Nelson's side : young Roberts of Burton Bradstock, nephew of Hardy's first captain. It was he who reported that other fine saying of the greatest of all seamen—his answer when he was asked not to wear his full uniform, because of the danger to which it exposed him—" I was never afraid of my honour." Roberts tells, too, how for every enemy ship that struck our men gave three cheers, "which was re-echoed by some of the poor wounded then in the cockpit, and it seemed to give new life to Lord Nelson."

Mr. Broadley commemorates other Dorset Trafalgar captains : Admiral of the Blue Sir Charles Bullen—who with his brother first went to sea under Marriott Arbuthnot and was instrumental in preventing the spread of the mutiny of the Nore—and Admiral of the Blue Sir Henry Digby, who likewise first served under a Dorset admiral, his kinsmen Robert Digby of Sherborne. Admiralty ran in the Dorset families.

Of the atmosphere on land in Dorset during the threatened Napoleonic invasion, apart from the personal interest of half of the county in its seamen individually, it would be useless to speak. *The Trumpet Major* and *The Dynasts* make any other comment, any general history, any further attempt to get into the spirit of the times, impertinent and unnecessary. It may be interesting to mention very briefly the practical steps taken for defence. Dumouriez, Pitt's adviser on coast-defence, recommended a certain number of batteries at the various river-mouths ; a camp on Ballard Down ; fairly strong fortification of Portland (" the western shore of Portland is not open to invasion " —God help an invader in Deadman's Bay !) and posts at Abbotsbury, Charmouth, and Lyme. He thought the geographical position of the country important—it was " the pivot on which the defence of the west of England turns." It ought to be defended " foot by foot with exceeding stubbornness." But he also thought it easy of defence. William Clavell (High Sheriff) and William Moreton Pitt, of

whom I shall speak later, put forward schemes for mobiliza-
tion which were rightly considered to be of more than local
value. Clavell's plan for moving stock and property in
case the invasion materialized was very like that secretly
circulated—officially—in 1914 to leading men in country
districts. George III himself thought the county " one of
the most valuable parts of the Kingdom," and mentioned
it in his letters. For the rest, Boney was the ogre, and
Dorset, not unique in its apprehensions, is unique in
possessing the intimate record of its feelings in Hardy's
great novel.

It must not be thought, however, that the French wars
and the great admirals were all the maritime preoccupation
of Dorset between Blake's battle off Portland and Trafalgar.
It is in the late seventeenth century and the eighteenth
that the direct relation between the sea and the land is
made most convincingly evident. Privateering, piracy, and
smuggling were not trades undertaken for fun, for adventure.
Those who took them up were in them for life or death : for
life, because the inhabitants of England needed desperately
many of the smuggled or captured goods, and because the
adventurers must themselves live by the seacraft they knew
so well ; and for death, because death, which mattered less
then than we esteem it to matter now, " will come when it
will come," whether by a chance shot, or by the power of
the sea, or by a Bridport dagger.

I deem it to be in something of that compulsion of
necessity, of the choice between life and death, that in 1695
a Poole man performed a singular act of valour. In May of
that year " William Thompson, master of a fishing boat,
when fishing near the Isle of Purbeck, accompanied by only
one man and a boy, perceived a privateer of Cherbourg
bearing down upon him. He did not avoid the enemy, but
prepared to defend himself in the best way he could, having
two small guns mounted and some small arms. He was so
successful in the encounter that in a short time he wounded
the captain, the lieutenant, and six more of the French, so

disheartening them that they bore away to avoid him.
But Thompson in his turn, encouraged by his success, gave
chase to the privateer, fired upon her incessantly for two
hours, and at length compelled the enemy to surrender.
He took possession of the sloop, and with fourteen prisoners
brought her into Poole harbour."

But Thompson was not the privateer's first assailant. The
day before, another Poole captain had taken the offensive
against the same enemy without hesitation. He might have
pleaded that he was really a coast defender ; but as a matter
of fact, I think, Captain Peter Joliffe was a privateer,
whether licensed or not : other of his exploits are recorded.
A ballad describes the action which preceded Thompson's,
and was cut short only by nightfall. It extols Joliffe's
powers :—

> " Whate'er he took in hand did thrive ;
>   Behold, this year of '95
>   Full twenty sail of fishermen
>   He freed from cruel Rovers then.

> " He had but one great gun aboard,
>   And two young lads, which did afford
>   But slender help, yet ne'er the less
>   They flew before him in distress.

> " This privateer which he forsook,
>   It was the same that Thompson took
>   Next day ; therefore it will appear
>   Few men like those of Dorsetshire."

I am reminded by that gallant rhyme of another which
was repeated to me by a mariner of Bridport Harbour
a great many years ago. He and I and other old friends had
had a sing-song in the parlour of the *George* inn (nursery
of many friendships) ; and this ballad is one which all the
fishermen knew, and sang with such sincere enjoyment
that I desired the (to me) unfamiliar words. Dick, in his
beautiful slow drawling voice, gave them to me the next
day, breaking involuntarily into a sort of chant as he repeated them. He said he had learnt the words and tune

from his grandfather, with whom he (as a boy) and his father used to go fishing off Bridport, especially at night. (They all had worked in the vanished shipyard.) I have been out with Dick on various errands, and I can see that little crew, picking up their lobster pots or letting down a line to the floor of the sea, whose every inch they knew by heart without ever having seen it, and finding their way back, by just smelling the wind, to the little dark difficult harbour. It was chiefly at night, Dick said, that they sang : perhaps not always such a holy and cheerful note as woke the unespied Bermudas, but anyhow good robust English. This is the song :—

" It was of two noble ships from England did set sail ;
   One's name was Prince of Lewis, and the other Prince of Wales.
      Blow high, blow low, and so sailèd we,
      Cruising down on the coast of New Barbaree.

" Look ahead, look astarn, look a-weather, look a-lee,
      Blow high, blow low, and so sailèd we,
   O weather look-out man, ' A lofty sail,' said he,
      Cruising down on the coast of New Barbaree.

" ' O hail her, O hail her,' our noble captain cried,
      Blow high, blow low, and so sailèd we :
   ' Are you a man of war, or a privateer you be,
      Cruising down on the coast of New Barbaree ? '

" ' I am no man of war, nor a privateer I be——'
      Blow high, blow low, and so sailèd we.
   ' But I am a noble pirate, a-cruising on the sea,
      Cruising down on the coast of New Barbaree.'

" 'Then it's quarters for quarters,' our noble captain cried,
      Blow high, blow low, and so sailèd we :
   And the quarters that we showed to them, we sank them in the sea,
      Cruising down on the coast of New Barbaree.

" So now this noble pirate is coming to an end,
      Blow high, blow low, and so sailèd we :
   With the ship she was their coffin, their grave it was the sea,
   Sunk down on the coast of New Barbaree."

It is taken down verbatim, grammar, syntax, and all. I sent a copy to Mr. John Masefield, who had recently published his admirable *Sailor's Garland*. *New Barbaree* is, of course, a well-known sea-song, of great age. If Dick's grandfather knew it as a boy, as I was told, he must have learnt it about the time of Trafalgar. But Mr. Masefield, whose book included a version of it, thought Dick's was older than his—probably going back, by oral tradition, almost to the seventeenth century, when the " noble pirate " from the coast of New Barbaree was a real and present menace.

" The ship she was their coffin, their grave it was the sea." Life and death are real upon the sea, whatever your lawful or unlawful occasions. A Dorset map of 1763 records three recent wrecks on the coast between Bridport and Abbotsbury—not, in many ways, a dangerous seaboard. In one case, off Swyre, " a Logwood ship taken by the *Culloden* was stranded here and the boat thrown over the beach on a wall."

The smuggling and privateering industries certainly prospered in Dorset during this period. I have spoken of the gipsies' adventures, and perhaps have given them an epic turn. But these tales are not romances. They are the warp and woof of the life of the people of Dorset, as well as of other counties. You do not risk your neck for the benefit of a novelist a hundred and fifty years later, and you do not become a criminal (even if the law is going to be altered sometime after you are dead, and realtered later by a Free Trade Prime Minister) for the mere love of adventure. The notorious and horrible Chater case brings a few realities to the surface. Certain smugglers in 1747 tried to land a large cargo of tea on the Dorset coast ; but it was seized and stored at Poole. Such was the power of the Free Traders that they attacked Poole Custom House openly in force and recovered the goods. But the channels of distribution on this occasion leaked. The tea was taken inland by way of Fordingbridge : I am inclined to conjecture, from comparison with the Canning case, that there was a

smugglers' clearing house in that district—probably near
"Tipput" (Tidpit, a deserted hamlet on a Neolithic trackway near the Avon before it leaves the Wiltshire downs) :
just as there was near Tonbridge on the Upper Medway
for Kent and East Sussex.   At Fordingbridge, Daniel
Chater—who acted, not wholly creditably, as a common
informer—recognized one of the carriers, and laid an
information. I need not go into the details of the proceedings which followed. The man recognized was arrested.
The smugglers took their revenge. They captured Chater
and a tide-waiter named Galley who had been officially
connected with him, and after dragging them across Hampshire beat them to death : or rather beat Galley to death
and Chater almost : Chater they finished off by dropping
him down a well. The later events took place in Sussex.
Eight of the smugglers were caught (not at all easily) and
hanged.

A story like it is remembered in Sussex to-day, I was told
in West Sussex, by one who owns the original documents of
the careful accounts kept by his smuggling ancestors during
that time : how a carrier received so much a journey, what
the journey was, to what centre (that is the important
point) ; and from that our casual talk—which was shared
with a number of small farmers—drifted to the general
question of smuggling. My companions all dwelt on the
local case (I had not mentioned Chater's). The scene of
the beating to death was Slindon, and they knew the inn
where it took place ; and they said that the murdered
man, then only half dead, was dragged eight or ten miles or
so to Parham, not far from where we were, and despatched.

This tale I have not troubled to pursue in detail : it is
duly chronicled elsewhere. The Chater case is recorded by
Messrs. Atton and Holland (in *The King's Customs*), who
have had access to official papers. It proves, I think, the
intensity and widespread influence of the Free Trade :
and the Sussex gossip, which also follows known fact, is
more than suggestive. In West Sussex, in oral tradition,

and in London and East Sussex in official documents, is the still sounding echo of deeds that took place a century and a half ago—a deed, in that special instance, commenced in Poole and consummated two counties away.

And this mixed evidence almost proves also, to my mind, what the Canning case suggests—the existence of a vast concealed machinery of distribution, well controlled, with well-chosen clearing houses, well-chosen routes, secret agents everywhere. Smuggling was not a question of a chance sea-captain knowing a chance longshoreman and running a cargo with a theatrical apparatus of lamps on a cliff. It was an industry, a huge organized industry, employing a large number of " workpeople." It is useless to smuggle —except in a pettifogging way, or except in connection with very precious small articles like diamonds, saccharine, and cocaine—unless you do it on an industrial scale.* I was told this, it is amusing to record, by a certain excise officer who at the same time boasted that he knew very well what came ashore at his little port, and nothing excisable could get past him. A skipper near by winked at me, and told me later that the tobacco " Customs " was then smoking, which he had bought in the inn, was itself smuggled ; and the next day I had the pleasure of seeing Customs lend the landlord a hand with a case of brandy (on which duty *had* been paid) up to the inn, without knowing that the case also contained other goods on which duty had not been paid. But this was only trivial and on a small scale : no life or death about it. (The persons concerned are all dead.)

But there were kindlier seafarers in Dorset than the smugglers, humbler men than the admirals, men with a little more vision, perhaps, than the privateers. One of them lives, I hope, for ever, even if his work may not : the creator of the Foundling Hospital.

Thomas Coram was born in Lyme Regis in 1668. How he spent all the eighty-four years of his active life is not

* See the Safeguarding of Industries Act, 1921. As Mr. Pecksniff said, " If anybody knows . . . an eligible opportunity now offers . . ."

fully known. He followed the sea in his early years, apparently, and then settled, appropriately enough for a Dorset
man, in Massachusetts, where he gave to the town of Taunton
land for a church or school, as occasion might arise : and
Mr. Speaker Onslow, a " warm friend " of his, gave, for the
use of the church subsequently built, a Book of Common
Prayer. Coram seems to have been a shipwright, and
eventually a shipowner, interested—again in the Dorset
manner—in the American fisheries. Indeed, that interest
gave him a title to fame not less authentic than his erection
of the Foundling Hospital. In 1735 he laid a memorial
before the King's Most Excellent Majesty in Council, re-
presenting that the cod-fisheries of Nova Scotia should be
developed, the country settled by " a competent number of
industrious Protestant families," and a suitable salt-station
for its benefit created in the Bahamas. After long considera-
tions and delay his project was carried out. There was no
noisy glory about this solid little achievement. It was a
quiet piece of what we have since been conjured to call
Empire-building.

As shipwright and shipmaster Coram prospered reasonably
and returned to England and settled in London about
1719. " While he lived in that part of this metropolis
which is the common residence of seafaring people "—
there are no further details : was it Ratcliffe or Wapping ?
I hope he lived near Captain Cook, his younger contemporary, in Stepney—" he used to come early into the city
and return late, according as his business required his
presence ; and both these circumstances afforded him frequent occasions of seeing young children exposed, sometimes
alive, sometimes dead, and sometimes dying, which affected
him extremely."

It took him seventeen years to affect other people extremely in this matter. Towards the end of these years of
effort, says his biographer, " this good man, whose head
was fertile in expedients, bethought himself at last of
applying to the ladies. He knew their nature, he knew their

influence, and soon found that he was in the right road.
They did not listen much to his arguments, for the sweetness
of their own tempers supplied a tenderness that rendered
arguments unnecessary." On October 17, 1729, he obtained
the charter of incorporation for an institution "for the
maintenance and education of deserted young children."

The charity is said to have been abused—not perhaps to
the extent of making illegitimate child-bearing a widespread habit, but at least enough to cause drastic revision
of the Foundling's rules, because the parish officers " emptied
their workhouses of the infant poor," dumping them in the
basket of reception hung outside the hospital. I have
attended the famous Sunday service there in these days,
and been shown the charming buildings by an obsequious
attendant ; and I do not like charitable institutions any
more than I like almshouses ; charity creates a multitude
of sins. Nevertheless, the name of Thomas Coram deserves
to live. He spent his hot-headed enthusiastic life in trying
to do good. He spent also his money—money indubitably
earned by his own exertions, for he was the son of a sea-
going ship's captain and did not start with wealth. He
died, as his epitaph says, " poor in worldly estate, rich in
good works." Towards the end of his life he himself was
kept by charity : a public subscription was opened for him,
and when he was asked if it would offend him, he answered
sturdily, " I have not wasted the little wealth I formerly
possessed in self-indulgence and vain expenses, and am not
ashamed to confess that, in this my old age, I am poor."
" He lived above the fear of anything but an unworthy
action." That is one eulogy of him : I think the simpler
and better is in the words I have quoted—"this good
man."

It is a curious and touching thing, the simplicity of the
seafaring life. The little " ports of stranded pride " seem
to preserve it, and its grandeur, too, in a more intimate
manner than the great harbours. In the homeliest terms
in daily use alongshore, there is often something large and

unexpected. Ask a creeping coaster whither he is bound.
He will not say to the Thames or London : he will say to
London River. It is a more majestic and spacious conception : it is geography in plain speech. Or look at the
humble voyages taken at a peradventure. I remember once
seeing a brand new Scandinavian ship come into Bridport
Harbour. It was her maiden voyage—just from Sweden
to this forgotten harbour, with timber. She was a lovely
boat, her decks shining, her paint all new, her tackle glistening, all her little bolts and blocks glorious. She was going
out in ballast to Cadiz, to pick up a cargo there : and thence
across the ocean to Rio, where the skipper hoped (but with
no certainty) to find some other load, and fare onwards
wherever the need might take him. All over the world on
chance.

I remember, too, one splendid land-fall in the autumn of
1914. It must have given to seafaring men some sense,
however dim, of the security which has been won in and by
England. On August 2nd a little schooner set out from
Archangel for Bridport. She was turned back from the
North Sea by reason of enemy mines, and she must voyage
all round the Shetlands and so into St. George's Channel
and round the Lizard. She touched at Lerwick and re-
provisioned for this longer journey. Down the western
coast she met with contrary winds, but she put in nowhere.
It was ten weeks before she turned well up Channel, and then
the tides and winds together were unfriendly ; for among
other hostile acts, Nature forbids entrance to Bridport
Harbour at low tide and when the wind is off shore. She
must beat on and off a few miles out for two days or more ;
and meanwhile every crumb of food on board was consumed. She could have made some Devon port without
trouble ; but West Bay was her journey's end, and to West
Bay alone in all the world would she go. And so at last,
after every known peril of the sea, starving but unconquered,
her crew of six brought her to the mark-buoy. The pilot
went aboard, and as the sun set she swayed slowly in ;

BRIDPORT HARBOUR

From an engraving of a drawing by J. M. W. Turner, R.A.

her Danish captain, a gay and gallant figure in bright blue trousers and a golden shirt, waving his hat in cheerful inarticulate triumph ; for though he had come safe to the one place in England he desired to reach, he could speak hardly a word of English.

If I want to feel really English, to draw into myself the life of the English sea, I will go to Bridport Harbour, and look at those little coasting vessels that have begun again to creep into the basin since the war. I will pat the large bollards—the wooden ones, like the wooden piles, are being changed for concrete—look once more at the painting of a three-decker on the rocket-house wall ; go into the Old Custom House—one of two " old " custom houses—and tread the stone flags and see again the faded lettering, " Long Room " and " Collector's Room," on the blackening doors : walk through Good's yard, up the brick and stone staircase climbing the enormous side of the barn, smell the timber and grain and rafters in the long upper floor with the square unglazed window looking over the Channel. And then I shall go up over the East Cliff, all among the horned sheep and the golfers, on a pilgrimage along the coast, past the villages that have bred so many seamen.

I shall not follow the shorter path inland, but the cliff edge, down into Port Coombe where the rabbits are, over the top and down to Burton Freshwater. O most desirable of places ! From nowhere are you not lovely. From the the road you are a green perspective for the golden beach and blue sea ; from the sea, beyond the carpet of pink thrift and yellow poppies, between your flaming cliffs, another green perspective for the stream (lined with comfrey and loosestrife) and the adorable village, with its grave simple church, its trees full of rooks, its meadows noisy with plover. This side the fields of asphodel, I want no more.

I come in due time by the field path alongside the magical river to Burton Bradstock itself : through Love Lane. Love Lane, a row of thatched cottages : life and love alike,

s

I daresay, are imperfect : no doubt these cottages also are imperfect : but not to me.

If you are a single-minded worshipper of external beauty you can stand a whole day in Burton in looking and looking and looking at the exterior of its cottages. There is not a bad building, from an æsthetic point of view, in the place, except the chief inn, and that is no worse than amusing. Your eye will wander over a wall and see here the amazing rich depth of gold in its stone : there the delicacy of the grey-green lichen : there the vivid blue of a periwinkle blossom, or the crimson of a fuchsia : here the admirable masonry of a dripstone, there the warm intimacy of a thatched eave. Or you can sit outside the inn, on the pavement, and see the narrow roads dropping away at your feet, or on the seats round the gossips' tree, and rest your eye always on peace and beauty.

From Love Lane go over the fields close to the two outrageous red villas half a mile away, just above the beach : hateful landmarks for many miles. Pass them and go up over the little hill to the decent yellow coastguard station, with its border, in the coastguard station manner of white-washed stones. After that you can choose either of two ways—along the shore, or a little higher, by the road.

Along the shore you pass Burton or Cogden Mere, a place for many kinds of waterfowl. It varies curiously in its wetness. Do not try to take short-cuts in this region. There is a straight track along the inside of the curve of the Chesil Bank. In some seasons it is good going on thin grass : in others you have to plough over slippery shingle ; the condition depends on the force and number of recent gales.

If you have a dog he will find and chase innumerable hares here ; yea, even on the beach itself. All these parts are full of them : I have seen as many as seventeen in a field at once, and I have also witnessed their fantastic March dances : once a party of friends caught a leveret with their bare hands.

You walk four miles or so to the roar of the sea. In the calmest weather there is always a roar as the waves slide back down the deep slope of the shingle. It is unwise to bathe here alone, especially just below Swyre, where in addition to the strong undertow, there is at times a dangerous current.* Between that point and Burton, probably, is one end of the tide that sweeps up from Start Point : but the whole bay, with the Race at Portland and the currents at Deadman's Bay and west of Lyme Cobb, is at times menacing, for all its calm appearance.

In due course you come to another seemly coastguard station, and pass below the farms of Bexington (which has an aisle all to itself in Puncknowle Church) and Labour-in-Vain, and then you must leave the shore before you reach the Fleet, and go by a footpath over the hill to the road that runs past Lord Ilchester's tropical gardens (full of exotic plants flourishing in the open all the year round), and so to the point where the main Burton road reaches level ground at last.

If you go by the road you see the same great bay from higher ground. You climb slowly uphill for a mile, and then down into the tail end of Swyre, where the base of the village cross still stands as a loafing pitch. You turn sharply to the right and sharply to the left (many cyclists have been injured or even killed here in past days : there is a concealed gate round a right angle), and are then faced by about four miles uphill along the most beautiful coast road I know. It runs over open rough land, once much more fully cultivated than now, unhedged, sloping gently to the sea half a mile or so away ; and all along is the immense smooth curve between Portland and Start Point, until at last you reach Abbotsbury Camp and look down on that still more glorious view which I have already described.

Looking back towards evening you get perhaps the finest

---

* In the last year of the war the current saved a man's life. He was lashed to a piece of wood and washed ashore there, and pulled out just in time, after nearly a day in the water. His ship had been sunk by an enemy submarine.

sight of all this pageantry of cliffs. You see the full majesty of the great hills which appear so noble from Lyme. From this Abbotsbury road, late in the day, you have them with the sun behind them, and they fall into a succession of sharp silhouettes, with purple dusk (deepening as it creeps westward) between each fold, and the sea like a lake at their feet.

Abbotsbury, like Swyre, Burton, and Bridport Harbour, is a stronghold of the mackerel industry. Many thousands may come ashore in one catch ; I have seen seven thousand at a time. Often they are preceded by still more multitudinous catches of sprats, so numerous that the packed seine looks like a silver furze bush from their protruding heads and tails. The sprats hunt the " bait "—little things an inch or two long who make the water close inshore black. The mackerel hunt the sprats. The porpoise, leaping joyously, hunt the mackerel, as may be seen on any fine August day.

At Abbotsbury, when the season is near, a watch is still kept up from immemorial times. A looker-out sits with a great horn upon St. Catherine's Hill, or on the Chesil Bank, and when the water grows dark with fish, winds his horn ; whereupon the nets and boats—mostly row-boats—are hastily got out. I do not know how they dispose of the catch at Abbotsbury ; but at Bridport, directly the news of the fishes' coming is hinted, the chief local fish dealer rushes down in his cart from the town with dozens of boxes of all kinds, and supernumerary vehicles if the season is good—nowadays sometimes with a motor lorry. If the catch is a big one, it is brought to the harbour steps in boats, and laboriously counted out into hundreds : for every hundred the boat owner puts aside a tally-fish—his account and his perquisite together. The price paid him varies : I have known it ten a penny. Odd fish—large, fresh, and good—can usually be bought by private persons for a penny or two—a few more or less do not matter to a big catch. The boxes are hastily loaded up and trundled up the hill to Bridport. A small proportion is kept for local sale : at a price usually differing *longo intervallo* from that paid at the harbour steps. The rest go off by rail or road to Bristol or Salisbury or Bournemouth or London. And there is mirth in the Harbour inns that night.

The mackerel, well cooked—in half a dozen different ways—and only half an hour dead, is as fair food as any man might seek. And if the trade were thoroughly organized, so that the fish reached small centres in the West directly and quickly, it might be made not only more profitable to the dealers than it is, but more profitable to the fishermen themselves. I will say nothing of the operations of a great trader who even in that remote region has tried to create better organization. Whether he succeeds or fails, I believe that this seasonal and uncertain trade *could* be put on a sounder footing. It requires three things it has not got : a sound and cheap and widespread telephone service, an efficient motor-lorry service (capable of other uses out of season), and a curing shed—for the kippered mackerel, properly treated, is as good as any kippered herring ; and at present fresh fish not quickly distributed have to be used as manure.

At Abbotsbury, according to Mr. H. J. Moule (in *Somerset and Dorset Notes and Queries*), there was, eighty or more years ago, a belief that boats could be bewitched : if so, they caught nothing. It is certainly strange how sometimes, when the sea is visibly swarming with fish, they will not be caught. The Abbotsbury men used to tie " holy stones "— pebbles with a natural hole in them—" to nails or staples in the bows, close beneath the gunwale," and they had a peculiar way of coiling their stern-ropes for the same purpose.

I have spoken of the Abbey at Abbotsbury, but not of the Swannery. This is, I believe, the largest in the world. Before the war it held 1200 monstrous fine birds, the contemplation of which made you ill content, afterwards, with the skinny fowl of other waters. The lovely creatures have been kept there continuously since Henry VIII's time, and possibly for many centuries earlier. They are very highly civilized. In the contrived walks you pass their nests and themselves at the closest quarters, not without awe ; because from elegant ornaments they may become fierce wild fowl. The veteran keeper once (outside the exhibition season—in spring) pulled an old cob off his nest for me (the male and female take turns on the eggs), to show his weapons of offence. The keeper wore thick leather gaiters. The angry bird hissed, and put all his hackles up : his neck became like a nutmeg-grater meant for cocoanuts. He pecked : and the sound on the gaiters was as that of a hammer. Then he spread his huge wings, and slapped with the outer pinions. It was as if a cane was being beaten on wood. And then he drew himself more erect. But at that the keeper for a moment deftly caught a wing pinion and pulled the wing out for me to see, the bird, still half tame, half wild, merely swearing. The keeper showed me the last weapon : a terrific knob, with a queer little hook in it, at the elbow joint (wrist joint, anatomically, for the pinions are our fingers ; but elbow is more natural). That had broken three ribs of an under-keeper not long ago. He drove the indignant father back to his nest, by gesticulation ; and he settled down sulkily. His lady was out shopping.

I observed, in the course of several visits, not only how tame they were, but how effete. In the nesting season, great parcels of twigs are brought to the walks and thrown down. A few birds will do their own furnishing. The rest require help. The keeper, seeing a couple anxious to set up house together, takes a bundle of twigs and throws it down in some likely haunt, and stirs it roughly into the form of a nest. Presently along comes Lord Cygnus, and notices the desirable mansion. He pulls a twig or two this way and that, and lo, a nest ! Exegit monumentum. And mighty proud he and his wife are of it.

It is a wonderful sight, that great lagoon covered by vast snowflakes : wonderful to behold the heavy uprising of a

flight of them, from the water, scuttering along like an aero-
plane before it lifts, for their bodies are heavy : wonderful
also to see the tremendous impetus with which they touch
the water again and rush through it till the resistance stops
them : most wonderful of all to hear the glorious metallic
clang of their wings as eight or ten in a V-shaped formation
fly over your head, their beautiful long necks straight,
their noble pinions flapping strongly in the tremendous
carriage of their body. English birds have many flights
more graceful, but none more impressive, nor, I think,
more splendid than the swan's, unless it be the heron's.

If you wander along from Abbotsbury on the inner
side of the Fleet, you will be near the scene of various
wrecks. The villages are chiefly a little inland, well sheltered
from the inhospitable beach. I may add two disasters to
those already mentioned. Below Fleet, in 1747, a Dutch
boat, the *Hope* of Amsterdam, went ashore : most of her
crew were saved. She carried about £50,000 in specie and
jewels. The whole neighbourhood swarmed to the spot
and carried off all they could lay hands upon. There were
furious combats over the possession of the property. No
one was killed in the tumult, but several perished of cold
and exposure on the inhospitable Bank, as they wearily
sought for loot. The military were called out, and eventually
about £20,000 or £30,000 was recovered and salvage paid
on it.

A grimmer record still is that of the transports which set
sail in 1795 under Abercrombie for the West Indies. They
met a gale, and were blown haphazard on to the Bank.
Two hundred and thirty-four bodies were recovered at
various points.

Just outside the entrance to the Swannery (down past
the glorious barn, which in length surpasses that of Fro-
cester, said by the invaluable Muirhead to be the largest
in England, by 92 feet) is a board on a post some three times
the height of a man. It tells how in 1824 the sea reached its
summit at that spot. The pole is nearly half a mile inland

from high-water mark. If you go down to the Chesil Beach
and look at the stones, now far larger than at any point
on your past walk, you will simply wonder : the only comment is "credo, quia incredibile." It did happen, because
a ship at the same time was deposited on top of the Bank.
This storm destroyed the old church at Fleet. That extraordinary effort of the sea was repeated in (I think) 1914,
when a biggish iron coaster, the *Dorothea*, was lifted up on
to the crest of the Beach by a huge sea. She lay there for
the best part of one winter, and various salvage companies
in turns sought to dislodge her, and lost their money. The
third or fourth thought of the device of putting rollers just
under her keel at the bows and digging the beach away :
whereupon she slid back into her element.

It is best not to pursue the coast here, but to walk on
from Abbotsbury to Portisham—Portesham or Possum :
a little square village sleeping beneath the chalk hills.
There is a pretty path across the fields to it. The best
summary of the compact and pretty place is the motto of
one of its sons—Sir Andrew Riccard, a great East India
merchant enriched in London by his own exertions, who
died in 1672. He punned : " Possum "—" I can." I do
not suggest that the village, with its rivulets and stone
houses, looks peculiarly efficient. But I am quite sure
that anyone who came out of these beautiful cottages or
worshipped in the beautiful church must be trustworthy—
in spite of all I have said about the smugglers.

Hardy and the smugglers and others commemorated in the
church showed that they lived up to the Latin pun—they
could and did. Here is buried a stout Royalist, not to be
withheld from politics even after death :—

> " William Weare lies here in dust
> As thou and I and all men must.
> Once plundered by Sabaean force—
> Some called it war, but others worse—
> With confidence he pleads his cause
> And King's to be above those laws.
> September's eighth day died he
> When near the date of 63,
> Anne Domini 1670."

His slab is now outside the church. Inside is a memorial to another of his family who died five years later, the wife of Robert Weare (the race intermarried with various local families of repute) :—

> " Underneath lies her whose actions pen'd
> The perfect copie of a friend :
> Whose good sweet heart did always shun
> Such things as ought not to be done.
> Rest there, for ever rest alone,
> Thy ashes can be touch'd by none."

Can they not ? There are Norman remains, including a font, in this venerable building, whose stone has weathered with a peculiar graciousness. But where are the dead Normans ? Where are the ashes or the bones of all the innumerable dead—innumerable even in a tiny village like this, whose written history goes back to Cnut ? I read that in excavating under St. Mary-le-Bow, in London, among structures several hundred years old, enquirers could dig no deeper than a few feet, because they came upon the underlying dead, whom they would not willingly disturb. But we know that many coffins and skeletons for which search has been made have vanished, along with the pious decrees of their tenants. Where, for instance, at Wimborne, is King Ethelred, who has two brasses and no coffin ? Where is the martyr at Shaftesbury ? Where is " the perfect copy of a friend " here at Portisham ? Where *are* all the dead ?

The rest of the country between Portisham and Weymouth, if you follow (approximately) the coast, is dull. Fleet, Langton Herring (" Alward held it in King Edward's time. Hugh son of Grip. . . ."), West Chickerel are negligible and uninteresting villages, and the country is undistinguished by anything except ordinary cultivation. Mohuns are buried at Fleet : their memorials record emphatically their own worthiness, the chastity of their wives, and the serenity of James I.

The roads hereabouts, before the days of charabancs, were good to walk upon for exercise, and no more. You can take a more desirable track either side of the railway from Portisham, to Upwey : one side along the little chalk ridge of Friar Waddon, the other past nowhere in particular : both to Upwey, where you begin to realize how loathsome the suburbs of a modern watering-place can be.

And so to Weymouth, which must have been much pleasanter in Farmer George's day than now. In the immortal phrase of Sam Lewis about Rome, "You can 'ave Weymouth."

And yet, if you go down to the unfailing interest of the quay—all quays are interesting—or ferry across to the Nothe, or stand near the statue—and look at the wonderful bay and the George III houses, it is impossible not to recapture some of the meaning of Weymouth. Here, in this place that the holidays of an urban population have made so disagreeable, the Romans built a temple to other gods than ours—if we have one. Here the Danes first slew a King's man. The town—itself for centuries torn by the rivalry between Melcombe and Weymouth, now one—stood up against the dominant Cinque Ports. It gave the Black Death to England. It sent ships to the Armada, and received their captures. It suffered in the usual way during the Civil War, and in the end grew, under the stimulus of George III's visit and the much later approach of the railways, into a large thriving aggregation of human beings.

What I complain of at Weymouth is not its prosperity or its efficiency, but the desperate ugliness, even sordidness of everything modern in it. Even its bridge is mean. The newer buildings have not so much as the credit of vulgarity on the grand scale. The amazing Jubilee clock is symbolical. It is of iron painted green and yellow, in the Public Lavatory Style, with a sort of bas-relief of Victoria on each of its sides.*

* This appalling erection is probably the inspiration of another in the public gardens at Dorchester, smaller, quite as ugly, but much funnier, because the Dorchester donor, an ex-mayor, whose image facially is not at all calculated to recall the Antinous or the Hermes, has caused his own likeness to appear on each of the green and gold sides. He was a good citizen and benefactor, but this clock tower is a mistake.

Will our handiwork of that age ever be thought beautiful, as we now think that of the Georgian era beautiful ? I hope so : but I fear not. But I am sure, on the other hand, that modern life, with all its swollen triviality and deformity, can still produce the spirit of the older centuries : produce it as surely and as gaily as Trumpet-Major Loveday, of Sutton Poyntz, near Weymouth : " The candle held by his father shed its waving light upon John's face and uniform as with a farewell smile he turned on the doorstone, backed by the black night ; and in another moment he had plunged into the darkness, the ring of his smart step dying away upon the bridge as he joined his companions in arms, and went off to blow his trumpet till silenced for ever upon one of the bloody battlefields of Spain."

XIII

" Britain, insignificant on the map of Europe, could scarcely sustain her
starving sons with bread and water, were it not for her trade, hitherto
secured in its pre-eminence by the operation of wise laws and institutions—by the character of a well-ordered and industrious population ; but, what are many of us now doing, let me ask you, my friends ?
I will answer this question, from the speech in the House of Commons,
of a gentleman whose ability to inform us, cannot be doubted, no
friend of the present ministers. He plainly tells us that monied men
will not remain to carry on trade and manufactures amongst a dis-
satisfied people, who are threatening to throw all into confusion ; they
are withdrawing themselves and their money into other countries.
. . . I beseech you, my friends, to return into the good old-fashioned
ways of common sense ; let us lay aside all these new-fangled notions
that have been put into our heads, and industriously pursue our proper
business. Let our behaviour to our superiors be decent, and respect-
ful, looking on them with goodwill and kindness, taking pleasure in
their prosperity—this as Christians."

The Friendly Fairy (Anon), 1820.

" The ostensible object of these associations was to keep a check on their
employers. . . . Every person, on being a member, bound himself by
an oath administered in the most solemn manner, not to disclose anything which might take place among them. That these associations
were most dangerous, no one could doubt ; it could not be proper that
the working orders of the people should meet together, and bind
themselves not to disclose their proceedings : it might be used for the
most dangerous purposes as regards the welfare of the state."

Counsel for prosecution in Rex v. Brice and others.
Annual Register, 1834.

THE SEQUESTERED VALE

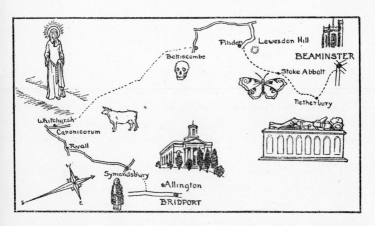

FARMER GEORGE had taken a genuine interest in agriculture, and, whether through his direct influence or not, his reign saw an immense improvement in methods of farming and stock-breeding. It was in the middle of the eighteenth century that the Dorset Horn sheep began to attract attention as a separate breed, and the Dorset Down sheep in 1743 was said by Gawler (a bad poet) to "keep half the nation warm." But the larger changes implied in the term "high farming" did not reach the county in any marked degree till after George III's death. The peasants as a whole lived the life of haphazard squalor described by Fielding : keeping a pig or a cow, if they could, on the common land which still existed. "We present," said the Manorial Court of Grimstone in 1728, "that Margaret Slowe hath a right to drive sheep and cattle to and from Grimstone Common to a close of Meadow

271

called Smithams, over the currant (*sic*) called Muckleford
Lake . . . and that John Sabbin and Robert Wood and
others the inhabitants of Muckleford have deprived the said
Margaret Slowe of the way by enlarging the said currant
about two foot wider than it antiently was, which was done
by cutting Grimstone Common."

Not an enclosure, perhaps ; but at least an attempt to
jump a communal claim of right. Here are communal
duties :

" 1753. We present that the tenants of this Manor shall
go out on the 6th day of March next, and shall dig and drain
the meadows, for carrying off the water, under a penalty
of 6s. 8d. for everyone neglecting. . . .

" 1781. We present that no pigs run about the streets
or other Commonable places of this said Liberty and Manor
under penalty of 5s."

It would be foolish to assert that the enclosure of common
land brought no benefits. It certainly made for better
crops : it might in a few good cases make for greater
amenities in village life. But it did not, as eulogists of
modern county society sometimes seem to hint, create
Arcadias watched over and mustered by a benevolent
squire : it simply deprived the pre-existing village of its
thousand-year-old rights and conveniences.

For with the enclosure independence became a greater
sham than before. The villager was still tied to one place
by the parish machinery, and he now lost the magic of his
little property in the seized common. It is possible, as was
claimed in a famous Somerset report, that that very property
had made him idle. But the right to any leisure he could
earn was hardly recognized : eighteenth-century landlords
were as keen as Carlyle on work—for the lower orders.
What happened was that without his pig or cow or fowls on
the common pasture the peasant had got to work solely
for a wage—a wage not likely to be made unduly high.
Prices rose steadily, and the growth of the larger industrial

centres, with their new machinery, killed the little local trades like weaving, baize-making, button-making, in which Dorset at least had been rich.

The wage-earning farm labourer . . . I know one alive now, a man of sixty or so, capable of begetting a strong progeny, who, on the estate of a good Dorset landlord, has never been able to afford to marry : he had to maintain his parents : and he is not a bad character ; on the contrary, his landlord respects him and aids him by gifts of comfort— of comfort to a single man—and of a friendly intercourse which is wholly admirable. A century and a quarter ago, in words which later he revised slightly so as to leave out the local application, Wordsworth (of all men—he who uttered nothing base !) told a little of the truth about the Dorset poor :

> " Auld Goody Blake was old and poor,
> Ill fed she was, and thinly clad ;
> And any man who pass'd her door
> Might see how poor a hut she had.

> " All day she spun in her poor dwelling,
> And then her three hours' work at night !
> Alas ! 'twas hardly worth the telling,
> It would not pay for candlelight.

> " —This woman dwelt in Dorsetshire,
> Her hut was on a cold hill-side,
> And in that country coals are dear,
> For they come far by wind and tide.*"

Wordsworth—in 1789, in the full glow of the Republican ardour which he lost with so much scorn in his later sonnets —was at least symptomatic, from a political point of view, of a possible change in public opinion and taste. The lower orders were attracting notice, almost becoming fashionable. On the other hand, a lesser poet hard by, William Crowe

* I suspect that the poet, not a rich man, may have suffered from that lack of coal at Racedown, on the edge of Marshwood Vale, the beautiful little house of the Pinneys in which he lived for a time : can it be that his removal to Nether Stowey brought him more coal and caused him to substitute in the poem the version now current, omitting all mention of fuel, and the name of the county.

T

of Oxford and Stoke Abbott, felt compelled to apologize
for doing what *Lyrical Ballads* did later without apology.
Crowe was wont (a wise habit) to sit on Lewesdon Hill
and admire the prospect ; and he wrote a poem, *Lewesdon
Hill*, " the fruit," as his epitaph at Stoke says, " of his
musings upon that eminence." It is not at all a bad poem,
by contemporary formal standards. The notes contain this
prophetic counterblast to Wordsworth and Coleridge :
" the author having ventured to introduce some provincial
and other terms, takes this occasion to say that it is a
liberty in which he has not indulged himself but when
he conceived it to be allowable for the sake of ornament
or expression."

That is the unhappy converse of the kindly Georgian
pomp—the emphatic ignoring of the misery of the poor in
so far as aristocratic benevolence did not touch it, and the
hardly less obvious conviction of the necessity of such misery,
which clearly, in so perfect a world, must be the natural
result and reward of insubordination or immorality. There
were, however, those who at least lifted up their voices
against the vices of establishment. William Moreton Pitt,
of the great family, M.P. for the county, and active in many
useful projects, addressed " the landed interest " in 1791,
on the subject of housing and fuel shortage. I do not feel
sure that his words are irrelevant to-day. " A large proportion of the poor," he said, " are absolutely precluded
from leaving the parishes in which they happen to reside ;
if those, who have been removed by the order of two justices,
again leave their place of legal settlement, they render
themselves liable to punishment, as rogues and vagabonds ;
and many, who have not been removed, but who have large
families, and who of course suffer the most, are least able
to change their places of residence, yet often cannot obtain
cottages to live in, though able and willing to pay rent.
. . . They have no resource but to be taken into a wretched
poor-house, there to associate with the old, the infirm, and
decrepid (*sic*), idiots and insane persons, the idle and

dissolute, loathsome from filth, and infested with vermin."
This Pitt (never mind the exact turn of his reasoning)
pleaded, virtually, for smallholdings to be created from
" rough, encumbered and uncultivated tracts of land " ;
for the brewing of small beer in every cottage ; the keeping
of pigs, the advancing of money in the form of purchased
material. " It seems to me that the feelings, and even the
prejudices of the poor, are entitled to the most full and
dispassionate consideration. These workhouses are un-
questionably *places of confinement*, and there can exist no
right to consign people, because they are poor, to a prison,
and to act towards them as if they were delinquents,
because they cannot maintain themselves without assistance." He appended to his " address " full and careful
plans of the cottages he wished to see built.

Quite a different type of landlord was a town-planner
of the same era—Lord Dorchester of Milton Abbas, whose
pompous and preposterous monument is in the exquisite
Abbey. Horace Walpole describes him with some bitterness :
"Lord Milton"—his first title: he became Earl of Dorchester
in 1792—" heir of Swift's old miser and usurer Damer, was
the most arrogant and proud of men, with no foundation
but great wealth and a match with the Duke of Dorset's
daughter. His birth and parts were equally mean and
contemptible."

This gentleman of England, acquiring the estate of Milton
Abbey, found the old village, which nestled beneath the
shadows of the great tower, an eyesore : it was close to the
windows of the ponderous neo-Gothic mansion Chambers
built him. So, like the African magician in the case of
Aladdin, he had it removed. He cared nothing for the
villagers' protests : his workmen might make jests of their
ancestors' bones in the old burial ground—he would build
them a fine new village : anyhow, he was not going to catch
sight of them every time he looked out of the window.

They were turned out neck and crop : the memory of the
arbitary act lived long. On the other hand, Lord Dorchester

built the present adorable village to receive them. But for
one or two new and ugly houses, and an unimpressive
church, it stands to-day as it was designed in 1786, a Noah's
Ark street of square yellow houses at regular intervals,
with chestnut trees in between and a backing of dark trees
up each side of the ravine in which they are so admirably
set.

It was not only definite tyranny of that type which the
labourers had to suffer. The agricultural reports of the
time are a record of little but hard work and starvation :
Eden's *State of the Poor* (1797) gives a labourer's
budget. A man at Blandford had two daughters and two
sons : his wife was dead. The elder daughter managed the
house : the rest earned nothing. House-rent was paid by
the parish. " The usual breakfast of the family is tea, or
bread and cheese ; their dinner, and supper, bread and
cheese, or potatoes sometimes mashed with fat taken from
broth, and sometimes with salt alone. Bullock's cheek is
generally bought every week to make broth. Treacle is used
to sweeten tea, instead of sugar. Very little milk or beer is
used. For clothing, both for himself and family, the man
is principally indebted to the charity of his neighbours."
His earnings that year were £17 9s. 6d.

The food of the poor, wrote Stevenson in 1812—in an
official report—" is wheaten bread, skim-milk cheese,
puddings, potatoes, and other vegetables, with a small
quantity of pickled pork and bacon." The potatoes they
probably grew on their employers' fallows, as they were
allowed to do. The concession was an ingenious device,
for it " affords a means of keeping the labourers more under
subjection, and prevents their leaving their master at least
during the summer, as in that case the crop would be
forfeited."

Stevenson says the land was badly farmed, as a rule.
The tendency was to amalgamate small farms, which should
have made for better methods. But John Claridge, reporting
to the Board of Agriculture and Internal Improvement in

1793, states the drawback to that process. He is an expert and moderate writer. "In many parts of Dorsetshire," he says, "one man occupies a whole hamlet, parish, or lordship; perhaps from 1500 to 2000 acres, which I fear has been too frequently made, by laying five or six farms together, and thereby striking a fatal blow at the little farmer, who is one of the most useful members of society.* The increase of large farms, evidently tends to place the great farmer at too wide a distance from the labourer, whom he considers a mere vassal, and though he employs him, and pays what he calls a customary price; still it is out of the power of the labourer, either by strength or ingenuity, or the most indefatigable industry, scarcely to supply his family with the common necessaries of life; and the moment his activity ceases, he becomes a pauper; the most he finds himself in possession of, is a cottage, seldom in good repair, a very small garden, and he can hire no land, even if he has a friend inclined to assist him with money or credit." That is from an official document. We have lately abolished the Agricultural Wages Board, to the unconcealed joy of the farmer, and once more he " pays what he calls a customary price."

If William IV had not been ready to create peers in 1831, to pass the Reform Bill, England might have had a revolution as bloody as the French one. Plans were ready for an armed rising. The agricultural labourer would not have been backward in such a movement. He had already begun to riot all over England.

"On the 22nd of November," wrote Mary Frampton of the year 1830, " the first risings took place in this county. Mr. Portman [of Bryanston: afterwards Viscount Portman] immediately promised to raise the wages of his labourers, and by doing this without concert with other gentlemen, greatly increased their difficulties." At Winfrith, " the mob, urged on from behind hedges, etc., by a number of women and children, advanced rather respectfully, and

* Perhaps; in 1793; to-day only if he is very competent.

with their hats in their hands, to demand increase of wages, but would not listen to the request that they would disperse."

There were many rick-burnings ; the authors were as a rule untraced. The diarist records her satisfaction with the result in cases where conviction was possible. " One of the motions made by Mr. Hunt on the first day of his appearance in the House of Commons, was for a petition to the King, to pardon all the unhappy men who had been convicted at the Special Assizes. Fortunately, however, as they were already on board the transports, and the wind fair, the petition would be too late. Care was taken . . . to send them to those parts of New Zealand and New Holland where their agricultural knowledge and labour might be useful—thus very probably at a future time rendering our disturbances here a blessing to our Antipodes."

But in spite of such measures, the discontent and the disorder remained. In 1831 the Dorset Yeomanry were re-enrolled to cope with the situation. A contested election of a member for the county that year showed the height of feeling. Mr. Ponsonby and Lord Ashley were the candidates, Lord Ashley standing for the gentry and farmers, Mr. Ponsonby for Reform. There was virtually a pitched battle at the poll at Poundbury. A house was destroyed at Blandford. Every pane of glass in Sherborne Castle was broken by rioters, as well as many in the town. A mob from Poole was expected to attack Corfe Castle and Encombe House, but the yeomanry were called out and held Wareham. " The minds of the common people," writes Mary Frampton, " are wickedly excited by persons of a somewhat higher class," who raised penny subscriptions to get reformers elected, and said that " 'Reform' would give them meat as well as bread in abundance by paying only a quarter, if so much, of the present price for those articles. How can the poor resist such tempting language ? " I should prefer to ask, why should they ?

All over the county, " bands of labourers assembled together, firing farmhouses, destroying machinery, and threatening the country houses of the gentry." Apart from the demonstration mentioned, there was a riot at Winfrith ; but Mr. James Frampton produced one hundred and forty mounted men, and charged the mob. The troops remained loyal ; as a eulogist wrote of the Blandford squadron :

" . . . Should the Demon of Intestine strife
　　Threat even our houses, our altar desecrate,
　Where is the Yeoman who would value life
　　To Guard from Rapine all that's good and great ? "

When the Reform Bill was first thrown out, there were further riots at Sherborne, quelled by the yeomanry. At Stour Provost rioters broke a threshing machine and surrounded the Rectory. The parson was an ex-officer of the Peninsular War. He had his own methods. He " singled out the ringleader, and having presented him with a sovereign, sent the rioters away well contented to spend it as they liked. The next day a detachment of Captain Jacob's troop from Sturminster Newton, under the command of a Non-Commissioned Officer named Harvey, came to the assistance of the Rector. The ringleader was apprehended, and sentenced to seven years' penal servitude."

The culmination, in Dorset, was the episode of the little band of poor peasants known to history as the Dorchester labourers.

The names of these unhappy men were George Loveless (who wrote a slightly rhetorical account of their sufferings), James Loveless, Thomas and John Stanfield (father and son ; John was the Loveless's nephew ; a family " conspiracy " !) James Hammett, and James Brine. James Loveless apparently was the leader. He seems to have invented the ritual of oaths, blindfoldings, and costume under which they " conspired." They certainly did " conspire," in a technical sense. Equally certainly, almost every one set in authority over them from the moment of their arrest treated them as the vilest of criminals, without regard to the extent or ferocity of their conspiracy.

Loveless gives this account of their grievances. " In the year 1831-2, there was a general movement of the working-classes for an increase of wages, and the labouring men in the parish where I lived (Tolpiddle) gathered together, and met their employers, to ask them for an advance of wages, and they came to a mutual agreement, the masters in Tolpiddle promising to give the men as much for their labour as the other masters in the district." He says there were no threats or intimidation, and that he himself, in view of the frequent incendiarism, was chosen as part of the watch against fires. But he was a Dissenter, and " by some in Tolpiddle, it is considered as the sin of witchcraft." " Shortly after, we learnt that, in almost every place around us, the masters were giving their men money, or money's worth, to the amount of ten shillings per week—we expected to be entitled to as much—but no—nine shillings must be our portion. After some months we were reduced to eight shillings per week." The wage or its equivalent was subsequently reduced to seven shillings and then six shillings was suggested. Thereupon " it was resolved to form a friendly society among the labourers, having sufficiently learnt that it would be vain [to] seek redress either of employers, magistrates, or parsons "—whom they had consulted already.

They did not know it was illegal to associate for such a purpose. On February 21, 1834, warning notices were posted by the magistrates. On February 29th the " conspirators " were all arrested, and walked peaceably with the constable to Dorchester, seven miles away. They were taken to the prison, identified, searched, and their heads shorn. Some days later they appeared before the magistrates and were committed for trial. The chaplain and "a Mr. Young, an attorney," tried to get Loveless to reveal their supposed plans. The authorities had the fear (not uncommon among authorities) of hidden plots of incredible magnitude.

On March 15th they were taken to the County Hall and
"ushered down some steps into a miserable dungeon,"
where they waited three days, and were then tried. "Our
masters were inquired of to know if we were not idle, or
attended public-houses, or some other fault in us ; and much
as they were opposed to us, they had common honesty
enough to declare that we were good labouring servants,
and that they never heard of any complaint against us."
Loveless says the judge was hostile. At any rate, he
sentenced them all to seven years' transportation, after he
had adjourned for two days to consider a protest by their
counsel.

On April 5th, with irons on his legs, Loveless was moved
to Portsmouth, where he worked for six weeks or so ; and
then on May 25th, in irons still, he sailed for Australia,
with twelve score other convicts. "A berth about five feet
six inches square was all that was allowed"—on a fourteen
weeks' voyage—"for six men to occupy day and night."

George Loveless was allotted to Tasmania. He "worked
on the roads with the chain-gang in the day," for a week or
so, and then on a Government farm. "Our hut was none
of the best : in fine weather we could lie in bed and view
the stars, in foul weather feel the wind and rain ; and this
added greatly to increase those rheumatic pains which were
first brought on by cold irons round the legs and hard
lying." The farm work continued till February, 1836,
when he was released on ticket-of-leave and told to find
work for himself. A month before he had been allowed to
write and ask his wife and children to come out to Tasmania,
at the Government expense : he did so with reluctance,
for he thought the life too hard and strange for them. He
got employment after a long search, and then learnt that
the home agitation against the harsh sentences was taking
effect. In October, 1836, he was given a free pardon and
offered a free passage home, but delayed accepting it till
he heard whether his wife was setting out or not. He arrived
in London on June 13th, 1837.

The other five offenders were sent to Sydney and assigned to different masters. John Stanfield was sent to a farm near his father, 150 miles up-country. A few weeks after he got there, he got leave to go and see his parent. " He [the older man] was then a dreadful spectacle, covered with sores from head to foot, and weak and helpless as a child." It is possible that his condition was caused by the custom of flogging shepherds and cattle-men who by accident let a beast or two of their huge herds go astray. Loveless quotes a bad master who got a magistrate's order to give fifty lashes to one such man. The culprit was then set to carry logs on his injured back, and, being unable to endure it, ran away, was caught, and got fifty more lashes. He ran away three times more, and received the same penalty each time ; again, and was sentenced to a sixth fifty—but this time, as his back " was in such a dreadful state," on another part of the body.

In 1836 John Stanfield and his father—chained together —were transferred, for some reason not explained to them, to Sydney gaol, being treated with the utmost severity and coarseness on the way. They were then set to work in a gang, where eventually James Loveless and Brine joined them. Stanfield petitioned successfully to be transferred back to his old master, and all four were so transferred. They were pardoned in 1837, and reached Plymouth on March 17, 1838. " The next day we proceeded through Exeter, where we were welcomed by a public meeting, to our native village, Tolpiddle, Dorsetshire, arriving in safety to the great joy of our relatives and friends."

The experiences of James Loveless were much the same. James Brine fared worse. He had the misfortune to be robbed, of all except some old clothes, by bushrangers, as he was on the way to his master, up-country. His master asked him where his provided " slops " and bedding were. He told him of the robbery. " He swore I was a liar, and said he would give me a ' d—d good flogging ' in the morning. ' You are one of the Dorsetshire machine-breakers,' said

he, ' but you are caught at last.' He gave me nothing to eat
until the following day." (Brine had had but one meal
during the three previous days.) And his master gave him
no clothes nor bedding for six months. "'If you ask me
for anything before the six months is expired, I will flog
you as often as I like.'" This man was a magistrate.

The sentence and the sufferings were long remembered :
long enough for the locality to set up, during the Great War
of 1914–1918, a monument to the sufferers. It was unveiled
by one of His Majesty's Ministers, a member of the War
Cabinet, who, like those he commemorated, was a labourer
and a Trade Unionist.

Their toil, and the toil of generations of their fathers,
made the England we see now. They mixed their labour
with that land ; but little of the goodly heritage is yet
theirs. See what they and others have made of Marshwood
Vale. Start at Beaminster.

The greater part of Beaminster was burnt down in 1781.
Hence the neat beauty of the little town now. It is just a
satisfactory large village, except for one thing in it—the
church, a dominant building fit for a town. The church by
some accident escaped the Puritan iconoclast, and the very
beautiful tower bears a cluster of images all up its surface,
gracious saints under canopies, in golden stone. It is the
most lovely tower in Dorset.

From its bells issue every three hours hymn tunes, as
elsewhere in the county. Within, it is spacious and decent.
It contains the monument of an Oglander of Parnham in
the theatrical style : that very old family succeeded, in
possession of the noble manor-house and its lands, the still
older family of Strode. Parnham House, half a mile away,
is a glory of Dorset.

The church also contains a pleasant punning epitaph,
hidden behind the organ : It is of 1653 :

> " 'Tis not because the woman's virtue dies,
>   That the brass tells us here Ann Hillary lies ;
>   Her name's long lov'd—she is in this commended,
>   The poor cry out, their Hillary term is ended."

There is a footpath to Netherbury which brings you out near its hardly less admirable church. Netherbury itself might be an emblem of much of Dorset's share in English history. Five miles away Bridport has clung to the great world by its ropes. Beaminster, with the church and its mart of incomparable cheeses, is as it were a secret metropolis. These two places are also joined by a road, along which a motor-bus service and motor-mail service of terrifying violence ply. But Netherbury is not upon that road. Netherbury is not really upon any road, though since a village, to exist, must be capable of being reached, some roads run to it. If you come by any way but the Beaminster footpath you find Netherbury by means of a map. You do not find it by direct vision or distant prospect. You turn down an unsuggestive lane with high banks west of the Bridport-Beaminster road : and in a quarter of a mile you are in the midst of a village compact, cheerful, reasonably active, and completely hidden from the traffic of the world.

Netherbury for centuries has had two industries : the making of sails and nets, and the growing of cider apples. Upon these homely slighted trades the village has maintained its peaceful existence. Once it was an abode of great folk : Beaminster formed part of Netherbury parish. High families lived there. It was " amoena sedes Gollopensis," as a memorial in Dorchester Parish Church calls the mansion of Strode, a pleasant residence. Nicholas Wadham, founder of the Oxford college, dwelt at Pomice, near by, now a farm. In the church are buried Mores of Melplash, ancestors of Sir Thomas. But now Netherbury is but a handful of yellow cottages, with one or two displeasing patches of brick, and a number of very fine box hedges, said to have been planted to stay infection of plague from house to house, when the village was ravaged by the scourge in 1666-8.

All the paths and roads converge upon the beautiful church (a very competent guide to which could once be purchased at the post office just below). It stands on the highest part of Netherbury's little hill, a golden pinnacle, gracious and lovely alike when it glows in sunlight and when its serene autumn colour shines through rain. Not Beaminster Church nor Sherborne Abbey itself is more finely weathered to unite in the yellow stone both life and venerable age. The tower is of well-proportioned Perpendicular work. Inside are graceful slender pillars, of early English design, an inlaid pulpit, two squints, four niches void of statues, a stoop, and a " crusader's " tomb of alabaster almost translucent in its purity. On it lies the mutilated figure of a knight. He wears armour of about the time of Henry V or Henry VI, and a collar of SS : once at his feet couched a dog or a lion, now headless. Above the canopy of the tomb is his helmet. Savages have carved their initials upon him : not only in the nineteenth and twentieth centuries. Of himself not so much as an initial is accurately known. He is said to be one of the Mores, whose crest is on the tomb. The guide to the church records a pretty local tradition that the knight slew an adversary in a duel, and that immediately a dove settled on his helmet, showing the justice and innocence of his quarrel : but the historian says that the bird is a moor-cock, the More totem.

I should like to think that this calm, strong marble face, so certain, in its quietness, of the Resurrection of the Dead, was that of a later knight buried a few yards away in the populous churchyard, with his wife beside him ; their Latin record tells that " Thomas Gollop of Strode, knight, and Martha his wife, bowed by the weariness of mortality, laid down here together, in the sure hope of resurrection, all that was mortal of them." They had gone through the Commonwealth, had twelve sons (one of whom lived in eight reigns), and died in 1664, just before the great plague of London and Netherbury.

If in days when even remote villages have fallen upon a period of change—not necessarily change for the worse— one wished to recapture those philosophic amenities which render Gray's Elegy still the most English of poems, I

think the slope of Netherbury churchyard would be a perfect
site for the philosopher's reflections. Wars and pestilence
have come upon the men who once found here the centre of
their world. Years have eaten the golden stone that faith
and the love of beauty moulded in such seemly fashion :
men have broken man's handiwork. No one can tell into
what fantastic lands the alabaster knight fared, what
temper in action won him his honourable collar : no one can
tell what impulses of wayward friendship or mean pride
cut letters upon his unknown form : no one can say whose
thought in stone the church is : no one can tell us any more
of Gollop of Strode than that, if epitaphs do not lie, he loved
his wife. The box and yew live on : silent. But they are
not more continuous than the unrecorded life of men in a
village. The reckoning bideth.

A hundred yards from the church, one autumn day, I
came into one reality of that almost dumb life. An old man,
digging potatoes in an allotment (last remnant of merry
socialist England) greeted me. It had been a wet summer,
followed by a fine autumn, so late that the harvests had been
gathered perforce before the sun reappeared. " We ought
to ha' waited," said the old man. " We hadn't patience.
The Lord A'mighty promised seedtime 'n' harvest so long
as the world do stand, and it come ; but not 'zackly so as to
please we sometimes."

Westwards from Netherbury there is a way to the great
hills of this region which might have baffled even the lamented
Mr. Walker Miles (whose work on field-paths all over England
deserves an eternal monument, for the open confusion of
wire-pulling landlords, builders, motorists, wealthy hermits,
embattled Americans, and every other legless monster).
Perhaps, as it is so utterly delightful a walk and so hard to
follow exactly, I had better hypostatize the true traveller
in the manner of Mr. Hope Moncrieff (that universal Black's
Guide) and name him P (Passenger ? Pedestrian ? Pro-
letarian ?). It seems a suitable artifice for this period.

The one-inch ordnance map shows P. how to leave

Netherbury.   The footpath goes past the narrow slip of allotments and downhill to a stream.   Across the stream, P. proceeds (P. always proceeds—he does not walk) through a wood, taking the right-hand path the other side of the footbridge, not the left (which is not on the map but is very insistent in fact).   Beyond the wood, the path, like so many on the Dorset map, vanishes on a hill-side.   Here P.'s nose, if of the usual shape, points straight ahead, not along corrugations which look like paths but are not.   Let P. follow his nose and ascend the hill at its steepest :   he will see at the top a gate, and thereafter a fenced or hedged track—the map's dotted " third class unmetalled road." Follow it.

P. has now come to a pathway of a kind peculiar to the edges of Marshwood Vale, and beyond description lovable. It is a little like the broad, disused, grass-grown roads of Kent :   but its hedges are ten or more feet thick.   It is, later, a little like the smugglers' ways of Sussex :   but it is much smoother, and, in a sense, more civilized.   At first it is open, with grass under foot :   a track seven or eight feet across.   On either side grow foxgloves and meadowsweet, and in due season periwinkle (its flowers blue stars, visible satellites, one cannot doubt, of a fabulous blue moon not to be seen by mortal eyes).   Blackberries of prodigious size and unspeakable lusciousness abound.   Upon the majority of blossoms, at the proper time of year, peacock butterflies of the largest possible dimensions, broader and more lustrous than even the Cornish giants of that tribe, are to be observed :   so fat and lethargic are they that an enthusiastic naturalist can catch, mutilate, or kill them with the naked hand.   Other flowers, shrubs, and insects occur in profusion.

This is the voice of prejudice.   The natural objects are those to be found in other parts of England.   But I love these better than those, as Ollendorff would say.   And when this grassy lane becomes a road-like track (not at all easy to walk upon in a wet winter, but admirable for about eight normal months in the year), it takes a character of

its own, for it sinks down between banks, and when the
summer has advanced the brambles meet overhead. The
sky is obscured : long, bleached, thornless bramble streamers
hang down from the leafy roof ; the walk becomes a green
thought in a green shade. You may reflect upon the action
of light in bleaching the prickly shrubs, or upon the careless-
ness of evolution in leaving them thornless where chance
cows might chew them, or upon the condition of soil which
produces such growths : or you may merely be entirely
contented by the silence and earthy fragrance of this long
green tunnel. If you descend upon Whitchurch Canonicorum, the capital of the Vale, from almost any point in the
hills around, you will find many such delicious alleys.

At present one does not descend. Return to P., who has
been left sniffing at those splendid flowers, or looking at a
map, or catching butterflies, for some time past. P. will
be in doubt when presently, by two trees high up, the path
divides. Nature and the map may suggest to him a short
cut if he takes the right-hand path. Not so. Let him shut
his right eye and go straight on. About a hundred yards
later, the information laid by H.M.'s Ordnance Survey will
prove true. P. must turn to the right : an oak tree and a
gully are signs : then over a stile and down into Stoke Abbot.
Here P. sees a church, and for the moment considering it
merely as a landmark, passes it on two sides. It is on the
right ; when the path reaches a road, P. turns to the right
and enters the churchyard and (with luck) the church.
Here P. may look upon the memorial to Dr. Crowe. The
church is not particularly interesting, but it is of a respectable antiquity : much of it is Early English, and the font
is Norman.

Anyone with a sense of historical decency would go from
here to Broadwindsor, along a pretty byroad, and look at
Thomas Fuller's pulpit in the (usually locked) church,
and meditate on Charles II and the other worthies already
mentioned : especially as Hutchins deals with Crowe under
Broadwindsor as well as Stoke. But just at this stage

I do not feel the need of second-rate authors or fugitive kings, and I prefer to go straight to Crowe's subject— Lewsdon Hill. Hutchins says that it is the highest hill in Dorset, being 960 feet above sea-level. I am afraid H.M. Ordnance Survey do not agree : 894 feet is all they give it, and to Pilsdon Pen they allot 907, and to Bulbarrow 905. Still, it is a considerable acclivity, to use the terms of th' period. And it is singularly beautiful, for its top is crowned with trees and bracken—not crowned only, but well clad. Dr. Crowe chose a good ground for his musings.

The path from Stoke over Lewsdon is easily found : it is another " third class unmetalled unfenced road " : that is to say, it is an ordinary green Down track along which a farm cart may pass once or twice a year.

Likewise the track to the main road is easy. The road here is good ; a fair high-hedged causeway. (Once a horse made a face at me here over a ten-foot high hedge : he *did :* a beastly ugly face, sardonic, in the derivative sense of that word. I do not know why he disliked and derided me : these Houyhnhnms——)

But you have got to be careful about THE highest hill in Dorset, Pilsdon Pen. If you go too far along the road, you will find certain notice-boards, directing you to go to a manor and ask leave to view a hill that was inhabited before manors were ever dreamed of. And then you will climb it from the west. But if . . . well, there is a gate on the east-ward side of the hill.

It is a great and fine hill. I rank it in Dorset next after Pentridge and equal with Creech Barrow ; Eggardon and Bulbarrow being first of all. Even people who know much of Southern England do not realize the spaciousness of these neglected hills, and are often not aware of the superb vision of domestic England which they afford. From Pilsdon you look back on hills I have enumerated more than once already : you see the whole wonderful curve of Marshwood Vale—shaggy Lewsdon, Lambert's Castle, Coney's Castle, Golden Cap, Thorncombe Beacon (the names alone ought to

U

defeat other counties) : you behold the Axe Valley spread out, and all that pageant which I have described as seen a little more distantly from Eggardon.

P. should go down from Pilsdon Pen towards Birdsmoor Gate on the main road. He can turn off, if he please, just below the great hill, and go south, past the old manor-house at Pilsdon itself : but personally I like the longer route, for it bears you round the high rim of the singular vale of Marshwood—a saucer with its seaward edge adorably chipped. P. should turn off at the byroad to Bettiscombe (unless he likes to look at the extraordinary modern buildings in speckled brick at Marshwood), and follow that byroad to Whitchurch.

At Bettiscombe is the Screaming Skull. (The only better title that I know for a really promising novel is *The Man with Three Thumbs* : and that, unhappily, has been wasted on a short story). The Bettiscombe Skull screams, and disaster overtakes the family, if you try to remove it. Quite jolly. Its history has been pursued by his Honour Judge Udal, of Antigua and Dorset, who in his West Indian dominion came by chance upon an estate known as Pinney's. Happily, possessing local knowledge of a penetrating kind, he hit on the solution of a mystery about which antiquarians would ordinarily have had to fill volumes of magazines. Mr. Udal traced the West Indian estate to a Pinney who was condemned to death, reprieved, sentenced to transportation, and apparently bought off, after Monmouth's rebellion. It seems that this Azariah Pinney, nevertheless, went to the West Indies : and his descendants returned in the eighteenth century to the ancestral district, bringing with them a negro servant, after the fashion of the times in which Samuel Johnson would serve his cat Hodge with oysters to prevent indignity to his black, Francis Barber. It is the anonymous black's skull, preserved by some whim, which screams.

P. can go all the way to Whitchurch Canonicorum from Bettiscombe by what is called a road (and indeed—*horresco referens*—I have been along it in a car). There is also, if you can hit it—I did it only by the graciousness of a country woman who carried her baby a quarter of a mile and left her house desolate to guide me—a path from below Duckpool across country : a mighty pleasant and wet path. This deep Vale country is no place for walkers, except in August or a dry September : you get either interminable curly lanes, or quaggy footpaths.

In due course P. arrives at Whitchurch of the Monks ; an ugly village with a venerable church. Here lies St. Wite or St. Candida, a saint of whom I have spoken : here are Norman arches ; here are a Grail and something like the Cretan *labrys* carved on stones embedded in the fine Perpendicular tower. This, like Powerstock and Bere Regis and Piddletown churches, is a building where intention has survived.

From Whitchurch a byroad takes P. to a little before Ryall, where a maddening confusion of roads awaits him. The only direction to give is that he should go almost due east, along a contour, so to speak—it is fairly easily recognized when he gets there ; it does not look promising, but it is right. By doing so he misses returning into the depths of the Vale, and also getting on to the main Bridport-Lyme road, and also going into a blind alley. Har Down (unaccountably called Sharedon and other vile names in eighteenth-century road-books) should be left dead due south, after a slight curve towards the south-east.

This track crosses the River Winniford, about which I will say no more than that it makes the road wet for an intolerable distance. Thereafter North Chideock is passed unobserved, and another green tunnel is entered.* This leads eventually to the fair village of Symondsbury, where are an ancient manor, an ancient inn, and a church which, until a year or two ago, would have been ancient if the

* See one-inch Ordnance Map. I will not guarantee that the little lanes will be roofed over in any one year. Farmers, for obvious reasons, have a habit of clearing lanes and ditches and hedges and copses from time to time.

eighteenth (or early nineteenth) century had tolerated such a Gothic survival.

The church is now being restored : I could almost wish it were not, for later centuries will certainly like to possess some monument of what 1818 thought of earlier ages, as well as of what 1922 thought of 1818.

What 1818 thought of its ancestors, the church as it was a few years ago showed. The period was still Augustan, and the nation—so far as Symondsbury is concerned— still knew its own mind. It may have been a narrow mind, for all that it prided itself upon its broad-bottomed wisdom : but it was a mind fully made-up and composed. When, therefore, it judged the " Gothick " of Symondsbury church, it found it bad : of course it may also have found it half-ruined, and have very rightly determined to arrest the decay ; but I doubt it.

The year 1818 covered the Gothic up : covered up the inside utterly and entirely, save where the immense and goodly Perpendicular shafts rose into the golden tower. High pews, with elegant wooden candlesticks—still in use before the new restoration—were so put in as to hide the bases of those columns. Much of the waggon roof was whitewashed and plastered. Two fine new galleries were inserted, one in the north transept, one all across the west end of the main aisle, cutting in half the light of an enormous window. To give entrance to this western gallery—which from the chancel steps, with a draped red window curtain in the big window and a neat projecting bay in the middle of the front row of seats, looked exactly like an enormous four-post bed—two stone staircases were erected *outside* the church. On the south a door was cut high up in the wall. On the north a window was bisected, and a wooden door substituted for half the Perpendicular arch. Another outside staircase was made for the northern gallery.

Below the gallery, at the extreme back of the church, were set unsmoothed, low, uncomfortable seats, doubtless for the poor and for children, with a raised seat in the middle for a beadle. Facing him stood that perfect emblem of Augustan pomp, a wooden font of a simple pseudo-Roman design, the wood painted to look like marble.

The gallery in the north transept was adorned at one side with a golden urn breathing stiff golden flowers. Over a high, graceful pulpit sat a seemly golden dove. The tables of the Law, the Creed, the Lord's Prayer, were blazoned on aggressively decent blue screens behind the holy table, around which, north and south, as well as west, ran a firm balustraded altar rail, so that communicants might draw near in a gentle domesticity.

All the stonework of the interior, except the central columns, was plastered over : and the plaster was given a pattern of lines to bear the semblance of joined and mortared stones. No transformation could have been more purposeful and complete, no breach with, or disregard of, the past and its continuity more determined.

A generation later two documents were added ; footnotes, as it were, confirming the taste of the restorers. One is the glass in the south transept window—a representation of the Evangelists which in design and colour can only be described as amazing. I have never seen, and wish never to see, anything like it. The other is an epitaph to a local worthy. His executors set it up. They were quite sure of his virtues. We might perhaps be surer of them to-day if they were a little less strenuously proclaimed. The panegyrists said that " he could not have been excelled in firmness of attachment to the existing institutions of his country both in Church and State." (Here follows a list of less exciting qualities.) " In his character were united all the *Christian Graces*, with all the *Sterling Virtues* of *True Patriotism*." He paid his labourers two shillings a day in 1812.

From Symondsbury P. makes his way east by a pleasant field-path entering the Bridport road just by the ironworks : than which nothing less like an ironworks has ever existed ; a graceful Georgian house with its own pond and garden visible from the road, its own decent ironwork, of the two patterns which adorn—adorn is the right word—half the good houses for miles round : no factory chimney, no coal, no dirt. . . . The eighteenth century here at least coped well with one ugliness of the industrial era.

And thus we come into Bridport again by way of Allington, where an unrestored church of almost the Symondsbury restoration period may be observed : formal, sedate, as certain of its convictions as of the even growth of its yew trees.

It is that certainty which contrasts so pitifully with the dim fumblings of the labourers towards freedom. They should have been content to make the earth beautiful and fruitful by their toil ; leaving it to the church builders and restorers to name their reward in this world—or the next. They should have known their place. . . .

XIV

" May our *Examples* influence All the rest of our *Country* to an *imitation*
of the like *Charity!* That if it be the *Will* of *God*, we may again
Enjoy the *Blessings* of peace, and see our *Jerusalem* once more
Established as a City *that is at Unity within itself.*
" *Now the* God of *Patience* and *Consolation, grant you to be likeminded
One towards Another, according to* Christ Jesus."

WILLIAM WAKE, afterwards Archbishop of Canterbury. *A Sermon Preach'd at the Reviving of the
Dorsetshire Feast,* 1690.

" In the black night, along the mud-deep roads,
    Amid the threatening boughs and ghostly streams,
Hark! Sounds that gird the darknesses like goads,
    Murmurs and rumours and reverberant dreams,
Trampling, breaths, movements, and a little light——
The Marching of the Army of the Night! "

FRANCIS ADAMS,
Songs of the Army of the Night.

HOLY AND HUMBLE MEN OF HEART

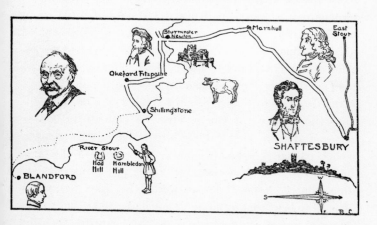

DORSET, as a rule, has not been backward in honouring her prophets in their own lifetime. Pride in local custom and tradition seems there to be both natural and evenly diffused. In 1859 William Barnes, a none too wealthy schoolmaster, was encouraged to give readings of his " dialect " poems to those who used the alleged dialect, in their very own towns and villages. It might have been imagined that his best audience would be polite gentry and students of folk-lore (a word he himself invented), and that his humbler hearers would suspect they were being exploited or turned into sentiment for foreign consumption. But in the result there was no high-brow atmosphere. The halls were packed with the people described in the poems, and the audiences were, by every account, enthusiastic.

Hardy has lamented the smothering of that good English

speech by the commonplace language of the State schools.
I certainly have met one striking instance of that crime.
I was being kindly shown over a certain fine place in the
county, outside the usual hours, by an under-bailiff : I
conjecture a peasant's son who had taken the advantage
of education. He spoke with the average middle-class
correctness and no local accent. He was a decent man, well
dressed in tweed, with a natural civility. We came into the
gardens of the house, and heard a thousand birds singing,
for it was spring. We both stopped to listen ; the sound was
an enchantment after the empty silences of the great mansion.
After a moment I said to him : " Have you ever heard that
little small song they whisper to one another in their nests
before dawn, before they get up ? " (It is the most excellent
noise the human ear can receive : a delicate intimacy of
tiny sound from the waking birds, the half-awake birds,
in their curiously wrought homes—more subtle and poignant
than all the beauty of their full voice. They utter it at no
other time.) " Yes," he answered, his face lighting up,
" I used to hear that at home : they had nests in our thatch."
Then his speech suddenly took on the beautiful vernacular
accent, which I cannot reproduce in print. He became the
peasant, the real Dorset man, again. " But they don't
sing so finely as when they've washed and dressed theirsen,
and that's rathe (early) in mornen now. Ah, they was all
of a charm at break of day." *Concentus avium.* . . . He
recollected himself and came back from the dawn to the
daylight rather guiltily : " I mean—they were singing
wonderfully."

But the local speech has not died out by any means, as
you can discover in any bar-parlour in a small village of
an evening. I once heard a perfect example of its strictly
correct use. I was in an inn near Badbury Rings, eating a
noble cheese for lunch (on its own runabout table of rough-
hewn wood), and drinking home-brewed cider, along with
five or six labourers. They were arguing down one of their
number, who seemed to be a sort of Joshua in his views

about the sun ; he wanted it in one particular place. He said it rose *there*, pointing : he could see it out of such and such windows. The discussion was long and curly, but the unanimous conclusion was simple : " You med (might) zee zun rise o'er Barbury, but not drough thic window." Apart from pronunciation, the point is " thic." It does not mean " this," as novelists who deal in local colour are apt to think. The men were talking of a number of windows— " Thic " is a collective adjective, and means " of this kind " —windows, magic casements, opening in one particular direction.   " Thic novelist " (like Mr. X——), " thic statesman " (like the Rt. Hon. Y——)—we want the word back in English. Was für ein ? . . .

The decay of this fine vernacular, as I have said, is not yet far advanced. Even the middle-classes in the little towns often revert to it in intimate conversation. The beauty of it, to me, is its clean simplicity : it is at once rich and plain. In the mouth of a good tale-teller the Dorset intonation makes it a perfect vehicle of direct romance.   " And with tha-a-at, he ups and he gies 'un a clout ower his head, *so* " : that is how stories should be told, so that you go off, as you listen, into a land where things may not always be what they seem, but where words mean what they mean, and nothing else.   It is a speech entirely English and entirely intelligible. It is as easy and beautiful as Chaucer's. Read Chaucer out loud with attention to the rhythm, and you can bid the philologers and glossarists go hang. Hear the Dorset " dialect " spoken, and as soon as you have got used to the inevitable change of tonic accent, it is clearer and better and robuster English than even the Cockney speaks.

Mr. Hardy need not despair of its survival. He himself has done enough to preserve its rhythm in books so long as books are read. And fortunately he also is not without honour—honour outside reading circles and dramatic and literary societies and the more exalted Press. That very under-bailiff, when I told him I had walked from Stinsford

that day, said, " You know that's Mellstock in Mr. Hardy's
book ? " I said, " Yes. Do you know *Under the Greenwood Tree?* " Yes," he answered, rather shyly ; " I've
read all his books. I read all I can. I know some of
the people in *Under the Greenwood Tree.*" And again, near
Bere Regis. A boy in a cart gave me a lift (oh, legless
motorists, when did you ever offer that unasked ? Not once
within my knowledge) : his mother was with him. Presently
after other conversation, she said, " I suppose you've read
Mr. Hardy's *Tess* ? " " Yes," I answered, " it was at
Bere she sheltered, wasn't it ? " " Yes," she replied :
" we know a lot of people in that book."

But it was really with an honour paid to a Dorset man
outside his county and outside his life that I meant to begin
this chapter on the Victorian aspect of the county. If I
deal with certain personalities rather more than with social
history at this point, it is because they are both a part and
a vehicle of that history. Alfred Stevens certainly was.

I was present at a curiously impressive ceremony at the
Tate Gallery in 1911. A number of elderly gentlemen in
red robes were gathered to meet the doyen of French
engravers, Legros, Sir William Richmond, the Keeper of the
National Gallery, and many distinguished men of art and
letters. They had all assembled to do honour to a
Blandford house-decorator's son, who fought with wild
beasts at the Office of Works, and was the greatest English
artist of his day, born at Blandford in 1817 ; and there
stood the Blandford Corporation waiting to hear their
dimly known fellow-citizen praised.

It was through the foresight and generosity of the vicar
of Blandford St. Mary's, Mr. Best, that Stevens first got
his chance. This wise man sent him at his own expense to
Italy to study, and there, probably, Stevens gained that
conception of the unity of all art which dominated his life.
He returned to Blandford in 1842, but not for long. He
became a master at the school which developed later into
the Royal College, and began forthwith to put into practice

PORTRAIT OF A CLERGYMAN
BELIEVED TO BE OF THE REV. THE HON. SAMUEL BEST
By Alfred Stevens
By permission of the Trustees of the Tate Gallery

his saying, " I know but one art." He designed stoves for a Sheffield firm, plates for Mintons, fine houses for the beautiful-and-good, lions for the British Museum, and finally the great Duke's monument for St. Paul's Cathedral, into which the Dean (Milman) was loth to allow even a sculptured horse to enter.

Sir William Armstrong's charming monograph on Stevens tells with much sympathy the story of his struggle with Mr. Ayrton (the First Commissioner of Works), who was capable of suggesting to an artist that if he did not complete his tale of bricks as per esteemed order, someone else would be set to round off the half-finished job. The essay brings out also the quality in Stevens which to me seems the essential part of his birthright—his extreme simplicity of soul. He had always a sincere purpose clear in his own mind, not necessarily believed in by others. And he saw and laboured for nothing else—except to be kind to puppies and poor people : he liked to have a puppy in his pocket, and was always being defrauded by beggars.

So likewise did William Barnes walk in simplicity through the wilderness of this world. Hardy, in a fine appreciation published when Barnes died in 1886, writes of " an aged clergyman, quaintly attired in caped cloak, knee-breeches, and buckled shoes, with a leather satchel slung over his shoulders, and a stout staff in his hand. He seemed usually to prefer the middle of the street to the pavement, and to be thinking of matters which had nothing to do with the scene before him."

A statue of him in that cloak now stands outside the parish church at Dorchester, by whose clock he was wont to set his watch. His association with Dorset was chiefly with the county town, except for his youth in Blackmore Vale. He kept a memorable school at Dorchester, and retired at length to the vicarage of Winterborne Came, three miles south. Dorchester to-day, indeed, in its external form, owes much to him. He was one of the little band of its citizens who prevented the railway companies from destroying

Maumbury Rings and Poundbury Camp. His zeal for the study of continuity with the past made him an original member of the Dorset Field Club, whose local antiquarian collections and investigations might be a model to all English counties.

His very perfect *genre* poetry apart, he is well known, perhaps even notorious, as an extreme enthusiast for Anglo-Saxon, and as a widely read but possibly too dogmatic philologist. He would have reduced the English speech of to-day almost to something like a system of monosyllables, by killing or banning Latinisms wherever a Saxon word existed or could be exhumed (" folk-wain " for " omnibus," for instance—and perhaps archaism *is* better than corrupted jargon in that case). What the reformed tongue should be at its best may be learnt from a few sentences of his which hold also his own ideal of life : " It often happens that so many of the earlier years of the worker for the minds of men are so ill paid that he dies almost breadless before he attains to well-paid fame ; or else, as a homely saying speaks, he cannot win bread till he has no teeth left to eat it. Yet it may be true that a work of fine art for the mind of man may not be always so truly rated by labour or transference as work for bodily life-gear. A great man's work is that of his own soul's thought, his own feeling, his own hand, his own skill, and no other man can give its like."*

The local sentiment—or parade of it—which might make unsympathetic persons suspect a fostered cult of Barnes was in fact a very genuine thing. He was loved. " No one was ever afraid of Mr. Barnes," said a child in his parish, not contemptuously. Perhaps she had experience of that cassock-coat pocket which besides prayer books or a " pocket font or communion service " would also hold dolls and sweets. After all, what *is* sentiment ? In the bad sense, it is hypertrophy of the lacrymal ducts by means of publicity campaigns which appeal to the most facile emotions : as when you raise your hat at the word " Mother."

* *Views on Labour and Gold*, 1859.

The answer to this is the ever-regretted Pelissier. In the good sense, it is an appeal to a simple and honourable emotion—against reason, perhaps, but quite often on the side of reason, for human beings are not all reasonable. Barnes had the gift of that appeal, and he could clothe it in the best of all coats of many colours—a rich living dialect.

Sentiment—I suppose Wordsworth's " Poor Susan " is as near the danger-line of sentimentality as most poems. Yet it happens to be true, and William Barnes proves it. He won for himself, in his lifetime, a tribute of which few writers could not be envious, ungrudgingly. His daughter records that one day in 1869 he received a letter " written in an uneducated round hand." The writer had had to dust some books. " Amongst them was your Poems in the Dorset Dialect. Sir, I shook hands with you in my heart, and I laughed and cried by turns. . . . Sometimes I sit down in the gloom of an underground London kitchen and shut my eyes, and try to fancy I am on Beaminster Down, where I have spent many a happy hour years ago. . . . May God bless you and all yours, is the true wish of an Old Domestic Servant, who loves the very name of Dorsetshire."

The urban temper of mind is apt to pride itself on its sense of the spirit of place ; I have, no doubt, given numerous examples of this form of self-conceit. What it too often fails to understand is the real *love* of place which is the life of the spirit, which has made it in the past, which will keep it alive when all the essayists of all the world are dead. A little aside in the Dorchester labourers' evidence— " They said we were as brothers " : the bitter memories of the uprooting of Milton village : the Old Domestic Servant's reverie of Beaminster Down—they are deeper things than sentiment or intellectual ecstasy. How deep in Dorset, it has taken Hardy to show us. It seems to me that in the dim courage of the labourers, in the simplicity of Stevens and Barnes, in the austere fire and profoundly human sense of the universe in Hardy, in the acceptance by the humble of the work of their own great ones, there is something central and permanent ; some kinship of spirit, linked, not distantly, to a fellowship with the very earth itself. Dorset men *love* Dorset. Here is a little of the peace I seek, a little continuity and permanence.

That spirit, I think, appears also in another well-known Dorset man of the nineteenth century. There moved to and fro about the county the handsome figure of General Pitt-Rivers ; moved a little irritably, at times, perhaps, for I am told he had the honourable affliction of the gout. I have already spoken of his wonderful excavations. He made munificent gifts to collections elsewhere, but he meant his work to carry its highest value locally. Accordingly he built a well-planned museum at Farnham, near the scene of his labours—ten miles from anywhere—and put most of his local finds in it, with elaborate models of the sites and cuttings and a collection of objects of peasant life from other countries, for purposes of comparison. It was a great idea, to let a few villages look on a pageant of the life of man, and study it closely, and feel it part of them-selves. Pitt-Rivers also built arbours in his grounds at Larmer Tree, close by, and encouraged excursions, and had a band at intervals, and wrote a vigorous guide to the place. He kept in his park reindeer, llamas (which bred), Indian cattle, yaks, and other exotic beasts and birds : all part of the same universal idea, if a little remote from it.

His fine books on the excavations are unfortunately accessible only in great libraries. They were privately printed, at great cost. Indeed, the expense of these under-takings was a serious burden on the family estates, which in Dorset covered not only the Chase, but land at Bridport Harbour and Cerne Abbas.

Over all these writings is the impression of a robust, self-willed, upright personality : I should have said, if Pitt-Rivers had not been a Conservative in politics, of what Stevenson called a Squirradical. Hear his rebuke to his fellow-landlords : * " The expense of conducting

* *Excavations in Cranborne Chase.* Vol. II, 1888.

explorations upon this system is considerable, but the wealth available in the county for the purpose is still ample, if only it could be turned into this channel. The number of county gentlemen of means, who are at a loss for intelligent occupation beyond hunting and shooting, must be considerable, and now that a paternal Government has made a present of their game to their tenants, and bids fair to deprive them of the part that some have hitherto taken, most advantageously to the public, in the management of local affairs, it may not perhaps be one of the least useful results of these volumes " . . . if the squires turn archæologists !

These few figures,* now outstanding, seem much more enduring, much more real, than those of the popular protagonists in the chief controversies of the time. Yet great and little things were going on round their lonely heads. It was the era of the Oxford movement, and the county trembled.

Walter Kerr Hamilton, Bishop of Salisbury from 1854 to his death in 1869, was an unafraid High Churchman in days before the nobility and gentry in general had recovered from Tract No. 90. (The opposite school of thought has always been strong in Dorset, especially in the eastern part of the county. I have heard of a celebrated Evangelical donkey . . .) Hamilton, in his episcopal charge of 1867, accepted the doctrines of the Real Presence and of priestly absolution. The matter was mentioned in the House of Lords. It was also mentioned at great length at a County Meeting held at Dorchester that year. "This meeting," the report of it says, "was specially important as having been convened and addressed by laymen only." The philanthropic Lord Shaftesbury was in the chair (" in his

---

* I may seem to speak of Mr. Hardy, among them, as if he were in the past ; but when I mention him I am really thinking of the living people and the vital ideas in his books, the first of which appeared in 1871 : he wrote, in his novels, as a rule, of that or an earlier period. His heresies of the nineteenth century have become our gospel : a faith, however, not yet mummified by full Establishment.

In this epoch also, in 1836, was born at Wareham (and there presented to the Princess, afterwards Queen, Victoria) the only begetter of the Daniel Press.

X

private capacity "), and was supported by the High Sheriff-elect, several M.P.'s, Lord Portman, Mr. Wingfield Digby, the Mayor of Dorchester, and many representatives of well-known county families. They protested vigorously. "When I have assisted at one of these [ritualistic] exhibitions," said the chairman, "I declare that I thought I was at Fordington Field, presiding at a review, rather than in an act of religion in a church." (I do not know whether to admire his lordship's conception of military science or of religion the more ; and this was ten years after the Crimean war.) It was admitted that Dorset itself was not seriously tainted. "There are here," said Lord Portman, "very few opportunities of showing off what I would call those nonsensical proceedings in the Church. (Loud applause.)" "The Church," cried the High Sheriff-elect, "if she protested against anything, did protest against the Bodily Presence of our Saviour in the Lord's Supper." (As who should say, "*Do* go away, dear Lord.") Eight hundred years before, the great abbot of Cerne, Ælfric, had put it differently and in better English : "Nothing is to be understood bodily, but all is to be understood spiritually. . . . Soothly it is Christ's body and blood, not bodily, but spiritually. Ye are not to ask how it is done, but to hold to your belief that it is so done."

"Thus, my lord, there are many panics in mankind besides merely that of fear. And thus is religion also panic." It was another Lord Shaftesbury who said that, the third Earl, the ingenious author of the *Characteristics*, with whom, writing quietly in his homes in Dorset and Chelsea and Hampstead, I am sorry that I have had no space to deal.

To-day, when the number of persons likely to become excited about either ritualism or methodism is appreciably diminished, the Dorchester meeting's feelings seem a little extravagant. It must not be imagined, however, that (save in the one respect of Popery) the chairman—at the time Lord Lieutenant of Dorset—was addicted to raging

furiously. The seventh Earl of Shaftesbury took up the
matter in the House of Lords, and mentioned the Dorchester
meeting (" I should not like to repeat the language used
on this subject ; it was, indeed, of the strongest description "). His mind was a convinced Protestant mind,
and in that regard, perhaps (to pervert a famous phrase),
was a little " clouded by enthusiasm," from a modern
point of view. But his deep love of justice and his passion
for reform, not to be quenched by failure nor to fail through
too facile investigation, carried with them an authentic
breadth of outlook. There is no trace of bitterness in his
attacks upon evil : the only bitter saying of his I have
noticed is about himself and his circumstances when he
succeeded to the earldom—" I came into an estate rife
with abominations without a farthing to set them right."*
His protests against the conditions of village life on his
family estate seem to have been vehement enough to cause
some slight estrangement from his father. In spite of limited
means, however, he succeeded, aided by his sister, in building model cottages at Wimborne St. Giles'. He had a real
respect for the agricultural labourer, and an admiration for
his genuine skill at his work, and a perception of its loneliness.
He advocated strongly the better education of the worker's
children, and the exclusion of young girls from field labour,
except at harvest time ; and he denounced in the House of
Lords, in moving terms which showed his knowledge of the
subject, the infamous " gangs " system.

He was not backward in reminding his own neighbours in
the county of some shortcomings. " The county of Dorset,"
he said at a dinner of the Sturminster Agricultural Society
in 1843, " is in every man's mouth ; we are within an ace
of becoming a by-word for poverty and oppression . . ."
He spoke of education and housing, and their interrelation.
" People go to their boards of guardians, and hear the long
catalogue of bastardy cases, and cry out ' sluts and pro-
fligates,' assuming that, when in early life these persons

* From the first Shaftesbury Lecture, by Sir John Kirk.

have been treated as swine, they are afterwards to walk
with the dignity of Christians."

Let his great-grandfather (appositely born at Exeter
House, on a site afterwards occupied by Exeter Hall) sum
up his characteristic, in his *Inquiry Concerning Virtue or
Merit* : " To have the natural, kindly, or generous affections
strong and powerful towards the good of the public, is to
have the chief means and power of self-enjoyment ; and to
want them, is certain misery and ill."

Literature in the nineteenth century was also represented
in Dorset by Motley, the historian of the Dutch, Solomon
Cæsar Malan (the Oriental scholar), and the beautiful
unhappy Mrs. Norton, whose pleasant facile pen has added
epitaphs to her kinsmen's graves at Frampton ; by George
Meredith, who lived near Lyme for some years, and Alfred
Russel Wallace, who retired to Parkstone and, later,
Broadstone, to conduct a highly diverting correspondence
with the County Council on smallholdings. He got the
local postman to certify his respectability in applying for
a holding, and stated that he had many years' experience
of agricultural science. How far he was in earnest I do not
know: but he pulled the Council's leg right well. He did
not get his smallholding.

That brings us back to the man whom Barnes and Hardy
have given to literature : the Dorset peasant and the land
upon which, like the bees, he toils for other people. Even
now he has not succeeded in making the land good for himself ; even now, after a thousand years of serfdom, he cannot
truly enjoy that with which he mixes his eternal labour.

The wholesale enclosures, as I have said, had completed,
by a series of rapid decisions, the slow inevitable progress
of the labourer from the position of a landholder or land-
sharer to that of one whose only property was in his labour.
And to Dorset the persecutions of 1831–1834 meant that he
must make no effort to lease or sell that property in combination or agreement with others who also possessed it.
He could bargain as an individual, but he must not form

a trust or association to protect his property, which, since it was his means of life, he must necessarily commit to the market.

But he must live, even like a hog. " At Milton Abbas [about 1870] on the average there were thirty-six persons in each house, and so crowded were they that cottagers with a desire for decency would combine and place all the males in one cottage and all the females in another." The labourer's wages in the 'sixties might be ten shillings or eleven shillings a week ; women on the land were paid sixpence or eightpence a day. The greater part of a family, women and children alike, had to work on the land, or starve ; or rather, work on the land and starve. I should like to define starvation as the point at which anyone, even if he were the poorest labourer, would feel hungry most of the time. It might be good for an employer, body and soul, to have that feeling. He might, after a trial of it, feel less inclined to write as Mr. Kebbel, a conscientious and sincere upholder of his chief Disraeli's conservatism, wrote in the year of the Empress of India's Jubilee. Mr. Kebbel observed (in his often admirable work on the village labourer) that the worst paid subject in Her Majesty's dominions was prospering : " the heart of the agricultural labourer has ' waxed fat with plenty.' " It is true that the rebellious fellow lived chiefly on bacon fat and bread and cheese : but " even in Wiltshire and Dorsetshire "—" even " is good—" the poor have money in the savings banks, and if they choose to deny themselves in point of diet, it is rather to their credit than otherwise." O excellent poor ! Stay with us always.

The position of the agricultural labourer is an anachronism. That is putting it temperately. Personally, I find that the story of his life in the nineteenth century, when the town labourer was winning a measure of freedom, turns me sick. In Dorset he was worse paid than anywhere else in England. He received payment in kind—cider, potatoes, flour— above the average. It kept him the more dependent. However prejudiced writers on the subject may be in various

ways, they all agree as to the low wage and the hard work
in Dorset ; and also as to the bad housing ; and to some
extent as to bad farming (due, no doubt, in many cases, to
impossible conditions at the worst period of agricultural
depression). The one bright spot in the county was the
extent to which allotments were provided. For the rest—
well, here is a not unique statement from the Poor Law
Commission report of 1843. At Stourpaine—a village of
ill-repute in those reports—a two-roomed cottage, in which
the upper room at its tallest was only seven feet high,
contained eleven persons whose combined earnings amounted
to 16s. 6d. a week. The bedroom was ten feet square.

Wages ranged between 8s. and 12s. a week for thirty
years or more. Nothing was paid, as a rule, during periods
of sickness, and the wage did not always include a cottage.
In 1874 came the great lock-out ; Dorset was involved
in it. The farmers and yeomen of England were not going
to pay more than two shillings a day anywhere. A
Beaminster man told Mr. F. E. Green that about that time
his father, with a wife and five children, lived on 7s. a week,
and had to walk four miles every day—seven days a week—
to work. The Commission on Agriculture of 1880 still shows
the Dorset labourer as the lowest-paid Englishman. The
average in England was 14s. 1¾d. a week ; the Dorset man
got 11s. Read Lady Cardigan's reminiscences (the half of
which was not told us) to see how the profiteers who
paid the average lived. By 1914 the wage had gone up to
16s. a week. But for the war there might have been serious
trouble then.

Mr. Green also found in Dorset the worst smallholding
estate he had seen. In the cottages the inhabitants did
not dare sleep upstairs, for the thatched roof might fall in.
The beds had to be placed to suit the strength of the floor.
In one cottage the window could not be opened " for fear
of the bricks falling down." In another a thistle was growing out of the parlour floor ; with a grim sense of humour
the tenant had tied it to the wall with bass, " as though it

were a precious hothouse plant." However, that was
exceptional. The county has been uneven in its delinquency.
I have spoken of the slugs of Cerne Abbas. In the more
neglected villages the cottages simply tumbled down.
Against that must be set the excellent work done of late
years at Iwerne Minster by Mr. Ismay, and on the Wimborne
estates, and by Mr. Debenham at Affpiddle, to name only a
few examples.

In 1919 the Agricultural Wages Board established a
minimum wage of 36s. 6d. a week for the county. The
Board was abolished in 1921 by the Government which was
to build Blake's new Jerusalem in England ; apparently
only for the upper-class Israelite. In the same year the
ex-mayor of a Dorset town was charged with a gross
infringement of an act dealing with wages, to which
he had himself agreed, and to whose scales the whole
of this particular trade locally had consented. A few years
before, the Education Committee of the County Council
approved a school History of Dorset : in many ways an
excellent work, full of heroes and historic scenes : but it
does not even mention the Dorchester Labourers.

" Clear your mind of cant," said Dr. Johnson ; and his
stress was upon " mind," not upon " cant." The absolute
prepossession in favour of the established order both of
things and of ideas is the most dangerous portent in the
world to-day. One blind force—the contented possessors,
good, well-meaning, sincere, in the main—is confronted with
another blind force, those who possess nothing but their
bodies and, to some extent, their souls. If ever they possess
their souls in full, they will break the opposing force as
Parliaments in the past have broken those who would
repress them. It is often clear enough, in times of industrial
trouble, that even the best employer and the best trade
unionist do not really understand and sympathize with one
another. There is a gap somewhere between the two types
of mind. How much more difficult is it to bridge the gulf
between the farmer, long inured to his routine of authority,

but not usually the possessor of his own land, and the inarticulate county labourer.

The impossibility of treating all the farmer's difficulties as uniform can be seen by walking through the different types of country. Start from Shaftesbury. Here till well into the nineteenth century was an old cloth industry, and also a button industry. The improvement of machinery and transport killed it. But till it expired, the farmers hated it. It kept the women and children and even some of the men away from labour in the fields. To-day we have to start leagues and institutes to revive such industries—in the farmer's interest. Without some such relief from monotony, the labourer and his family will not stay on the land.

Shaftesbury is on the chalk (upper greensand, strictly). It is an island in a sea of Kimmeridge Clay, which merges into other clays in Blackmore Vale, lying sheer beneath the town's feet. The sheep bells tell you what the farmer of the hill has to think about.

If you like a good road, you can leave Shaftesbury by the great Sherborne Causeway, perhaps the oldest main road, as such, in Dorset : even in Henry VIII's reign its repair was a matter of Government concern. In that case follow it as far as East Stour* and then turn south. Many names round here suggest a new factor in life, which Shaftesbury does not possess—the river. This is a Vale of Dairies.

A straighter way to the heart of the Vale is by either of the byroads running south-west from Shaston—through Todber or Margaret Marsh—to Marnhull. That is the village where Hardy placed Tess and her noble father. It looks down on the Stour, and has a fine church, but is not otherwise interesting.

A road runs south through the close weald country to yet another town named from the river—Sturminster

* Where Fielding lived with his first wife and wasted his estate. It is said that the curate of Motcombe, not far off, Fielding's tutor in boyhood, was the original of Parson Trulliber. Hutchins reports that the redoubtable divine " dearly loved a bit of good victuals and a drop of drink." The original of Parson Adams was also a Dorset man.

Newton. Just west of the stream here is the country of
Barnes' childhood—Bagber Common, the large farmhouse called Woodlands (the scene of " Fanny's Birthday "
and the home of " Gruffmoody Grim "), and the Lydden
Brook.

Sturminster is a pretty, open little town. Sir Frederick
Treves speaks affectionately of one of its two attractive-
looking inns. I have stayed at both. It is unusual to find
so small a place so well furnished with reasonable accommodation. The church is handsome, but no more. The bridge
is likewise handsome. It leads across the curly river (few
streams writhe so unceasingly as the Stour) to the former
" new town," which no longer exists. Not even the Middle
Age castle stands, except for a few steep grassy mounds.
For mediæval warfare it was well placed, being only a few
miles north of the gap where the river cuts clean through the
hills. The railway follows the river's lead.

That gap is very impressive when you are in it at
Shillingstone or Child Okeford. Hambledon and Hod Hills
rise very steeply almost out of the river on the east, and to
the west is the enormous lump of Shillingstone Hill, rising
equally steeply into the noble ridge of which Bulbarrow,
about three miles away, is the summit. The Vale is abruptly
walled off, with only a door half a mile wide in the ramparts.
Neolithic man and Rome too must have appreciated the
gap. The hills are full of their remains.

The road running direct to Blandford is not very interesting. A pleasanter but longer way is to cross the river again,
and go through Child Okeford up to the top of the hills
and along them. The view over the river is exceptionally
charming. There are various tracks over the chalk downs to
Blandford.*

The outskirts of Blandford, especially along the Salisbury
road, are not pleasing. But the central streets are as good
Georgian as one could wish to see. It is not uniform in the

* I do not know how far the war-time occupation of the hills—the Naval
Divisions were trained here—still persists.

details of its architecture, but it is all in the Georgian spirit, for the greater part of the buildings arose together—after the great fire of 1731, which destroyed most of the town. It left untouched, however, a beautiful Tudor mansion of red brick in the higher part of the place.

Here the farmer would not now have much chance. Blandford "Forum" (there is no reason to believe it has a Roman origin) stands on a slim spit of alluvial land, and houses cluster along it. It is, however, the site of an important fair — the Dorset Horn Sheep Fair, to which monstrous rams are brought from all over the county, as well as from the neighbouring hills. At one time it was celebrated for its point lace, which Defoe said was the finest in England : but that industry, too, has vanished. The town has a curious reputation for high prices, as Hardy, all-observant, notes. I came across an example of the complaint (before the war) in an inn a few miles away. A woman going home from marketing produced a wizened little cucumber from her bag. " They charged me ninepence for that to Blandford," she told the landlady, " and 'tisn't so big as a vinegar bottle. But they do say things is always dear in Blandford."

By this route you will have trodden upon seven different soils—Kimmeridge and Corallian beds of the Jurassic system, chalk, Upper and Lower Greensand and Gault of the Cretaceous strata, and alluvium of the geological present. To rear the sheep on the hills and the kine in the valleys, to give the land its look of settled old content, their inhabitants were paid, before the war, about 16s. a week. Is it wonderful that Jude the stonemason echoed Æschylus when little " Father Time " hanged himself—" things are as they are, and will be brought to their destined issue " ?

XV

" And now being to take our leave of this County, I should, according to our usual custom, wish it somewhat for the completing of its happiness. But it affording in itself all necessaries for man's subsistence, and being thorough the conveniency of the sea, supplied with foreign commodities, I am at a loss what to beg any way additional thereunto. Yet, seeing great possessions may be diminished by *robbery*, may the *hemp* (the instrument of common execution) growing herein be a constant *monitor* unto such who are *thievishly given*, whither their destructive *ways* tend ; and mind them of that *end* which is due unto them, that they, leaving so *bad*, may embrace a *better* (*some industrious*) course of living ! "

THOMAS FULLER,
The History of the Worthies of England.

" Magnus ab integro saeclorum nascitur ordo.
Jam redit et virgo, redeunt Saturnia regna ;
Jam nova progenies caelo demittitur alto. . . .
Non rastros patietur humus, non vinea falcem ;
Robustus quoque jam tauris juga solvit aratro ;
Nec varios discet mentiri lana colores,
Ipse sed in pratis aries jam sauve rubenti
Murice, jam croceo mutabit vellera luto ;
Sponte sua sandyx pascentes vestiet agnos."

PUBLIUS VERGILIUS MARO,
Ecloga.

AN EXCEEDING HIGH PLACE

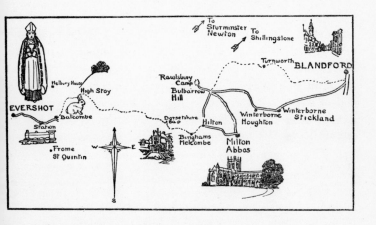

I WILL begin this last chapter in the reverse order to that followed hitherto in this book; by walking, in print, half across Dorset—the noblest walk, in my belief, in the south of England.

There is a good little inn at Evershot, to which many naval men from Portland repair for hunting with the Cattistock. Start from there, first visiting the church to look at the brass of a priest in vestments, holding a chalice and host. It is of William Grey, once rector of the parish, to whose soul his Creator was besought to be gracious in the year 1524.

The old house opposite the inn is a pleasant building, and so are others in this village, for which I feel hardly the mild tolerance that Sir Frederick Treves expresses, but rather affection and admiration. Near the east end of the long street is the Old Rectory, which indeed is an old and graceful edifice of the beautiful local stone, but not, I am told, the old rectory. That habitation, in which Crabbe would have lived if he had not been an absentee,* is said to be represented by some fragments of wall in the garden of the present house.

The curious thing about Evershot is its recondite importance. It is technically a hamlet in the parish of Frome St. Quintin (Little Frome). But Hutchins says Evershot "was formerly a small market town"; and it was large enough in the eighteenth century to be a station on the fine new turnpike-road built in 1754. It was the repository of a drum of a company of the first Dorset Volunteers, seventy-five strong in 1803. It kept a wake after the great Woodbury Hill fair. It maintained archery butts till the end of the sixteenth century. And it has a railway station named after it—a mile away—which is more than can be said of Frome St. Quintin; though on the other hand Little Frome is mentioned in Domesday—the King held it—and Evershot is not.

Following the road east, you pass the gates of Melbury House: I have spoken more than once of its owners, the family of Strangways, whose old and honourable name is so closely connected with the larger issues in Dorset history. There is probably no dynasty in the county which can show a more vigorous continuity, more active life, than the Strangways', who have held Melbury Sampford for so many generations. To-day, the semi-patriarchal position of such families may be threatened by the Agricultural Workers Union, and, no doubt, in the long run, rightly threatened: but it is usually based on something deeper and better than habitual authority.

On the road past the station, climbing slowly uphill—with tributary lanes on either side, into the intricate weald on the north, over the hills and valleys to the chalk on the south—grow in due season wild raspberries and yellow mullein, most glorious of English wildflowers. At the top of the ridge is an amazing profusion of blackberries, exceeded

* But he preached at Evershot at least once.

in size only by the Eggardon monsters. And when you reach
what is clearly the summit (a number of cross "roads"
with a small copse), you are once more at the most beautiful
place in Dorset—Batcombe Hill.

I have been up many high hills in many parts of England ;
and there is even in Dorset a more spacious view than
Batcombe Hill affords. But I know nothing more satisfying,
even overwhelming, than the pageant of English country
below you here. The gorse not merely never ceases to bloom,
in its kindly solicitude for lovers ; acres of it flame all the
year round. You will seldom fail to find some heather out :
the bracken is yellow or green or golden in turn : foxgloves,
honeysuckle, wild roses, harebells—all the flowers that are
most excellently English abound. Yew and holly lie in the
dark, almost menacing, southward valleys ; and all round
on every side stretches England, for as far as any human
eye can see—England, the real England.

A little further on, at the wildest and most desolate part
of the upland, stands the strange monument known as
Cross in Hand, to which Tess came in one of her wanderings. It is a shaft of wrought stone, four feet or so high.
To me it certainly bears the shape of a strong arm ending in a
fist clenched upon a bar. No one knows its origin. There
are various legends, stored in *Somerset and Dorset Notes and
Queries* and elsewhere. An old inhabitant told Mr. H. J.
Moule that it was set up to mark the spot where a criminal
was hung for highway robbery and murder. Another
story is that a priest, bearing the Sacrament to a dying
man by night, lost the pyx here. He was directed to it by
a supernatural pillar of fire, and found it surrounded by
cattle, all kneeling, save one—the Devil in the guise of a
black horse. Yet another suggestion is that it marks the
first spot from which the inhabitants of Minterne, who had
formerly no church and were in the parish of Yetminster,
could catch sight of Yetminster Church and bury their dead
there within range of it. A more prosaic explanation is that
it is a moot-stone.

The track all along this glorious ridge is, I think, the old turnpike-road, as I have said. It curves with the contour, through the Great Ditch, and past the trees of High Stoy, down to a brief gap in the height, above Minterne. You will see little sign of human life along it, but a million rabbits. You will have alongside you all the way the same spacious view.

Above Minterne, after going south-east along Little Minterne Hill, it is best to bear due east again, along Rake Hill, down into the deep valley by Alton Pancras, up over Church Hill, down again to the Mappowder road, up to Nettlecomb Tout and the Dorsetshire Gap.

The Gap is a network of small paths. It is perhaps the central point in the watershed of these high hills. On one side the River Lydden starts, flowing nearly due north until, as a stream of some size, it joins the Stour above Sturminster, to turn abruptly south with the larger river and pierce, at Shillingstone, the ridge from which it first sprang. On the south slope springs the goodly River Piddle, who makes no attempt on the hills, but runs cheerfully between the ridges of the Great Heath to join the Frome at Wareham.

From the Gap there is a pleasant path down to Melcombe Horsey, where gracious Perpendicular stone mullions and mouldings, perhaps remains of the old manor of the De Horseys, or of a church, still exist in the later walls of the farmhouse.

Here, at the road, there are several choices. The object of this walk is to reach the top of Bulbarrow. The direct way is to go straight up the road north-east. But a longer way, involving a sight of one of the most beautiful of all stone manor-houses, is to continue east through Bingham's Melcombe, and then across to Hilton (by a footpath not marked on the map), to look at the painted panels of the Apostles in the church. They come from Milton Abbey; and it is worth while to go further and take the road across the Park so as to see the Abbey beyond the lawn, shining in grey beauty against a background of dark trees. From either Hilton or from the westernmost lodge of the park there is a road up to the top of the ridge.

And here, before I speak of Bulbarrow, I will say how to get away from it, for it is eight miles from any resources of civilization. One method is to walk along the ridge and drop into the pretty village of Ibberton, past Belchalwell, and by the footpath over Okeford Common (very heavy going in a wet season) to Sturminster. Another is to take the direct road down to Sturminster through Woolland. Another is go by the equally direct road through Okeford Fitzpaine to Shillingstone. Yet another is to go to Blandford through two of the Winterbornes (at Stickland take the secret-looking track running east, rather than the north-by-east road—the drive across Bryanston Park has forbidding notices). This is a good way, because from the road you get enchanting glimpses of the Isle of Wight through gaps in the hedge. A more devious but fine way of escape is along the ridge north-north-east towards Ibberton, turning a point east above that village, along Bell Hill, bending back south-east at Turnworth Hill and so by infinitely wavering paths to Durweston and eventually Blandford.

When you reach Bulbarrow it is worth while to turn off westwards for a few hundred yards to look at Rawlsbury Camp. It juts out over Blackmore Vale, one more promontory fort, like a threat.

But the height of Bulbarrow itself is the place to rest. This, I think, is the steepest hill in Dorset ; and the view is the most spacious in the south of England. From the high ground near Winchester to the hills of Devon, from the Isle of Wight to the Mendips, from Purbeck to Salisbury Plain and Mere, you can look with no limit but the strength of your eyes.

And here, too, you are within sight of everything that has happened in Dorset. Rawlsbury gives you the Stone Age. On the road to Sturminster, at Fifehead Neville, almost at your feet, is a Roman villa. You can see Alfred's

Y

town of Shaftesbury only a few miles away. Many of the
village names are half-Norman—Fitzpaine (Okeford is in
Domesday), Neville, de Horsey, Bryan. Milton Abbey is
only just behind you. The Clubmen met at Shaftesbury
and surrendered on Hambledon Hill. The road you are on
is a mid-eighteenth-century turnpike. William Barnes
walked the lanes and paths below you. Until almost the
end of the great war Shillingstone held the record of having
sent more of its sons to fight, in proportion to its population
than any other village in England.

That at least is one permanent thing in Dorset folk.
"Who's afeard?" is one of the county mottoes; not the
men of Dorset, at any rate. They stood up against
the Roman and the Saxon: they fell at Hastings: they
resisted Spain and Boney equally: they tried to stop
the Civil War: they were sent overseas in chains
for their courage. It was a Dorset man who died to
blow up the Cashmere Gate at Delhi in the Indian
Mutiny—Salkeld of Fontmell Magna. It was a Dorset
man who first won a V.C. in the air—Rhodes-Moorhouse
of Parnham.

The history of the County regiment, creditable enough,
is a record of hard fighting in many lands. It was summed
up in a *Times* leading article during the war. The regiment
was in the great retreat: it died. It lost four hundred
men in a battalion. *The Times* took one of its nameless
actions as typical, and spoke of it as the kind of unadvertised
regiment which makes the backbone of the British Army.
I should have said, rather, the ever-flowing life-blood.
The 39th Regiment of Foot, now the Dorsets, bears the proud
and unique motto of "Primus in Indis," for it was the first
King's regiment to be employed in the India won by John
Company: in token of which the county Territorials were
placed at the head of their fellow-regiments when English
troops first landed in India in the Great War—once more
"Primus in Indis." On their colour are (among others)
the names of Plassey, Gibraltar (for the four years' siege—

its colonel "was the soul of the defence," and is buried there), Vittoria, Peninsula, Albuera.

They were likewise, apart from the honourable inscriptions on the colours, in almost all places where the arms of England ventured : at Dettingen, at Culloden, Martinique, Badajoz, Sevastopol, the Tirah Campaign, the Relief of Ladysmith (the last three are also on the colours). Once, on the way to India—where it served so lately as during the Moplah rising —the regiment came near to disaster : its detachment was on the *Sarah Sands*, the famous ship that caught fire in the Indian Ocean, in 1857, when she was laden with troops to deal with the Mutiny. The vessel was only held together by chains. The last survivor of that event, a Dorset man, died in 1912.

The Territorials stretch back to the old Volunteers, formed in 1794–98. The Yeomanry have a fine record, especially during the late war, when they had the unique distinction of bringing off three successful cavalry charges—in the desert against the Senoussi, in Palestine, and in Mesopotamia. They had a further singular distinction, which is best described in the words of Mr. Winston Churchill. " The Arab army," said Mr. Churchill to the House of Commons in June, 1921, " is already partly formed under the administration of Ja'afar Pasha, the present Mesopotamian Secretary of State for War. I do not know whether the Committee have in their minds the romantic career of this man. He began the war fighting against us at the Dardanelles, and he received a German Iron Cross. He then came round to the Western Desert, where he commanded the army of the Senoussi against us. He fought, I believe, three battles, in two of which he was victorious, but the third went amiss from his point of view, and he was wounded and pursued by the Dorsetshire Yeomanry and finally caught in the open field, taken to Cairo as prisoner of war and confined in the citadel. He endeavoured to escape, but, being (*sic*) a somewhat ample personage, the rope by which he was descending from the wall of the citadel broke and precipitated him into a ditch, where his leg was broken. While he was in hospital recovering from these injuries he read in the papers that King Hussein, the Sheriff of Mecca, had declared war upon the Turks, and he immediately saw that he was on the other side to what he had hitherto thought. He therefore made representations to the Arab leaders at Mecca, and after some hesitation he was given a command in their army. He very speedily rose to a position of high confidence and distinguished himself greatly in the fighting which took place in the next two years. He was finally given the commandership of St. Michael and St. George by Lord Allenby in a hollow square of British troops composed almost entirely of the same Dorsetshire Yeomanry which had ridden him down."

In courage, at least, we are no worse than our fathers. Are we as good or better in other ways? More people perhaps are comfortable and law-abiding; but then there *are* more people. Natural needs are more easily supplied, with better wares drawn from an infinitely wider world. But are there proportionately more good and happy people than there were at any one period in the long pageant of history? Was a Celt in a wolf-skin, huddled in a wattle hut or awaiting battle on Rawlsbury ramparts, less free, more miserable, than a Dorset peasant in a Flanders dugout?

But for the war, I should have said that in one respect, at any rate, we are better. We are or should be less ready to take life, and we are kinder to animals, which is another aspect of the same feeling. And we certainly are cleaner and know more about sanitation. Probably also, on the whole, more people have a chance of prosperity than before. Perhaps—and this is where I doubt whether any change which has taken place is relative or absolute—perhaps we have a slightly stronger sense of brotherhood. I do not feel sure; we have got rid of legal slavery and serfdom and enforced obedience to an overlord. But I am not at all certain whether we have advanced far enough towards getting rid of virtual serfdom. It is the agricultural labourer in a county like Dorset who stirs that doubt.

As I sat on Bulbarrow one day, a rabbit passed me, within a foot or so. She was sweating, going heavily like a thing very nigh foundered. A few minutes later—it was at least three or four minutes, even in that remote stillness where time might well have stopped—came the stoat. He did not see me at first, in his intentness : but a couple of yards away he became aware of a foreign body, sat up on his haunches, his forepaws just resting on the ground, and looked at me —angrily, defiantly, it seemed : at least with no fear. Then he dropped his lithe, beautiful body, made a detour round me, picked up the scent again, and went off at a steady, certain lope.

I have seen rabbits in that worse stage, the horrible coma which seems to envelop them when the pursuit is nearly ended : their great eyes are larger than ever, they sweat, they are rigid. I remember that I called my dog off one (and he came, good beast) which he was about to worry : it never stirred. And the admirable Bedlington cast about, and found why. He snuffed the air openly for a minute, and then—then a stoat had the run of its life. He got away. In the meantime, as Jeremy (the Bedlington) went conveniently in another direction, I could look at the wretched coney. I had to strike it to make it move : then it went rather clumsily into some brambles and vanished. I once found a rabbit in a noose near Smedmore, which was similarly hypnotized (if that is the right word), it was unhurt. I set it free, but had to slap it to make it aware of freedom. And I also found a blackbird numbed in the same way in a trap.

Shall I " moralize " the tale, or make emblems as Bunyan or Quarles ? Perhaps : but with a difference. " Not 'zackly so as to please we "—should that brave acquiescence in an age-long faith still be treated as natural and sacred ? Is there no escape, in country life, from the hypnotism of immemorial custom ? There is all the long history of both individual and corporate effort behind the agricultural labourer—still, for all the machine-shops, the most numerous and healthy wage-earner in England : all the history of slavery to Celts and Romans and Saxons, of serfdom under the Normans, of land-bondage from then until to-day. Where can they go, these poor men, what money can they earn, if the freedom of their village (quite often, may be, no more insanitary than a town slum) is not enough for their hopes, if they do not want to accept traditions and beliefs out of which their lords have—very reluctantly— educated them ? There is only one place to which they can go, and that is to hell : the hell of urban labour, or the slower hell of urban money-making if they have a gift for it.

But, like the rabbit, they do not know it is hell. And in spite of the fury which consumes me when I see a bent rheumatic old labourer, in frowsy tatters that would turn a scarecrow into an aristocrat, rather drunk, rather illiterate, vaguely pious, skilled at his eternal job—when I see him going into even a decent modern cottage I cling to the faint belief that things *are* a little better than in 1831, and even during the Civil War, and the Black Death, and when the Anarchy killed men like flies, and when the Saxons and Romans and Celts came : a little better, but not much. At least the labourers have had the courage to form unions, whose activities irritate parliamentary candidates of un- favourable views. But nineteen centuries after Christ we ought to have got further than that in making our civic and moral conduct keep pace without material improvements. It ought not to be beyond the wit of man to farm so com- petently as to make the rural housing problem (the con- clusion of the whole matter) no problem.

I know that is an easily given opinion, and that the question is not easy, nor all the arguments necessarily on one side. The points seem to be these. The landlord, not always directly interested in the land, and often only through a paid agent, knows the farmer more intimately than the labourer, but all the same—society being what it is, or at any rate was until recently—has a position to keep up and wants his rents. The farmer is not necessarily a man with fluid capital, nor is he always ready to acquire new knowledge, even if he has the capacity or time (a good farmer works very hard, remember). The weak point in his case, since agriculture has really become an industry, is his preference for paying income-tax upon double his rent (which he knows) rather than upon his real income, which he can't and won't compute. But that again is also a point for him : his money is locked up in solid things which one unforeseeable season may destroy, whose value he can never really tell at any moment, whose market value is affected by a hundred different systems of weights and measures, by deals in kind, by his own use of his own produce. On the other hand, in a county like Dorset, he has often the opportunity of direct dealing with the retailer— the publican, the butcher, the greengrocer, the milkman (who all may be farmers themselves)—without a middle-man's or market's intervention on many occasions. He *ought* to be a business man. Yet he seems seldom to be capitalist enough (nor is the landlord) to be able to sink enough money in the land or in stock or machinery to make it, so to speak, an up-to-date factory. He cannot—at any rate does not—go to the public and ask them to take up shares in Cows Limited or Amalgamated Wheat Producers Limited : and I am not sure that the shares would be underwritten if he did. We have not evolved a satisfactory system of agricultural banks yet.

At the same time, I do not believe England is adequately farmed even under existing methods : only a little more knowledge would make a great deal of difference—did, when during the war there was a little more money to be made out of it without really developing new activities and new modes of thoughts and new vitality.

The labourer sees fresh amenities being provided for him : clubs, institutes, an occasional day off, village cinemas. But he does not see his lot changed in essence. He is still another man's man. He sees also that many Acts of Parliament " have a catch in them " : particularly that one of compulsory powers which are never used. He cannot often put up the little capital for a smallholding, and he has no backer to lend him the money, even if, with a grooved knowledge of the work of cultivation, he is really likely to understand its principles and be successful. And he is still expected to know his place,* and to work like a negro in the plantations—if his employers can only get rid of the eight-hour day, as they openly wish to do.

As I write this, the Trade Unionists of the country have begged the agricultural unionists not to go back to the pre-war rates, at whatever cost they resist : and the organs of big money have said they must go back, or agriculture will be impossible. It seems to me the solution will only come when the genuine expert and enthusiast—and the Ministry of Agriculture is not now a body of amateurs and pedants—is given power and backed by a Government with real driving force and money to sink in ultimately reproductive work. At one time, with a fairly active Development Commission, with the close inspection of methods and distribution of material during a brief period of the war, with the additional labour of willing if not always skilled women and German prisoners (fas est et ab hoste doceri), with some attempt at a housing policy, and a dozen suggestive reconstruction schemes, it seemed as if there was hope. Now there is not much more than fear of conflict.

The material improvements in methods have certainly been great and continuous for two centuries past, though the late war standard of production may now have been lowered. The best features of the new age are its genuine interest in the science of rural life, its careful investigation of ways and means, its willingness to consider agriculture as an intricate and highly skilled industry. Its worst

---

* It is not strictly relevant, but I cannot help quoting it : " It is a fine thing for me that I have lived all this time and have not once heard any Englishman or any Englishwoman of my acquaintance say anything aggressively disloyal" (Mr. Stephen Paget : *I have Reason to Believe*, 1921).

feature is the still-surviving deep-rooted antagonism of standpoint between master and man (I use those terms for convenience only ; they beg my question, really). The misunderstanding is mainly on the master's side. You cannot read (say) the election address or speeches of a Dorset conservative candidate for Parliament without becoming aware of it. At the back of *his* mind is a profound inability to understand change of mind. Few of the employing classes in a purely agricultural county realize fully that men—human beings, *men*—will never again, even in the remotest country districts, be really willing to accept betterment of physical conditions as a substitute for absolute independence. Labourers will not believe they must always be poor. They will not sell their labour, or lease their property in it, in exchange only for good drains, neat roads, post offices, even for higher wages : they will not accept the market as the sole condition of existence. There are those in the country for whom a poor man, like a rich man or a middle-class man, can feel an immense personal respect amounting almost to an acknowledgment of a right to command. But that is quite a different pre-eminence from what the average landlord even now still expects as a right. Whatever may be the landlord's difficulties over housing, over second-rate tenants farming his soil imperfectly, over bad seasons and capricious prices, the one thing he has got to do is to change his mind—his *mind :* to rend his heart, and not his garments. His is the mind of the old world, and, at that, not of the golden age of the old world. He is no longer lord, whatever his legal rights. He is trustee-administrator, and his humblest tenant is his equal as a man and as a citizen. He can say, if he please, " this is mine " ; but the claim is no longer admittedly valid if it is based upon inheritance. If it is based upon purchase—well, financiers go to the lamp-post early in revolutions.

It remains to be seen whether the new owners of to-day— for a major part of England has changed hands in the last few years—will learn what industry has learnt. The great industrial employers at least respect the great industrial leaders, as well as their men. They know now that even well-paid workmen do not down tools and risk starvation for themselves and their families—no bleating about agitators and strike pay and doles really disproves that risk—without at least some substance in their cause. The better sort of employer knows also that behind whatever may be the substance of a supposed injustice, there is now a new point of view.

There is also a new point of view, probably, in the minds of those who have freshly acquired the soil of England : the earth that lives on English flesh and blood, hides English bones. I do not know what they think. I could wish that when they are, as often, men who have made money honourably by business, they would view the culture of the land as a business. I believe that not only a revolution of the spirit but a revolution of financial outlook is needed. A great deal of hard money is needed to render backward soil fertile, to reclaim waste land, to breed scientific crops as well as stock, to pay for agricultural education (from top to bottom), to improve communications, to build good houses—and, while the financier waits for the returns which a vast outlay in industry will command when the spade work is done, to pay good wages.

" Landlord," " farmer," " publican " : a comparison of the derivative meaning of those words with their modern colloquial sense is a lesson in economics. The only word in the agricultural " Who's Who " which does not change its true connotation much is " labourer."*

Have I found peace in demi-paradise ? For my selfish self, yes, and infinite happiness. But for the self which loves England, no. It seems to me that there are half a dozen points of view which one may take about a county like Dorset, and about the lives of those who make it a dwelling-

---

* " One who labours."—N.E.D.

place for humanity ; and all of them are only half-true, and
more or less contradictory. One can sit on a high empty
hill in the sun, and wonder at the simple beauty of England :
the light, the green grass, the careful hedges, sheep, a brook,
an elm or oak, a vociferous magpie, a yellowhammer, the
concert of homely birds. And then a labourer comes in
sight ; labouring. It is not only of an English economic
problem that he is the emblem. He is Man, and a much
better man than many of us. He is the heir of all the ages :
he has conquered the difficult earth. Upon him, and upon
him only, in the first instance, rest our life, our civilization,
our arts, our peace. Men who have become enlarged
through his labour have used their brains to give him more
efficient tools. Associations of men, which we call towns
or cities, have been formed, through greed or necessity or
ambition, to supply him, by way of middlemen—the landlord, the farmer, the shopkeeper—with the means of his
arduous life. You cannot live on coal or iron ore : you can
live on the work done by the agricultural labourer—the
peasant, the pagan, the man of the country, the man who
makes and has made the world habitable. His is the most
enduring of all crafts, the most inevitable. He makes it
possible for me to write a book. He lets me hear the night-
ingale (but very rarely in Dorset). He enables me to play
cricket, to drink good Dorchester ale, to walk the field-paths
and roads, to eat Blue Vinney. He also crucifies jays, and
is often very dirty.

And is he English ? What in this county of the Western
Marches *is* an Englishman ? Scientists will define him by
his cranial index, his hair, his physique, his speech. You
can trace a line of Danes from Wareham to Severn Sea, by
that kind of mark. You can find in Ireland men more
" Irish " than the Celtic Irish, with not a drop of Celtic
blood in their veins. There is something perdurable in
the associations and creative effect of place : in the climate,
may be, in the arts and crafts to which the particular soil
forces its parasites, and in the accumulated mind of genera-

tions on the same spot. You become English by living in
England, whether you trace your descent to Athelstan or to
yesterday's alien or to a nameless Neolithic shepherd.

That mixture of blood may be the dim cause of our troubles
in rural England ; the old incompatibilities of race may not
yet be sufficiently softened and fused. I doubt it : all
history, with its story of common intercourse and inter-
changed, ever-changing lordship by men of each and every
stock, is against such a view. It seems to me that our
difficulties are deep-rooted in the mind of man, to be
destroyed only by that psychical change which the religious
name conversion. I do not profess and call myself a Christian
in any dogmatic sense ; but I believe that the pale Galilean
must conquer in spirit if we are to have, at long last, an
earth worthy of its human victor. We are but the paragon
of animals, so far. We can have no true peace till we become
as gods—all of us. We know quite enough (for to-day's
moment) about practical reforms, methods, applied science :
we do not know enough about one another. "This is My
commandment, that ye love one another " : is that the
answer ?

APPENDIX

HOW TO LINK ALL THE RUTTERS INTO ONE

THE following notes will show how by a slight transposition here and there and the interpolation of an extra walk or two, the scenes described in this book may be linked up in a continuous walking tour which will cover the greater part of Dorset.

A word as to the inns. I have inserted their names as a matter of convenience, not of commendation. I have had meals and in many cases slept at all those mentioned; usually in reasonable comfort. But conditions are changing and have changed much of late: not all have recovered from the war, and a new tenant may turn a good inn into a bad one, and vice versa. For general observations on inns see Chapter XI, pages 236-238 and below. Inclusion here does not mean there are no others as good.

This is the itinerary. References to "map" mean the one-inch Ordnance Map.

Route 1. From Studland to Lulworth as described fully in the text of Chapter II. Before the war there was an excellent little hotel at Sandbanks, across the harbour mouth, and a ferry to and fro. This also would be a good starting-place. But I do not know that either facility is yet fully re-established. Till they are, it is best to go to Studland ("Banks Arms") so as to arrive in the early afternoon, and visit Little Sea and the Heath before starting on the longer walk next day. Swanage is the station for Studland (walk 2 miles, drive 3-4). The total distance from Studland to West Lulworth and Lulworth Cove ("Cove Hotel," "Castle") is a good sixteen miles: rather more if you visit most of the places mentioned in Chapter II. The last half of Chapter II I leave till later (Route 12).

At Lulworth there are alternatives: (a) to walk or drive a dreary five miles to Wool and catch a train to Dorchester for

APPENDIX

HOW TO LINK ALL THE RUTTIERS INTO ONE

THE following notes will show how by a slight transposition here and there and the interpolation of an
extra walk or two, the scenes described in this book
may be linked up in a continuous walking tour which will cover
the greater part of Dorset.

A word as to the inns. I have inserted their names as a matter
of convenience, not of confident recommendation. I have had
meals and in many cases slept at all those mentioned : usually
in reasonable comfort. But conditions are changing and have
changed much of late : not all have recovered from the war ;
and a new tenant may turn a good inn into a bad one, and vice
versa. For general observations on inns see Chapter XI, pages
236-238 and below. Inclusion here does not mean there are no
others as good.

This is the itinerary. References to "map" mean the one-inch
Ordnance Map.

ROUTE 1. From Studland to Lulworth, as described fully
in the text of Chapter II. Before the war there was an excellent
little hotel at Sandbanks, across the harbour mouth, and a ferry
to and fro. This also would be a good starting-place. But I do
not know that either facility is yet fully re-established. Till
they are, it is best to go to Studland (" Bankes Arms ") so as to
arrive in the early afternoon, and visit Little Sea and the Heath
before starting on the longer walk next day. Swanage is the
station for Studland (walk 2 miles, drive 3–4). The total
distance from Studland to West Lulworth and Lulworth Cove
(" Cove Hotel," " Castle ") is a good sixteen miles : rather more
if you visit most of the places mentioned in Chapter II. The last
half of Chapter II I leave till later (Route 12).

At Lulworth there are alternatives : (a) to walk or drive a
dreary five miles to Wool and catch a train to Dorchester for

the night : in that event, if there is time, Wool Bridge and Manor should be looked at and Bindon Abbey (6d.) visited : (b) to stay at Lulworth and add an extra walk, thus :

ROUTE 1A. Lulworth Cove to Weymouth along the coast—a stiff ten miles of magnificent cliff scenery. Train to Dorchester (" King's Arms," " Antelope. ")

ROUTE 2. Dorchester to Abbotsbury, as described in Chapter III. If it is fine the Down route is better than the road. To take this, follow the Weymouth road to the cemetery ; turn right, past Maiden Castle. When the grass track has passed a sheep dip and joined the Martinstown-Weymouth road, follow it a few yards and then turn up the slope between two cottages (gate). Near the top of the slope bear to the right, and when you see a number of tumuli in front of you and the Hardy monument further on, follow your nose due west. After the Monument, if you are going on to Abbotsbury Camp, at the point where the road curves down to Abbotsbury go through the southernmost of several gates in a group in the corner—*not* the one marked " to Gorwell "—and follow the highest contour (along the hedge at first). From the Camp turn back down the road for Abbotsbury itself (" Ilchester Arms "). Distance in all about twelve miles. Return to Dorchester by train or by one of the cross-country ways that can be worked out from the ordnance map—all good.

ROUTE 3. Dorchester to Eggardon and Bridport as in Chapter IV (latter part). From Eggardon you can follow the road through Spyway on to the main road, or, more pleasantly, turn off it (see map) to Matravers and Uploders. At the right-angle turn in Uploders, where there is a spring, turn left up the dark path. At one point you join something like a road for a few hundred yards : leave this where it curves south, take a gate on the right, and turn sharp left along the left-hand side of the field uphill. This brings you out to Lee Lane (see Chap. IX, page 176). Distance by this route to Bridport Town (" Grey-hound," " Bull ") about eighteen miles ; 1¾ miles more to Bridport Harbour (" George," " West Bay Hotel," " Bridport Arms "). The way by the main road after Spyway takes a mile or two off ; a fine road, but infested by motors. A much shorter way is to end the journey just after Eggardon, and go down to Powerstock Station and take a train (*not* from Powerstock village—see map, and Chap. VI).

ROUTE 4. To get to the Saxons, the journey described in Chapter XII must be interpolated here—Bridport Harbour to Weymouth. About twenty-six miles. Train from Weymouth to Corfe Castle (" Greyhound," " Bankes Arms.")

ROUTE 5. Corfe Castle to Shaftesbury (" Grosvenor Arms," where they brew their own beer), as in Chapter V. This probably ought to be a two-day journey broken at Blandford. The pleasantest way, in my opinion, is Wareham (see Church and walls and bridge)—Lytchett Matravers—Sturminster Marshall (see Church)—Shapwick—the Tarrants—Blandford ; then along the Salisbury road to the cemetery, and left over the downs ; lonely byroads almost all the way. If opportunity occurs, go down to the village of Iwerne Minster (pronounced " you-ern "—" Talbot ")and see it and the church, of which William of Wykeham was once vicar : it adds two miles to the distance, which is about thirty-five miles. If you go by way of the Roman road and Wimborne (the Minster is worth it, but to me the journey is less attractive), a train from Wimborne to Blandford will be helpful.

ROUTE 6. Interpolate the walk from Shaftesbury to Blandford here (see Chap. XIV for details). Distance according to alternative chosen—16 to 25 miles.

ROUTE 7. Blandford to Dorchester along the Roman road. Walk or train to Spettisbury (see Crawford Bridge), up over the Rings, and by winding byroads (see map) to join the Roman track at Bushes Barn. Route quite clear on map to Tolpiddle. Thence main road to Piddletown (" King's Arms," " Blue Vinney ") : turn left at entrance to village, over White Hill, round Rainbarrow ; left at cross roads to Lower Bockhampton, then footpath by stream to the main road close to Dorchester. 20–21 miles in all.

ROUTE 8. Train to Maiden Newton (" White Horse," "Station Hotel ") : Maiden Newton to Powerstock (see Chapter VI for details). For Frome Vauchurch, which deserves a digression, turn to the left as you face the " White Horse," and take the first turning to the right ; left across the river. Seven or eight miles with much room for more.

Accommodation here may be difficult, as it is limited, though all the little inns are friendly : it is probably best to take a train (or walk) to Evershot (" Acorn ") or Dorchester and return to Maiden Newton the next day.

z

ROUTE 9.   Maiden Newton to Bere Regis (" Royal Oak," also a home brewer), through Sydling, Cerne, and the Piddle villages ; see all the churches.   From 16 to 22 miles according to path chosen.   The main road is alive with motors : the other roads all lonely.

Accommodation at Bere Regis is also limited.   This is the most difficult stage of the progress.   If you cannot get in at Bere you had better walk or drive (cars on hire) either back to Dorchester or on to Wareham (" Red Lion," " Black Bear ").   The next stage begins at Burton Bradstock (" Anchor "), near Bridport. It is quite easy, if there is room at Bere, to devise a noble walk over the Heath and back by train (the next day—Route 9A) ; say, by the path up past the cemetery, by the middle track across Bere Heath to Turner's Puddle ; so to Throop Clump and the high ridge by which lies Culpepper's Dish—one of several strange cup-like subsidences in this region.   Thence either by Moreton (" Frampton Arms," by station) or Tincleton to Dorchester, and on by train or motor-bus to Bridport.   A motor carrier runs on certain days between Dorchester and Bere ; on others from Bere to Poole.   Enquire at Dorchester about this.   Messrs. Ling of Dorchester issue a useful list of such facilities.

ROUTE 10.   Walk to Burton from Bridport or West Bay (unless you stayed the night there already—there are lodgings as well as the inn : so also at most of the seaside villages). Burton to Sherborne (" Digby Arms ") (see Chapter VIII) (Puncknowle is pronounced Punnle, and Leigh Lie) ; 20–27 miles according to route.   Sandwiches are necessary.

Stay the night either at Sherborne or Yeovil (" Three Choughs," " Mermaid ").   Motor-bus next day to South Perrott.   Follow the gipsies' route (see Chap. X) to Abbotsbury, and if possible on to Dorchester (or train to Dorchester), and back by train or motor-bus to Bridport.   Distances are given in the text.

ROUTE 11.   Motor-bus Bridport (or Bridport Harbour) to Beaminster (" White Hart ").   Beaminster to Netherbury, Whitchurch, Symondsbury, and Bridport ; see text for details and distances.   Inns at all three villages.

ROUTE 12.   Bridport Harbour to Lyme Regis (" Royal Lion," " Three Caps ") and back : outwards, over Golden Cap (see Chap. II, end) : return, along the main road (see Chap. IX). Eighteen long miles in all.   Whatever you do *do not leave the*

cliff route to form the second half of the journey. The easiest way
to take it is to miss Eype's* Mouth, and the descent to sea-level
there. Go up over the west cliff between the new houses, and make
for Eype church, past Cliff Cottage : then along the road to Eype
Down, round it on the far side, over a gate in the right-hand
south corner, along the left-hand edge to the back of Thorncombe Beacon. The track then runs west one hundred yards
or so inland. At Sea Town (" Anchor ") observe the directions
in Chapter II. On Golden Cap get the country in front of you
well into your mind's eye, and steer for Upcot and Frenchay
Farm : *do not go along the coast edge after Stanton St. Gabriel.*
On Stonebarrow Hill you can either turn to the left just above
Frenchay Farm and so to Char Mouth, or go on into Charmouth
village (" Coach and Horses ") at its east end ; and from Char
Mouth by fields without going into the village at all. There is
another obvious short cut across the fields into Lyme itself, from
the summit of the road. The very short quiet walk round Lyme
described in Chapter XI may be taken after a judicious luncheon
and rest.

ROUTE 13. Evershot to Blandford (train up to Evershot the
night before or early in the morning) (see Chapter XV for
details). The longest route described there (by Hilton, Milton,
and Turnworth Down) is about thirty-eight miles : the shortest
direct to Sturminster (" Swan," " White Hart "), about twenty.
Sandwiches essential on this journey.

ROUTE 14. Train from Blandford or Sturminster to Spettisbury : thence to Pentridge and Cranborne (" Fleur-de-Lys "—
locally known as Flower de Luce) (see Chapter IV for much
of the route). Cross Crawford Bridge to Shapwick, and so to
Badbury Rings. Thence by the straight Ackling Dyke (see map
and text) up to the border of the county. Turn rather more
than a right angle by a footpath over Pentridge Hill to Cranborne, where the lovely manor-house can be seen at close quarters,
and the church, with curious wall-paintings, visited. About
15–18 miles in all. Sandwiches desirable. From here you can
easily get to the railway at Daggon's Road or Verwood, and so
farewell to Dorset.

I ought to add to this Ruttier some geographical reference to
the works of Thomas Hardy, my deep love of which has, I hope,

* Pronounced Eep.

become apparent. There is an exhaustive, even exhausting, book on Hardy topography, by Mr. Hermann Lea (Macmillan), and a less exhausting one by Sir Bertram Windle (Lane); and a well-arranged " Hardy Dictionary " by Mr. F. O. Saxelby (Routledge). There has sprung up, inevitably, a topographical cult of his novels which may temporarily identify one of England's most universal writers with purely local conditions—though no writer has transmuted more splendidly the local into the national. For the benefit of those who regard local conditions as more interesting than great literature, I append a few notes showing which of Hardy's works deal with the chief places I mention. I do not include small casual references.

CHAPTER I. Bridport Harbour (" Port Bredy "). See *Wessex Tales* (" Fellow Townsmen "), *Tess* and *The Mayor of Casterbridge*.

CHAPTER II. Studland to Lulworth. See *The Hand of Ethelberta* for Swanage (" Knollsea ") and Corfe Castle (" Corvesgate Castle "); *Far from the Madding Crowd* (references also elsewhere) for West Lulworth (" Lulstead ").

CHAPTER III. Dorchester to Abbotsbury. *The Mayor of Casterbridge* (and many other references, especially in the Poems), for Dorchester (" Casterbridge "), and Fordington (" Durnover "); the Poems, *passim*, for Maiden Castle and Blackdown. It is possible that the Great Barn, in *Far from the Madding Crowd*, is the Abbotsbury barn, an infinitely more impressive building than that at Cerne, which Mr. Lea suggests as the original.

CHAPTER IV. The Roman roads. Dorchester as above. " Long Ash Lane," of *Tess* and other works, is the stretch near Maiden Newton. Eggardon (" Eggar ") and Poundbury (" Pummery ") come into the Poems, and Poundbury into *The Mayor of Casterbridge*. A portion of the road near Milborne St. Andrew is hinted at in *Two on a Tower*, and the country just east of Dorchester is described intimately in *Far from the Madding Crowd*.

CHAPTER V. Studland to Shaftesbury. For Corfe, see Chapter II. Wareham is the " Anglebury " of *The Hand of Ethelberta* (Lytchett Minster appears here) and *The Return of the Native*, in which the Great Heath is described in imperishable words. Wimborne (" Warborne ") is in *Two on a Tower*, Blandford (" Shottsford ") in *The Woodlanders* and *Far from the Madding*

Crowd. Shaftesbury is the scene of much of *Jude the Obscure:* and Tess crossed this country in her unhappy journey from Marnhull ("Marlott") to Cranborne (possibly "Chaseborough").

CHAPTER VI. Maiden Newton to Powerstock. Maiden Newton is "Chalk Newton" of *Wessex Tales :* in which my surname has the honour of appearing; but I am afraid I do not own a farm there like my namesake. So far as I know, the other places are not mentioned by Hardy.

CHAPTER VII. Maiden Newton to Bere Regis. Maiden Newton as above. Piddletown is "Weatherbury" of *Far from the Madding Crowd :* the "Vale of Great Dairies" of *Tess* also lies in this region. Bere Regis ("Kingsbere") is likewise in *Tess*. On Woodbury Hill close by is held the wasp-haunted fair described in *Far from the Madding Crowd.*

CHAPTER VIII. Burton to Sherborne. Sherborne is the "Sherton Abbas" of *The Woodlanders*, which describes the Blackmore Vale country generally (as *Tess* also does). Other places are not mentioned.

CHAPTERS IX and X. The only Hardy "site" is Beaminster ("Emminster," of *Tess*).

CHAPTERS XI and XII deal with the scene of *The Trumpet Major;* "Budmouth," of course, is Weymouth, and most of the sites can be very easily identified. Chapter XIII covers the Blackmore Vale country already mentioned.

CHAPTER XIV starts at "Evershead" (Evershot, of *Tess*). The Cross-in-Hand is the subject of one of the poems, *The Lost Pyx*, and appears in *Tess*. High Stoy appears in a preface quoted in the text—that of *The Woodlanders*, which also contains other places (Okeford Fitzpaine—"Oakbury Fitzpiers") mentioned here and elsewhere.

Hardy is, of course, the great name in Dorset literature. I have spoken of other Dorset writers in the course of this book, and works of local application are abundant. Modern fiction about the county is represented by a number of novels by Mrs. M. E. Francis, Mr. Orme Agnus, and Miss G. MacFadden.

Sixteen walks, seventeen days; say, three weeks. It is worth it, even if you do not find all the inns comfortable : possibly not all immaculately clean. You must not expect too much. You may expect civility and kindness in abundant measure : lonely roads, empty footpaths, adorably varied and unforbidden country.

The one-inch ordnance maps are essential ; five cover virtually the whole county. Any smaller scale is useless in a county like Dorset. The road standard is not (thank God) that of motorists. Many alleged third-class roads on the one-inch map are not roads at all, but a couple of ruts in turf : many paths marked are very indistinct. There are only three main roads which motorists use virulently, and they are often not good (I gather that the local stone is too friable for road surfaces)—from Poole and Wareham to Dorchester, from Poole, Wimborne and Bland-ford to Dorchester, all uniting in the Dorchester-Bridport-Axminster-Exeter road ; and from Shaftesbury to Sherborne, Yeovil and Axminster to the same end : the Dorchester to Weymouth branch is also contagious. Many motor-bus and motor carrier services (more than I can keep pace with) are growing up on the chief minor roads. They are badly needed for agricultural transport. But even when they are fully developed, there will still be a thousand lanes and footpaths " the world forgetting, by the world forgot." I would only say to those who use them, use them decently and reasonably. Trespass is a small thing in itself : few good farmers or landowners in an open country really mind it : abused, it is a great evil, the enemy of society as well as of sound farming.

I hesitate to add any practical advice to walkers. But for those who have yet to learn by experience I would say this. Have a bag or trunk with plenty of clean clothes sent on by rail every two or three days to one of your calling-places. Carry with you, if you use a rucksack, whatever else it contains, a clean extra pair of thick socks (undarned if possible), which put on immediately the walk is ended, and a pair of comfortable slippers. Let all your clothing be loose enough for ease but not so loose as to sag and catch dust and rain. Use a sound ointment like lanoline or vaseline for your feet before and after walking, whether you feel tired or not. Wear thick boots (the use of rubber pads is a matter of taste : I like them). If you can manage it, carry with you in your rucksack the smallest possible tongue in a glass, some biscuits or a roll, and a flask of some cordial : you may get lost, and Dorset is a desolate county in places. I recommend brown sherry a little diluted (I know it is a vile suggestion, but I have tried most things). If you use tobacco, take as much of your fancy as you can store : Dorchester, Weymouth, and Sherborne are good centres for it, the rest poor. Carry a crooked ash stick : it will not break, and the crook is useful.

You will not find, if you are of civil address (as all who read this book must be), that even the good hotels in the towns are (as yet) exigent in the matter of dress ; nor are they (with one exception, and that is worth it) unduly high, as a rule, in prices. At the lesser inns in villages you may only be able to get beer or cider and cheese, and eggs, and tea : not bad fare. At the larger hotels in the towns you may get a three-or four-course English dinner and a corresponding lunch. Bathrooms are not universal, but more frequent than legend suggests. If you only know how to find out—the ostler is the best starting-place, especially if you still know a little about horses—there are plenty of conveniences in the way of carriers and station buses and farm carts and milkmen, to aid you with your burden. The railway services cut the county into cubes, more or less : Cranborne Chase and the Bulbarrow ridge are the worst places for desolation. Cross-country connections are very bad. Avoid trying to make them at the three stations at Yeovil as you would the Devil, and pray for the soul and recent good intention of Sir Eric Geddes. God rest you.

INDEX

Abbotsbury, 48–49, 41, 45, 170, 201, 205, 222, 247, 251
— Abbey, 48, 76, 95, 112–113
— Camp, 47–49, 259
— Church, 48–49
— Swannery, 261–263
— Tithe-Barn, 48, 263
Ackling Dyke, the, 218
Adams, Parson, 312
Aelfric, 75, 118, 306
Affpiddle, 122, 116, 311
Agglestone, the, 19–20
Agincourt, 114
Agricultural Wages Board, 311
Aiulf, 76
Alban's Head, St., 22
Aldhelm, saint and bishop, 22, 74, 77, 153
Aldhelm's Head, St., 21–22
Alford, Gregory, 177–180
Alfred, King, 74–75, 77, 83
Alington, Lord, 148
Allington, 175, 294
Almar, 98
Almer, 134
Alton Pancras, 320
Aluric, 149
Alward, Chap. VI *passim*, 265
Amber in Dorset, 44
Ancren Riwle, the, 113–114
Angel, James, 211–212
Anning, Mary, 33–34, 232
Antelope, The (Dorchester), 197, 202, 237
Anvil Point, 22
Arbuthnot, Admiral Marriott, 244, 245, 247
Argyle, Duke of, 179
Arish Mell Gap, 30–31, 57–58
Armada, Spanish, 141–143
Armstrong, Sir William, 301
Arne Bay, 18
Arnold, Melchisedech, 212–213
" Arripay," 109–110
Arthur, King, 63, 19, 28
Arundel, Roger, 100
Askatham, 176
Askerswell, 176–177
Assize, the Bloody, 41, 183–185
Athelhampton, 121, 133
Athelstan, 10, 40, 75
Augustine, St., 119
Austen, Jane, 233 ; quoted, 230, 232, 234
Austin, St., 119
Avalon, 27
Axe Valley, the, 290
Axminster, 142, 172, 176, 227
Ayrton, the Rt. Hon. A. S., 300–301

Badbury Rings, 61–63, 28, 55, 56, 73, 166–168, 298–299
Badonicus, Mons, 73
Bagber Common, 313
Bailey, John, 213
Baker, Hugh, 163
Ballard Down, 20, 247
Bance, Mr., 196
Bancks, Jacob, 191, 204
Bankes, Henry, M.P., 199
Barbary pirates, 110, 139, 250–251
Barnes, William, 301–303, 41, 94, 297, 313
Barneston Manor, 29
Bartlett, Robert Abram, 140
Basingstoke, 219–220
Bastard, the Rev. Thomas, 134–136
Batcombe, 151–152, 118
Batcombe Hill, 319, 151
Bath, 184
Beach, Mr., of Bridport, 173, 175
Beaminster, 283–284, 57, 191, 310
Beaminster Down, 303
Beckford, Peter, 203
Bedford family, 145–147
Bell, Dr. Andrew, 228–229
Bell Hill, 321
Bennett, John, 184
Bere Regis, 123–127, 56, 67, 78, 95, 96, 111, 131, 134–135
Bermudas, the, 143–145, 194, 250
Bertufus, 48, 54
Berwick farm, 146–147
Best, the Rev. and Hon. Samuel, 300
Bettiscombe, 290
Bewley, Francis, 215–216
Bexington, 48, 148, 259
Bickley, Francis, 235
Bindon Abbey, 111–112, 119
Bindon Hill, 30–31, 57
Bingham's Melcombe, 134, 320
Birdsmoor Gate, 290
Black Death, the, 77, 107, 114–115, 266
Blackdown, 44–46, 31
Blackmore Vale, 151–152, 80, 95, 312–313, 321–323
Blagdon, 228
Blake, Admiral, 165, 248
Blandford, 313–314, 9, 126, 165, 191, 203–204, 276, 278–279, 300
Blandford St. Mary's, 193, 300
Bloody Assize, the, 183–185, 41
Bloody Bank (Wareham), 185
Bloody Lane (Bothenhampton), 180
Bokerly Dyke, 43, 53–54, 56, 218
Bond, family of, 29

345